The
Ghosts
on
87th
Lane

About the Author

M. L. Woelm has experienced paranormal phenomena since she was a little girl. A grandmother, she enjoys exploring popular haunts around the world. She lives with her husband and their dog Max, who loyally alerts her of every ghostly visitor.

The Ghosts on 87th Lane

on

87th Lane

a true story

M. L. Woelm

Llewellyn Publications
Woodbury, Minnesota

First Edition
First Printing, 2007

Book design and layout by Joanna Willis
Cover design by Gavin Dayton Duffy
Cover image © PictureQuest
Interior photographs by the author

Llewellyn is a registered trademark of Llewellyn Worldwide, Ltd.

Library of Congress Cataloging-in-Publication Data
Woelm, M. L. (Marlene L.), 1941–
    The ghosts on 87th Lane : a true story / M.L. Woelm.
        p. cm.
    ISBN: 978-0-7387-1031-0
    1. Ghosts—Minnesota—Blaine. 2. Haunted places—Minnesota—Blaine.
    3. Woelm, M. L. (Marlene L.), 1941– I. Title.
    BF1472.U6W64 2007
    133.109776'65—dc22   2007013068

Llewellyn Worldwide does not participate in, endorse, or have any authority or responsibility concerning private business transactions between our authors and the
public.
    All mail addressed to the author is forwarded but the publisher cannot, unless spe-
cifically instructed by the author, give out an address or phone number.
    Any Internet references contained in this work are current at publication time, but
the publisher cannot guarantee that a specific location will continue to be maintained. Please refer to the publisher's website for links to authors' websites and other
sources.

Llewellyn Publications
A Division of Llewellyn Worldwide, Ltd.
2143 Wooddale Drive, Dept. 978-0-7387-1031-0
Woodbury, MN 55125-2989, U.S.A.
www.llewellyn.com

Printed in the United States of America

Contents

Preface

It's fairly quiet these days, but back in May of 1968, the first night we spent in our house was anything but quiet. For the next several years, almost every night was filled with supernatural mischief. There were nights when my body was paralyzed with fear, yet other evenings would find me laughing nervously at the paranormal antics going on all over the place. Until my daughter became an adult, I had no one within my immediate family to lean on for support. I rode this psychic roller coaster all alone—quietly screaming to myself and hanging on for dear life, never knowing what to expect. I tried to put my experiences down on paper many times, but something always stopped me.

My home is not a glamorous Hollywood mansion or classic English country estate with long, sweeping staircases down which ghosts silently glide. It has no fireplaces, hidden passages, balconies, or walled-up skeletons. This is why I wanted to tell my story: to prove that ghosts can and will haunt anywhere they wish. Location, style, or size of home does not concern them.

During the years of 1968 to 1978, when I was experiencing the heaviest ghostly activity in my house, I avidly sought information on the subject. Of all the books I read, my favorite was *Spindrift: Spray from a Psychic Sea*, by Jan Bryant Bartell. Ms. Bartell's story helped me deal with my scary days and nights. Granted, she was a stage actress and writer married to a successful restaurateur and living in a third-floor walkup in a Greenwich Village brownstone, and I was a housewife and mother married to a munitions-plant worker and living in a small house in a Minneapolis suburb, but we had a close, psychic bond. We had shared many of the same experiences as we reluctantly began our separate journeys into the world of the paranormal. Each of us had hoped to find a credible explanation for what was occurring in our respective homes. In the end, logic escaped us, and both Ms. Bartell and I had to reluctantly accept the fact that our homes were inhabited by something we could not see. It was a tremendous relief knowing I was not the only one being drawn into the baffling world of the supernatural without my consent. I wanted to write to Ms. Bartell and tell her how her experiences helped me cope, but unfortunately she crossed over to the Other Side in the early seventies—after she completed her book. (Although our lives followed parallel paths up to a point, I do not wish to share that final coincidence with her, at least not yet.)

At some point, things here quieted down quite a bit. I thought my ghost had finally tired of tormenting me and had moved on, but in the autumn of 1995, several more incidents occurred, which resulted in my decision to finish this book. Some names have been changed to protect the identities of persons who wish to remain anonymous, especially the skeptics in my life. I also changed the names of those who have crossed over during the writing of this book, on the off chance they didn't wish to be identified. There are enough spirits haunting me now as it is!

Dedication

I dedicate this book to my daughter, Kristen, who deals with phenomena more sensibly than I ever will; to Nancy Letson and my other special friends who never shut me up nor shut me out; and, finally, to Ms. Bartell, who unknowingly held my hand through some scary times. I also wish to thank Grandma Gladys, who encouraged me for decades. Her earthly journey has ceased, but her enthusiasm remains tucked away in my heart. I also want to acknowledge the skeptics I encountered along the way—especially my husband, Paul, and son, Scott. Roadblocks, although exasperating, often serve a useful purpose. In my case, these hurdles were real character builders.

Everyone has a right to his or her own opinion. I believe in the psychic presence that I've seen, felt, and heard over the years, and no one will ever convince me that ghosts don't exist. Whether you're a believer or not, I invite you to enjoy my own personal ghost story, which is part memoir and part journal.

Back Story

The year is 1995, and I'm determined to publish my story. It's become my own personal quest, my Holy Grail. Around midnight some weeks ago, after far too much caffeine, I was lying awake upstairs in bed and recalling all the events that have happened in this house over the years. I remembered what I could and decided to go for it.

Back in 1968, I started writing twenty-page letters to a family friend who lived in Omaha, Nebraska, documenting each occurrence on the precise date and time it happened. He kept the letters in a three-ring binder and teased me that he was going to publish them. We'd often argue over whose property the letters were—the author's or the recipient's. In the end, he refused to return them to me for my own documentation, despite my shameless begging. Unfortunately, our family lost track of him in 1984, so I must start the memoir section of this book over from scratch. I am not amused!

In the late sixties, while nervously typing those letters, it felt like someone was watching me. That eerie feeling was often followed by unusual noises behind my back, often loud enough to make me jump. The simple act of putting past events down on paper seems to deepen my sensitivity. This, in turn, attracts the noises and unsettling feelings, which still invade my quiet time at the computer now. However, these days I refuse to be manipulated by them. Oh, they still scare me—but I'll fight through my fear to finish the account of my life in this house.

Despite the hazy dates and times, the activity of those early years is burned into my brain as if it were a cattle brand. Funny enough, the events from 1979 to 1995 are less clear. Since I've been working outside the home for a number of years, keeping track of odd occurrences seems trivial, because I need every brain cell I have to keep my life on schedule. Oh, each little trick and each little treat is just as annoying as it was years ago, but my world has become larger and my time more precious. As a matter of fact, my spiritual border might have faded into oblivion without me taking note had it not burst back into my life a few months ago. I found myself sucked back into the whirlpool of the unexplained, totally against my will, once again.

A Memoir of the Early Years

1: My First Look Around

March 1968: House Hunting Is a Drag

My story began the first day Paul walked into our apartment and announced that he had found a house for us. We had been house hunting for several weeks. Each trip began with eager anticipation and ended with the words, "We just can't afford this one." The houses I loved were always out of our price range.

We were a one-income family, period. Although many wives and mothers were carving out a nice spot for themselves in the workplace, Paul didn't want me to join them. He had a troubled childhood and seriously believed that children raised by a stay-at-home mom would fare better than those with a mother who worked outside the home. This meant less money, fewer material things, and the frustration connected with both. I stayed home with our two small children just to keep peace in the family, even though it meant living without a lot of things we needed and many things we wanted—including my dream house.

At first, we dragged the kids with us on the numerous house-hunting trips. The weather was still cold and snowy, so this meant boots, scarves, and lots of whining—and that was just me! Finally, to simplify matters, Paul began going out by himself. I didn't like that arrangement at all, but back in 1968 the assertiveness movement was still in its infancy. Come to think of it, I hadn't even heard the A-word yet. The afternoon Paul came home saying he'd found a house, I was overjoyed, in a suspicious sort of way. "Where is it? How much is it? When can I see it?" It was in Blaine, Minnesota, and the asking price was $16,500. We could just barely swing it. Paul called Jack, the Realtor, to set up a date for me to see the house. I arranged for a babysitter. I was so excited.

By the time Jack and Paul took me to see the house, the FHA people had already looked at it, given the owners a list of repairs that needed to be made, and assessed the value of the home at $12,500. When I called to share this good fortune with my best friend, Carrie, she asked, "What do you think is wrong with it?" I laughed and blurted out, "Maybe it's haunted!" Why I said that, I'll never know. Those prophetic words just popped out of my mouth. We cackled over my silly joke like our cartoon role models, Wilma Flintstone and Betty Rubble, and then got down to the business of discussing my long-overdue move. By this time, all my friends had abandoned apartment living and settled in new or nearly new homes in the 'burbs.

En route to my first tour of the place, the Realtor explained that the house was an older, two-bedroom expansion model. This style made its debut around the end of the Korean War, when these homes sprang up all over the country to accommodate returning war veterans. These structures were designed to be starter homes—built quickly and cheaply.

Is This Really My Home Sweet Home?

I'll never forget pulling up in front of the small clapboard house. I couldn't understand why anyone would paint this style of house in two colors, since it only accentuated how small it is. It looked like a sad little orphan in tattered clothes. Yet there it stood, proudly holding its head high, adorned with peeling white paint on its top portion and cracked aqua blue on its bottom half. I actually felt sorry for it. This was the awkward child in the orphanage whom no one wanted, the child always left behind after his pretty playmates were placed in good homes. I've always been a sucker for a hard-luck story, and now the orphan belonged to me. Although it's difficult to admit, I was embarrassed to end up with the worst-looking house in my circle of friends. Apparently, history really is destined to repeat itself—especially my history—because I grew up in a house that always looked shabby and rundown. My family never had any money, and even though my darling dad did his best to provide for the family, ours was the worst-looking of all my friends' houses back in those days too. I'd hoped for something better when I grew up.

Everything in Minnesota looks its scruffiest in March. I sighed as I gazed at my future home sitting on its bleak piece of property. There was no garage, but apartment living during the past six years had rarely afforded us a garage, so that was no big deal. There were a couple of massive oak trees in the front yard that looked pretty friendly despite their dormant state. I pictured the gnarled giants covered with leaves and flanked all around by green grass, flower gardens, shrubs, and maybe a white picket fence. I'd had my heart set on a house with a picket fence for as long as I could remember. Here was my chance to make that dream come true. If only I'd had a fairy godmother who could turn this melancholy property into a sweet little cottage with one grand sweep of her magic wand.

Two huge elms stood guard in the backyard, surrounded on three sides by an odd assortment of neighbors' fences. This poor little house had to wear hand-me-down fences too. How unfair! There were clusters of dormant shrubs around the property line. I hoped they would magically become lilacs when the sun warmed everything in the spring. The scent of lilacs wafting through the springtime air is delightful, and it stirs up wonderful memories. The old elm trees would give off lots of shade, and there was plenty of room for a swing set and sandbox. I could finally have the vegetable garden I'd always wanted. I made up my mind to dwell on the positives. There was no other option.

As we entered the house, we found ourselves on a small landing, looking down the basement steps; I wondered if we'd have to put up a gate to keep the kids from falling down there. Then we entered the plain-looking kitchen. The smell of coffee brewing on the stove welcomed us. It actually made this dour little house seem friendly. Years later, I learned that this was the oldest real-estate trick in the book, designed to give prospective buyers a "welcome home" kind of feeling. The friendly smell did nothing to change the size of the room, however. I was soon to discover the kitchen was approximately nine by thirteen feet. The area adjacent to the back door was completely wasted space: possibly enough room for our drop-leaf table and two chairs, but there were four of us! The fridge wouldn't fit there because of the south-facing window. There was a traffic area through the room that ended with a very narrow opening into the hallway, flanked on either side by the stove and the cupboards. This opening was eighteen inches. I made a mental note never to gain weight.

The other window in the kitchen had been located over the sink, facing east. It had been turned into a pass-through and knickknack shelf when an addition was built. After stepping inside the back door, it was plain to see the previous owner loved bland colors. The floors in entryway and kitchen were covered with gray tile speckled with white and pink dots—typical forties and fifties fare. The walls were grayish taupe, and pink and white organdy curtains adorned the window. It was certainly not my taste. The badly stained sink had residue stuck in the drain basket. Even if you couldn't afford new appliances, you could at least keep the old ones clean, I thought.

The addition was called a family room, and it was thirteen feet square. This room was painted the same color as the kitchen and sported the same organdy curtains and the same blah tile. It was furnished with a couple of armchairs, end tables, and lamps, as well as the kitchen table with chairs and a toaster. As we gazed into the dull, drab room, Jack quickly pointed out that most two-bedroom expansion homes didn't have a nice-sized addition like this. I had to admit it had possibilities. A fireplace and a pair of wingback chairs would look great in here. Maybe cozy shutters over the four small corner windows—or better yet, larger windows could change this gloomy living space into something more cheery and transform this room into a perfect place for growing plants, since it got the morning sun.

The biggest drawback was money. So for now, we'd leave the ugly tile, replace the curtains, and paint over the boring walls as soon as possible. I couldn't say anything about the color scheme, because the current owner, Agnes Miller, stuck to us like glue. Home owners are usually not around when their properties are being shown, as a courtesy to the prospective buyers. Apparently, Agnes didn't know how to drive, had nowhere to go, or was just plain nosy, so the chubby, rosy-cheeked woman was always in the way. This house was so small that she became a hindrance during the showing. Our group pressed onward as Jack walked us through the rest of the house.

Next, we moved into the living room. This room was roughly eleven by seventeen feet in size. It had one average-sized window on the south side and a large picture window facing west. This room also had a tiny coat closet located opposite the front door. The doors could not be opened at the same time without banging one into the other. Although I'm sure the architect's plans were followed to the letter, it's a structural aberration if you ask me.

This room was a mournful dirge of brown. A thin mud-colored carpet rested loosely atop the floor while light brown paint covered the walls. The focal point was the large picture window, dressed with boring Austrian poufs. They were made from a milk-chocolate-colored fabric. I stared at them with genuine disbelief. Agnes proudly proclaimed, "I made the curtains myself." I think Jack mistook my stunned expression for one of admiration, because he stated with confidence, "Marlene, those curtains will stay with the house." I thought to myself, *Oh no, they won't.* Jack confirmed that the carpet was staying with the house as well. Lucky us!

This room was sparsely furnished with a nondescript couch and armchair (both in the tan color family) and a couple of end tables, but what caught my eye was the monstrosity against the short north wall. It was an oversized, cumbersome chair made from ornately carved wood with a very dark finish. This chair most definitely had spent a previous life as a gargoyle. In a museum, this huge piece of furniture would have looked quite interesting; however, in a room this size, it was seriously out of place. Agnes said it was a genuine antique throne dating from the eighteenth century. Antique or not, it was genuinely unattractive. Trust me.

Virtually everything in this room was some shade of brown. I couldn't explain why, but something about the monochromatic color scheme disturbed me. So did the air in the living room—it felt heavy. The coffeepot was still perking on the stove, and the smell of over-cooked coffee wafting in from the kitchen added to the dense composition of the air, giving the room a suffocating quality.

The bathroom was grungy and cramped. Neither Paul nor I were large people; however, the two of us could barely squeeze into the tiny room to look it over. It was approximately the size of a small walk-in closet—about nine by six feet. With the tub, toilet, and sink, it became much smaller, making it a one-person room. It looked as if someone could dangle their legs in the bathtub while sitting on the toilet.

Generally speaking, when someone puts their home on the market, they make sure it is as clean and shiny as possible. This poor little house smacked of gross indifference, neglect, and apathy both inside and out. Dirty pink tile extended halfway up the painted pink walls. Several of the tiles were chipped on the edges, and the toilet bowl needed a lot of work. It was quite apparent that Agnes preferred to spend her quality time with her garish throne in the living room rather than with its china cousin in here. The sink was almost as bad, and there was precious little porcelain left in the bathtub; the yellowish brown scum and the black cast-iron spots seemed to battle for squatters' rights along its bottom. The tub, toilet, and sink would be difficult to restore to an acceptable level of cleanliness. If I'd had my druthers, there would have been a junkyard in this trio's future, but some good old-fashioned elbow grease would have to work its magic in the meantime.

Some time ago, cupboards had been installed above the tub, so anyone over five feet ten inches was unable to comfortably stand upright in the shower. I drew attention to them, saying, "There isn't much headroom for taking a shower." Jack, who was standing in the hall, pointed out that the cupboards take the place of the linen closet. Agnes laughed and said, "It's a good thing that we're short people." She told me her husband was five foot six and she was only five foot two. I knew, at five-four, that I'd have no headroom concerns, but my husband wouldn't be very comfortable in here. And at that point in time, we had no way of knowing the height our children would reach in the coming years. To add inconvenience to the mix, I'd have to balance on the rim of the tub to put towels away. I knew that could get tricky, since I'm not a graceful creature.

At the end of the short hallway—which was covered with brown asbestos tile—and to the right of the bathroom door stood my son's future bedroom; it was about nine by ten feet. The walls were an uninspired tan color, and the floor was covered with the same asbestos tile as the hallway. I thought it a little strange to have cold tile in a bedroom, without even so much as a throw rug for warmth. This room held a twin bed covered with a patchwork quilt, some toys, and a dresser. Since it needed a lot of work, I decided to have the kids bunk upstairs and make this a playroom for the time being.

The Millers' bedroom was located kitty-corner from the bath. This room looked a bit larger, but not by much. Agnes was finally introducing some heavy-duty color into her home decorating: these walls were covered with eye-popping fuchsia paint, which gave the room an odd luminosity. After that shocking surprise, my eyes were drawn to the throw rugs that covered the taupe tile floor. Oh boy, more tile! The rugs were bright red acrylic shag. I blinked several times before my eyes bounced from the French provincial gold-trimmed bed to the windows and back to the floor. Screaming red curtains and a matching bedspread completed her decor. If snapping my fingers could transform this garish room into a living human being, it would have instantly become a painted French floozy loitering under a streetlight and waiting for some action to come her way . . . but that's just my opinion.

When we'd first entered the house, I thought there had been a glow emanating from this room. Now that I was standing in it, I could see why. Paul blurted out, "You need sunglasses in here!" and Jack laughed. I didn't look at Agnes, but I'm sure she didn't appreciate that remark. From my perspective, it's puzzling why she used such bland colors in the other rooms and then put fuchsia and bright red in here. I assured Paul that the color would change as soon as possible.

On the tall dresser sat a jewelry box, a clock, and a picture of a little boy. Agnes had referred to the tan bedroom next door as her youngest daughter's room. She said the older girls slept upstairs, so I didn't know where this little fellow fit in; maybe he was a godson or a favorite nephew. After I saw his sweet little face, I wanted to ask about him later, but that shocking assault of fuchsia knocked me for a loop and I completely forgot.

Jack was prattling on and on about how this house was a true handyman special. Now, that would be a good thing *if* Paul were a handyman. Trust me, he's not! I thought maybe my father-in-law would help us fix this house up. He was a bona fide handyman. I just hoped he'd be agreeable to it. I pressed my fingers tightly against the paneled walls for stability. The more I saw of this house, the more I disliked it, but it was my only chance to get out of the apartment and get settled before Krissy started kindergarten that fall.

Jack was eager to show us the second floor. We took a leap of faith and trekked up the creaky steps behind him. The threadbare carpet on the risers shifted with every step we took, and there was no hand railing to grab in case one of us lost our footing. Halfway up the steps, Jack directed our attention to the cheap paneling on the stairway walls, as if to convince himself that it was a selling feature. It looked like it had been slapped up in a hurry. The stairs groaned under our combined weight. A couple of the steps didn't feel safe, but with new carpet, some new boards, and a couple of handrails, this could become a good, sturdy flight of stairs. We'd have to deal with the ugly paneling later. Paul liked the paneling on the walls, but then he's a paneling freak. We looked at one home in another sub-urb that was completely paneled—even the kitchen and bath. Paul loved it. Thank God the asking price was beyond our price range, or I would have ended up in the loony bin.

As we passed the storage area on our left, Jack pulled aside a drab gray curtain to reveal several suitcases. "Here you will find ample storage. The cubbyholes that open onto this space run along the entire length of the house." I peered into the storage area. Just be-yond the suitcases, I saw a wooden door that Jack opened to reveal a cubbyhole with a small floor inside. I felt very cold and prickly as we stood in that area. This hostile space made it quite clear that it did not want to hold anything that belonged to us. I made a mental note to respect its wishes. The cubbyhole on the other side of the room had a friendlier attitude. We could store a lot of belongings in there if we wished. At the time, our little family didn't have much in the way of storable possessions, but when we did, I knew which cubby to use.

One interesting feature in this style of home is the layout of the second floor. The walls were only four feet high, and then they an-gled up to form a slanted ceiling. The most headroom up there is a strip down the center of the ceiling that runs the length of the room; it's about three and half feet wide. Veering away from that area could result in a nasty bump to the head. This was a perfect room for small children or gnomes—and a bloody inconvenience for everyone else. I planned on putting our two small kids up there until they required separate bedrooms. One thing that bothered me was the fact that there was no two-way light switch at the bottom of the steps. (I'm embarrassed to say there still isn't.) Every trip taken up or down the steps after dark would have to be made in the dark. The first light switch was located about seven feet into the room *after* you'd climbed the stairs. This large bedroom took up the entire second floor and consisted of three distinct spaces. The smallest, at the head of the stairs, was about six by ten feet; the next area, which included the closet, measured nine by ten feet; and the largest and most usable area was eleven and a half by ten feet.

Due to the structure of the walls, the pint-sized closet was a squatty kind of space. The rod would accommodate adult shirts, but anything longer, such as a dress, would hit the floor. This bedroom had a melancholy feel to it in spite of the cozy ceiling. The absence of color could have been the culprit. Color makes almost any space livable and attractive. Eons ago, the cavemen worked wonders with it, and in this case I thought it couldn't hurt. I had spent the first six years of my marriage in apartments with white walls. I couldn't wait to start painting this house.

This dreary space had grayish walls, an unstained hardwood floor, a couple of unmatched metal beds, and two dressers in it. Agnes said her two older daughters bunked up here. Jack fell all over himself pointing out the hardwood floor. He was getting on my nerves. I silently wondered how many prospective buyers had tramped through this gloomy little property and turned it down flat. I wished we could have as well. But since that wasn't an option, I focused on ideas for sprucing up the house with paint and accessories. It had to work. This house was in our price range, and Paul had already put earnest money down on it. That was two strikes against me.

Our return trip down the stairs was eerie. I felt a cold, prickly sensation as we passed the hostile cubbyhole. I whispered to Paul how chilly this house felt. Jack must have overheard me, because, sensing my displeasure, he interrupted our private conversation by loudly declaring, "It's March, what do you expect?" Good ol' Jack must have felt very sure of himself when he uttered that sarcastic remark, knowing he'd already made the sale. He could finally take this fixer-upper out of his inventory. While his insensitive words hung in the air, the back of my neck felt like it was being bombarded with thousands of tiny needles. As I made my way down the steps, I knew right then and there something was amiss in this melancholy place, and it couldn't all be blamed on the cold dampness of March. Strike number three!

Our tour wouldn't have been complete without a trip to the basement. It was unfinished, but the Millers had furnished the first room at the bottom of the steps with a couch, a couple of cast-off chairs, a television set, and an old upright piano. From the odor in the air, we could tell the cement floor had been freshly painted: a lovely battleship gray. Impertinence is contagious! The cement block walls were sporting a coat of deep carnation pink. Does anybody want to guess what Mrs. Miller's favorite colors were? Jack directed our attention to the exposed joists supporting the living-room floor, claiming that the excellent craftsmanship would keep the floor from squeaking. As if on cue, Agnes, who was still underfoot, chimed in by saying, "My father was very impressed with those two-by-fours. This kind of quality workmanship isn't done anymore these days." Why she made that remark, I'll never know. As long as we've lived here, that floor has always creaked.

Our Realtor opened an ill-fitting door held shut by a hook-and-eye lock located at the top, and we saw the other half of the basement. In this space, the floor was painted in that same fuchsia paint Agnes had used in her bedroom. These people wasted nothing. This area was home to the furnace as well as the washer and dryer. More fixer-upper talk spewed from Jack's mouth. His phony enthusiasm annoyed me. I wanted to blurt out, "So when are you coming over to start working on this dump, Jack?" Tucked around in back, on the other side of the living space, was a room filled with tools. Paul seemed very pleased to have his own work room, but I wasn't comfortable down here. The basement didn't feel as hostile as the cubbyhole upstairs, but it didn't radiate warmth either.

When we arrived back at our apartment, Paul told me his mother and stepfather had already looked at the house. "What?" I exclaimed. I was quite disappointed that they had seen my future home before I had. They advised him to buy it, because it could always be fixed up. The main thing was to get in and get settled. Then Paul cautioned, "This is the only house I'm ever going to buy you. You better not start any fights with the neighbors, because we're not moving." That just about covers the dual decision-making in our family back in the sixties.

I called my mother-in-law to see what she *really* thought of the place. Their home was beautifully furnished, so I didn't believe she approved of our little orphan by any stretch of the imagination. In a semi-sarcastic tone of voice, Dora admitted she'd never live in a house like that, but she said that with decent decorating and much-needed repairs, it wouldn't be half bad for a starter home. She emphasized the word "starter." Dora said we could always move into something better in a few years. Paul's words—"This is the only house I'm ever going to buy you"—reverberated in my mind after she made that remark. I asked if the kids were home when they looked at the house. She said they were, so I asked her if she saw a little boy. She replied, "That's a sad story. He died six years ago of a ruptured bowel. There is a picture of him on her bedroom dresser."

I could hardly wait to hang up. I immediately called Carrie with that piece of news and added, "Maybe my house has a ghost after all!" She whined, "My house didn't come with one. I'm jealous." Wilma and Betty laughed again while Carrie and I made plans for the upcoming move. She and her husband volunteered to help.

A closing date was set, and late one afternoon in a cramped office downtown, we signed the papers with our two small children scuffling on the floor at our feet. The adoption was complete. We were first-time owners of a small house with very strange vibes. I was overwhelmed with happiness, though it was tempered with misgivings.

Does This Look Like a Haunted House?
I had many reservations about buying this house, but nonetheless our kids, Kristen and Scott, stand outside our new home in Blaine, Minnesota, in 1968.

Paul had qualified for a GI loan, so several repairs had to be made before we could take possession. It would have been perfect if new bathroom appliances and a new kitchen sink had made the fix-up list, but that didn't happen. The septic tank was replaced with a sewer, and upgrades were made to the furnace to bring the house up to code. After the new sewer pipe was installed, we were left with three huge mounds of dirt in the front yard, and it was up to us to dispose of it. Somebody told Paul that watering the soil would eventually blend it back into the ground. Guess who got that job? I could imagine the neighbors saying, "Hey, have you seen the crazy lady who moved into the rundown blue and white house? She waters those piles of dirt in her front yard every single night." Boy, did I feel foolish standing out there, hose in hand, making mounds of mud. It made no sense. One evening, a neighbor walked by and asked me what I was growing in those mounds. That did it. After that bit of humiliation, I ended up shoveling the stubborn dirt around the base of the oak trees and against the foundation. But I've jumped ahead of myself.

Although the Millers had legal rights to the house till month's end, they moved out in mid-April, as soon as we closed on it. I'm sure they weren't happy about having to sink more money into the place, as they were getting over a thousand less than their asking price. They left behind an old junky car and said they'd be back for it, but they never returned.

On a positive note, their hasty departure gave us a rare opportunity to get in early and paint. I could hardly wait to get at it. Paul worked nights, so I spent my mornings hauling small loads of nonessentials from our apartment in Fridley to the house. Since we were a one-vehicle family, it was imperative that I return before Paul had to leave for work. I painted or cleaned as time permitted during those visits. Krissy, my social butterfly, was in her glory. She was busy meeting all the neighbors. Scott played with his trucks in the empty, echoing rooms while I did battle with the fuchsia floozy in the bedroom. It was quite a nasty scuffle, but after three coats of soft avocado paint, the room was habitable. It was the first room I painted, because no one could have slept in there without suffering permanent brain damage.

While I rolled paint, my little daughter ran around the neighborhood and then raced back to tell me the names of all the housewives on the block. She brought with her their invitations to come for coffee as soon as we were settled. She also rattled off all the new friends she had made. Scott was perfectly happy playing in the house by me, and I was thankful for my three-year-old's company, because it kept me from working in the stone-cold silence. I didn't feel comfortable in the house quite yet, and I wondered if I ever would.

The tiny kitchen got a coat of pale coral paint before we moved in. That wasn't a favorite color of mine, but it coordinated with the ugly floor tile. I was no fan of the blond pine woodwork and cupboards either, but with one income, we had to pace ourselves on redecorating. The rest of the rooms would just have to wait their turn.

2: Getting Acquainted

Our Ghost Says "Hi"

And so it began. On a fine May morning, we moved in lock, stock, barrel, and mortgage. The birds were singing, the sun was shining, and everything was going according to schedule. Paul's parents took the kids for the day, and we had two couples helping us move. We worked very hard all day, setting up beds and putting away the toys, clothing, and kitchen items. By late afternoon, the house was in order. Our helpers went home, our children were returned, and we were thoroughly exhausted.

I took Kris and Scott up the stairs, settled them in their beds, and plugged in their little fifteen-watt night lamp. We said prayers and shared kisses and hugs. Scott asked if we were going to sleep in our other house tomorrow night. I smiled at my sleepy little son's question. "This is our house now, honey."

He said, "No, our real house. I don't like this house."

I wanted to say, "Me, neither," but I assured him things would look differently in the morning, when he could bring out all his toys. I left the cheerful circle of light and made my way past the creepy cubbyhole and down the dark stairway, sliding my hands along the paneling for stability. *We have to get a handrail up as soon as possible*, I thought. *These steps are an accident waiting to happen.*

Paul nursed a beer, and I gulped down a bottle of Diet Rite before we fell into bed. My husband is usually asleep before his head hits the pillow. I, on the other hand, have had trouble falling asleep since the kids were born. Although we were bone-tired, we sleepily discussed the phone company coming out the next morning and then kissed good-night.

As we dozed off, our ears were bombarded with the sounds of boxes moving around and objects hitting the floor above us.

"What's wrong with those darn kids?" Paul asked. "Why aren't they asleep? It sounds like they are up there playing."

I replied, "They are in a strange house, you know. I'll go up and see what's going on."

I climbed those awful steps and headed to the opposite side of the long room, only to find both children sound asleep. (Hint: If you suspect your children are playing possum, try leaning over them till your face is about a half-inch away from theirs. If they are goofing around, they will open their eyes and giggle. If they are fast asleep, they won't move.) I left the glow of their friendly night-light once more and trudged ever so carefully down the stairs.

This scene was repeated two more times within the next five minutes. Paul was getting more short-tempered by the second. The noises were growing louder, and he was actually having trouble falling asleep. He threatened to go upstairs and paddle the kids' behinds, so I made one more trip and still found no explanation for the noises. When I crawled back into bed for the third time, I informed my irritated husband, "The kids are sound asleep, and for your information there are no boxes up there. Everything was put away. Go up there and see for yourself!" I don't think he heard me, though. He was snoring away like crazy. Great, another noise to keep me awake. I racked my brain wondering how it could be so quiet upstairs and so noisy down here. While the loud thumps and scratching noises cavorted above our bedroom, I explored every plausible explanation till I fell asleep. The next thing I knew, someone was pounding on the back door, the sun was streaming in the windows, and the kids were in our bedroom announcing that there was a phone truck in the driveway.

Lights Out!

A few days later, a little after eleven p.m., a second unusual experience occurred. After a relaxing bath, I was towel-drying my hair in the living room. There were two lamps on in the house—one in the living room and another in our bedroom. Other than that, the remainder of the downstairs was completely dark. As I sat in the swivel rocker and calculated the amount of time it would take to drive into Minneapolis the following morning, the living-room lamp abruptly went off, leaving me in the dark. It definitely took my mind off my yearly Pap test. I immediately checked the hallway and discovered that the lamp in the bedroom was still on. Thank God the power hadn't gone off, because I had no idea which box held the flashlights and candles. The kids would have been terrified if they had awakened to find themselves in a pitch-black room—but not as terrified as their panic-stricken mother, who would have to climb that spooky stairway to comfort them. I sat there shaking for what seemed like a lifetime.

Finally, I got up and started toward the lamp in the far corner of the room. As I reached for the switch, the light suddenly popped back on! I jumped backward, bumping into the wall. My heart began pounding in my throat.

I checked the bulb. It was screwed securely into the socket.

I checked the plug. It was firmly inserted into the outlet.

I grabbed the cord and wiggled it every which way imaginable to see if there was a short. The bulb stayed on.

For some reason, I glanced at the clock. It was almost 11:20. Unfortunately, this event was the beginning of an assortment of occurrences that were to plague me every night for the next few years. The activity would change slightly, but each evening at approximately 11:20, the light in whichever room I sat would flicker or dim for a second or two. As my personal witching hour approached, I'd call friends whose husbands worked the night shift. I desperately needed company while awaiting this curious ritual.

I wasn't about to admit that a ghost might be the cause of this peculiar event. Actually, I believed in them, but it's always been my nature to look for practical explanations: I will accept a paranormal reason only after every rational idea has been checked out. Although I'd forgotten this conversation from a couple months ago, my silly remark to Carrie popped into my head: "Maybe we have a ghost after all." Oh, brother!

Nobody wants to know anyone who lives with ghosts. (Just ask me—I could write a book about it. As a matter of fact, this is the book!) Some of my so-called best friends disappeared into the woodwork during this miserable time of my life. But worst of all, my husband would not listen to any of it. He knew I didn't like the house and thought I was trying to force a move, as if we had a choice. Even if he had teased me about my alleged ghost, it would have made my life bearable. But not to acknowledge it at all—to leave me twisting in the wind, as it were—was inexcusable. From my perspective, it seemed like he didn't give a damn about my mental health, although I'm sure he didn't see it that way. I knew we couldn't afford to move. I just needed him on my side—emotionally, if nothing else—and his no-nonsense character just wouldn't permit it.

In addition to the flickering lights each evening, I heard boxes moving inside the hostile cubbyhole, much like the noises Paul and I both heard that first night. The floor in this cubbyhole is located above the kitchen stove. At first, I heard the scraping, dragging noises only at night, but they soon invaded my daylight hours as well. The phenomena slowly intensified as the days and weeks rolled by. The noises never began until Paul left for work at three o'clock each afternoon. To make matters worse, the noises seemed to take the weekends off, when he was home. Oh, great! Maybe I *was* imagining things . . . but why would I torment myself like that?

As the mysterious routine escalated, I began hearing what sounded like little items dropping on the floor inside the cubbyhole door. I decided it was mice. The only thing that destroyed that perfectly sensible explanation was this: the bits and pieces seemed to fall, get picked up, and then drop again. Mice are monotonous nibblers and gnaw for long periods of time. They don't pick things up and drop them every few seconds. Each sound I heard was different from the time before. Okay, so it's not mice. Might it be squirrels? Bats, perhaps? Ghosts?

Anybody got a better suggestion?

I began doubting my sanity. How many roles could I possibly play in this drama? Happy, well-adjusted wife? Loving mother? Pleasant neighbor? Although I could have easily played the other roles, the part of terror-stricken woman fit me like a glove. Every night after the kids went to sleep, I silently cried, wondering if I was losing my mind. I telephoned my friends for support. At first, I'd chat about any old thing, just to have the luxury of hearing a voice on the other end of the line. However, as the days went by, I could no longer contain my fear. I tried as hard as I could to keep the unpopular idea of living in a haunted house to myself, but it managed to slip out. That's when my friends' true personalities emerged.

I couldn't believe the indifference shown by these women. These were good friends—friends that I had known for years, the kind of women you would never expect to desert you when you needed them. My former roommates humored me by feigning interest, but I could tell they didn't believe me. One dear friend said she believed in ESP because her entire family intuitively knew when one of them was ill or in trouble. However, she didn't think she could go as far as including ghosts in that belief. Yet another friend, who I felt was sophisticated enough to understand the paranormal, told me never to call her again and slammed the receiver in my ear. Worst of all, Carrie, who believed in the paranormal and, better yet, believed me, was getting a divorce and moving out to Utah. One afternoon before she left, she called and asked if I had talked to the neighbors to see what they had to say about my house. I choked back my tears and said, "I can't ask them, Carrie, I just can't. If my own husband and friends have turned their backs on me, what chance do I have with total strangers?"

As each day dawned, I became aware of more noises—noises that could not be explained through rational means. By this time, I had dark circles under my eyes and was becoming more and more jittery. Although weeks had passed since we had moved in, I didn't feel like meeting any neighbors, so I didn't leave the house except to hang out laundry and shop for groceries. I felt like everyone outside these four walls could take one look at me and *know* there was something amiss in my house. It was awful. I was losing patience with the kids and snapping at Paul, and then there was my health. My normal pack-a-day cigarette habit had doubled—and sometimes even tripled, depending on the amount of stress in my day. That can't have been good.

One evening while writing to some friends in Kansas, I heard scratching sounds on the other side of my kitchen door. The door was open a couple of inches, so I immediately kicked it shut, thinking I'd scare whatever it was away. The scratching continued.

I held my foot against the door for what seemed like an eternity. I didn't know what was on the other side, but I was damn sure going to keep it there. I slammed the chain lock in place and waited. My pulse was exploding in my eardrums, and the scream I was holding down in my throat was slowly inching its way to freedom.

Within a few minutes, the scratching stopped. It wasn't quite 11:20, so the lights weren't going to dim yet—thank God. I took in a deep breath to steady my nerves. Seconds later, I heard someone coming down the steps from the kids' bedroom. To be more precise, I heard a *noise* coming down the steps. It sounded like someone with the sniffles. My children rarely get out of bed once they are tucked in, so I wondered if Kristen needed something. She didn't have a cold; however, her sniffling was a nervous habit. From the table, I called out, "Krissy?" The sniffling continued slowly down the stairs, one deliberate step at a time. My little daughter didn't answer me, but she was half-asleep, so that was no surprise. Although still reeling from the scratching sounds, I had to get to my sleepy daughter in case she missed a step. On the way to the upstairs doorway, I called out, "Kris, what's the matter? Do you have to go potty? Do you have a tummy ache?"

Sniff, sniff!

Her lack of response raised a red flag. I quickly stepped into the hall and peered up into the black stairway. "Kris, why don't you answer Mama?" At that moment, the sniffling stopped. The dark stairway was empty. It was only then that I realized her bare heels hadn't thudded across the hardwood floor before the noise began.

As I peered into that black abyss, I must have gone white as a ghost—excuse the supernatural simile. I wanted so badly to slam that door shut, but it had to remain open at night so we could hear if the kids needed us. It would terrify them if they ever found it closed. On the other hand, I was scared stiff because it had to remain open. Talk about the sacrifices parents make for their children!

Scratching and Sniffing
In addition to flickering lights, unexplained noises—like a children's sniffling coming from this empty stairway—began to terrify me in our early days in the house.

After those bizarre occurrences ganged up on me, I couldn't get my letter-writing momentum back. After all, I was trying my best to give our friends a rosy picture of our new home and was failing miserably. Me, a writer of fiction? I think not. I couldn't have lied about loving this house even if my very life depended on it, not on that night, anyway. There was no way my nerves were going to settle down enough to finish my letter, so I put it away, lit up a cigarette, and went into the living room to ponder what had just happened. I glanced up at the clock and realized that the flickering lights hadn't performed their nightly ritual. For a split second, I wondered why, but I quickly decided to let it go and savor this small victory.

Okay, I Take a Chance!

My self-imposed isolation was almost worse than the creepy things going on in the house, and after a few weeks of being shut in with the noises and flickering lights, I couldn't deal with it any longer. I had absolutely no one to confide in, so one sunny afternoon after Paul left for work, I ventured outside to meet my next-door neighbor, Martha. She seemed friendly enough, because she always waved at me when she saw me. I had seen her outside with her four children almost every day, but up until that very moment I had not found the courage to meet her.

We introduced ourselves and exchanged pleasantries; then I brought the social amenities to a screeching halt by blurting out, "Did the little boy who lived here die in this house?" Paul's warning to get along with the neighbors flew right out the window. If asking questions about this house would result in bad relations between our houses, so be it. From my perspective, things couldn't get any worse. After my socially inept question, I expected Martha to grab her children and storm into her house to get away from the crazy neighbor lady in the driveway. But that didn't happen. Her pale blue eyes grew enormous behind her eyeglasses as she whispered, "Why do you ask that?" Her expression was caring and sympathetic, and I took her response to be a positive sign.

Martha showed genuine interest and compassion, two emotions so desperately missing in my life in those days. Something about her face told me I could trust her, which made this woman the answer to my unspoken prayer. She smiled and said, "Come in for coffee. I don't want the kids to hear us." I ran back to my house to grab my cigarettes. As I trotted back to her house, I wondered what I was about to hear. Our kids played in the yard, occasionally running in and out of the house, as kids are known to do. Of course, the topic of our conversation immediately changed each time they burst through the front door to update us on what they were doing outside.

Martha's Story

Martha and her husband, Earl, had known the Miller family very well. The guys each worked the night shift in downtown Minneapolis, and their respective jobs were in close proximity to each other, so they often drove together. Martha began by telling me the Millers' little son, Johnny, was six years old when he died in a downtown hospital of a bowel obstruction, just as my mother-in-law had said. Since the guys had ridden together that night, Martha's husband was at the hospital with the family when it happened. He later told Martha that the last words little Johnny spoke were, "I don't want to die. I want to go home and play." Those words chilled my bones.

I was faced with conflicting emotions: fear and empathy. My eyes filled with tears. What an awful tragedy: their only son, dead at the tender age of six. My older brother was murdered when he was five years old, and I know how that affected our family, especially my poor mother. I almost hated to ask, "Do you remember what time of night he died?"

She thought for a moment and then replied, "It was close to the end of their shifts, if I remember correctly. I'd say it happened sometime between eleven p.m. and midnight."

"Then that explains it."

She leaned toward me as her eyes grew enormous again. "Explains what? What have you *seen*?"

Martha had just opened the door, and I marched across the threshold, dragging my insecurities and fears behind me and giving no thought to the consequences. I began telling her about the incidents that had been plaguing me since we'd moved in. I started out with the noises we heard our first night and how the lights had either dimmed or flickered at 11:20 every night since; then I finished up with the most recent occurrences.

She replied in a whispery voice, "I wouldn't live in your house if someone paid me to live there." Martha went on to say that the neighborhood kids referred to our home as "the haunted house" because the Miller girls had freely talked about their brother's ghost at school. Apparently, everyone in the entire neighborhood knew our house was haunted. Everyone but me, that is.

I sat there dumbfounded. For a minute or two, Martha and I just stared at each other across her dining table. She broke the silence by saying, "Do you want to hear more?" I thought about it for a few seconds, and then nodded. I pushed my cigarettes and matches toward her. She thanked me, pulled out a cigarette and lit it, and inhaled deeply. When she exhaled, streams of smoke became tangled up in her words. "Agnes was so devastated when her son died that for three days afterward, she locked herself upstairs and would not even come down to eat." She told me that the grieving woman had actually sat up there in the bedroom and wished him back.

I looked at her in total disbelief. "Wished . . . him . . . back?" I had never heard of such a thing. I unconsciously removed another cigarette from the pack and lit up. *Mrs. Miller had wished him back.* I just couldn't get my head around that explanation.

Martha poured us each another cup of coffee and continued, "That's what she said. Agnes told me it worked, too, because little Johnny came back home. They were all very happy to have him living with them again."

"Was she nuts?"

"Maybe so, but how else do you explain all the things that have happened in your house over the years?"

"Like what?" I quietly whispered.

It was Martha's turn to unburden her mind of pent-up information. It was obvious that this woman had been waiting for me to ask her, and words almost literally flew out of her mouth. "Like their first Christmas after Johnny died. That morning, they found some gifts opened and paper strewn all over the living room. And they always left that cubbyhole door open so he could get in and out of it. According to the girls, he lived in the cubbyhole after he died." I shook my head in amazement as I watched goose bumps form on my arms. Although I was sitting in a stifling dining room with the afternoon sun beating in through the west window, I began shivering. Up until this very moment, I had hoped that the things happening in my house were just some kind of weird coincidence. Even though I was truly scared, I had to ask, "By any chance, do you remember which cubbyhole they said he lived in?"

Martha pointed to the side of my house where the noisy cubbyhole was located.

My skin was crawling by this time. "Are you putting me on?"

She shook her head slowly as she took another long drag off her cigarette. Her words again punched their way through the puffs of smoke streaming from her nose and mouth. "I wouldn't live in your house if it were the last house on earth." We sat in silence, listening to our kids laughing and yelling in the front yard. While those healthy, boisterous children were running around in the bright summer sunlight, a ghost child was quietly playing in a dark nook all alone. How surreal is that?

We changed the subject every time the kids came in to tattle on each other or get lemonade refills, but that afternoon Martha also managed to tell me how Agnes would rarely go down in the basement—and never, ever after dark. Her husband often did the laundry for her. Also, I learned how one night Agnes's little son's ghost woke her up by grabbing the big toe on her left foot, which she always left uncovered while she slept—a habit, I'm sorry to say, I share with her. That particular night, she asked Johnny if she could please get a glimpse of him. He allegedly replied, "No, Mommy, I look horrible now."

I sat there soaking in all the unbelievable things Martha was telling me. If he lived in the cubbyhole, it would be the perfect explanation for the noises I heard above me when I was in the kitchen. It would also explain why I felt that icy, prickly sensation each time I went up and down the stairs, and why that cubbyhole door slowly opened at odd times of the day or night. Lord, I hated that spooky *crrr-eeeeak*.

Was the ghost child responsible for opening that little door, or was gravity the culprit? I was fighting to hang on to some kind of logic, because Paul would never buy Martha's story. He would think I put her up to it, because his skepticism is rock solid. Either I had to come up with a sensible explanation for the occurrences or quit telling him about them. After going over the two choices spinning around in my head, I decided on the latter. My new friend and I each lit up another cigarette and stared at each other in silence for another long moment.

I finally spoke. "Martha, might there be an electrical anomaly in our area each night around the time my lights flicker? You know, like a power surge or an overload on a transmitter?"

She considered this and then said, "The surrounding homes are on the same transformer, and my lights never dim or flicker at 11:20. If you'd like, I'll discreetly ask a few of the other neighbors to see if theirs do. Meanwhile, since Earl and Paul both work nights, feel free to call me when you need to talk to someone." As she gathered up the empty cups from the table, Martha said Johnny had always been very fond of her. Then she told me she hadn't stepped foot in our house since he died because she believed Johnny's ghost would follow her home if she ever did.

She was embarrassed to confess that to me, but I assured her that I totally understood fear. I grinned and said, "I'm the poster child for fear."

Then Martha added, "I refuse to come over there, but I'll gladly keep you company over the phone."

I thanked her for the information, the coffee, and her offer to help as best she could. As I got ready to leave, I said, "Let me know if I'm becoming a nuisance, though, okay? I am so relieved to have someone to talk to that I don't want to wear out my welcome."

I left my pack of smokes with her, because earlier she'd let it slip that her husband refused to buy them for her. She thanked me and then added, "Anytime you want to call, it's okay with me. I have no idea how you can stand to live in that house . . . none at all."

I Look for Answers in the Only Place I Can

That summer, I began taking my children to the Anoka County Public Library after Paul left for work. It became one of our favorite weekly rituals. The library was conveniently located about ten minutes from our house by foot. Those unnerving noises would start up above the kitchen the minute Paul pulled out of the driveway. That was my cue to load the kids into their red wagon and haul them up to the library. Although Krissy and Scott were fortunate enough to own scads of books, the library offered hundreds of new titles for their reading pleasure. I let them check out ten to twelve books each, enough to last for the week. As I saw it, I was cultivating their love of reading while giving myself a break from the ghostly activity in our home—for a few blissful hours, anyway. Another plus: the library was air-conditioned!

My reading material had a much different flavor than my kids' did. I began devouring book after book on poltergeists, residual hauntings, true experiences, and parapsychologists' theories—whatever I could get my hands on. The selection was not as comprehensive as I would have liked, but that first summer, I read all the paranormal books the library had to offer, and some more than once. Back then, the irony escaped me, but while I was losing myself in others' ghostly experiences, my own were being written—page by page—every single night.

After my initial visit with Martha, I finally had to admit the things that were happening in my house had to be caused by a spirit. And if she was correct, that spirit was the Millers' little son.

Heeeere's Johnny!

Since Martha knew how much I hated being alone in the house at night, she often invited us over for supper. She and I took turns making the meals, but we'd always eat at her house. After the dishes were cleaned up, we would entertain ourselves with a lively game of Scrabble while our kids played upstairs. Scott and Kris looked forward to the evenings we spent with Martha and her children as much as I. Sometimes my kids would fall asleep over there, and Paul and I would carry them up to bed after he got home at 12:15 a.m. One summer night during one of our next-door suppers, my ghost made itself known in a most flamboyant way.

A mixed-breed puppy had joined our family a few weeks earlier. Krissy had named him Shaggy. He was an adorable pup, full of life and roly-poly fun. Although I think Paul loved the little critter, he always said Shag was the most neurotic dog he had ever seen.

I was in the throes of potty-training the little guy, and on this particular evening, I went home every couple of hours to bring him outside for his bathroom chores. Each time I unlocked the door, he met me in the entryway with fear in his eyes. I felt guilty leaving him all alone, but Martha didn't allow pets in her house, so I had no choice. After he peed, I'd sit in the entryway and play with him for a couple of minutes; then he'd get a big hug before I put him back in the house. The third time I went home was at about ten o'clock. When I opened up the back door, Shaggy raced out between my legs, yelping into the night. He stopped just beyond the glow of the yard light and refused to come back to me. I chased him down and put him on his chain. This time I went all the way into the house, completely unprepared for what I was about to see.

Every kitchen cupboard door and drawer was standing wide open. On the floor below the dishtowel drawer was a little pile of towels, and another was barely clinging to the side of the drawer. There was also a dishtowel draped over the ironing board in the family room. I couldn't believe my eyes! I looked into the bathroom and saw a trail of toilet paper that had been pulled off the roll. I rolled it back on and then checked the living room, where one lamp was on the floor with its shade removed. A few tissues had even been pulled from the box on the end table and flung around the room. What was going on? I knew Shaggy couldn't have engineered this whole mess, so I guessed the spirit child had to be the main instigator.

The door to the living-room closet was wide open, revealing several items of clothing that had been pulled off the hangers and lay strewn on the floor. A few of the wire hangers were actually bent from the force of the pull. I turned around and tried the front door. It was locked. In fact, every door and window was shut and locked. I ran down into the basement and found those windows locked as well. Back on the main floor, the toy room was a disaster. I shut that door and decided against going upstairs.

Then I turned to look in our bedroom. Aha—the pièce de résistance! This door, which normally stood wide open, was shut. I turned the knob and pushed on the door. It would only budge about four inches, which was just enough for me to reach in and flip on the light switch. Through this narrow opening, I could see that the large box that had been sitting in the far corner of the room was missing. From my limited range of vision, I spied the contents of the box scattered on the floor. Something was blocking the door, so I reached in as far as I could and discovered the missing box turned upside-down and wedged between the bedroom and closet doors. Unfortunately, my fingers couldn't reach in far enough to get a grip on it. The covers had been partially pulled off the bed. Had we been robbed? In the back of my mind, I kept thinking a burglar couldn't have done this. For one thing, how would he have gotten *out* of this room? The shade was pulled down on the only window within my line of vision. I pushed against the door again, but the box wouldn't budge. Paul would have to pit his strength against it if we were going to sleep in there that night.

Since getting into my bedroom was impossible, I haphazardly straightened the living room and picked up some of the smaller messes. The entire time I was in the house, I had the most uncomfortable feeling that I was trespassing, like someone or something was watching me. It was eerie and overpowering. It finally got the better of me, and I had to get out of there. I tried to pull Shaggy back into the house, but he braced his little legs on the door frame and flatly refused. Since the evening was mild and dry, I left him outside.

I ran across our driveway, back to Martha's house. My heart was pounding in my ears. She was standing in her front door when I got there. "What took you so long?" she asked. "I was just going to come over to see what happened." She held for the door for me and I rushed passed her. With shaking hands, I grabbed my pack of cigarettes, pulled one out, and lit it. I began rattling on and on about what I had seen. I heard my disjointed sentences collide with each other and then veer off in opposite directions, making absolutely no sense at all. I don't know if I even took a breath except to inhale another lungful of smoke, which resulted in a nasty coughing fit.

"You are going to wait here till Paul comes home. I don't want you going back in there alone."

"The whole house is a mess. I have to get it picked up."

"Let him see it. Then he'll have to believe you."

I reluctantly yielded to her judgment, nodding my head as I gulped down a giant swig of Diet Rite. When my nerves calmed down, I said, "You are right, Martha. Let him see it." To my knowledge, my skeptical spouse had never seen or heard anything supernatural in our house since that awful racket the first night. If he had, he'd never told me about it, and if he hadn't, he'd have to believe me now.

At exactly 12:15 a.m., Paul pulled into the driveway. I ran out to tell him we were next door. Then I started telling him about the mess inside. He had to admit we were living with something supernatural, right? No such luck. Paul blamed Shaggy for everything. He offered no logical explanation for how our puppy—who was too short to reach the handles—had opened the kitchen drawers. As for the top cupboard doors, well, Paul didn't get to see them. I had closed them as I walked through the kitchen. In retrospect, I should have left them alone. Shag couldn't have draped the towel over the ironing board either. Even if he had ransacked our bedroom, I'd like to hear Paul's explanation of how the puppy had tipped that huge box completely over, wedged it between two doors, and then escaped through a four-inch opening while closing the door behind him. A frightened animal could have easily knocked over a lamp, but unscrewing the shade? And how did the pooch open the closet door? I supposed he could have pulled clothing off the hangers, but I seriously doubted he had. In his terror, I'm sure our little puppy added to the chaos in some way, but with the amount of carnage in the house, it couldn't all have been his doing. I'm sure Paul was as bewildered as I, but his male bravado wouldn't allow him to back down. He just blamed it all on "that damn neurotic dog."

After we straightened up the rest of the mess, we brought our sleeping children home and nothing more was said about it. I was crushed. So was Martha when I filled her in the following morning. What would it take for Paul to admit something out of the ordinary was happening? The utter defeat I suffered that night was indescribable. I decided that from now on, I'd continue to write to our friend in Omaha and tell him about the weird things happening here. Whether he really believed this ghost theory was immaterial to me; at least he was willing to listen. For the record, he said if it were his house, he'd move out as soon as possible. He would call once a month to chat, and one night he even offered a place in his home for the children and me if I wanted to leave. I thanked him with a ton of gratitude in my voice but said that was not an option.

More Shaggy-Dog Stories

Shag was held responsible for several other incidents before he finally ran away. For one, Paul always left his tennis shoes underneath the end table in the living room—side by side, with the laces draped over the side of each shoe. One Saturday morning, a shoe was gone.

He wasn't very happy about this at all. The kids and I were pressed into service to help search the house. After we had gone through the bedrooms, the toy box, the upstairs, and the basement, Paul blamed Shaggy. Exactly one week later, the shoe reappeared right next to its mate, with the laces draped the way Paul had left them. You could always count on Shag to remember the tiniest of details, and apparently our ghost child's memory wasn't half bad either. The miraculous reappearance of the shoe was lost on Paul. He just put them on and said no more about it.

Another baffling incident took place one weeknight after I had gone to bed. I was hunkered down under the covers, hoping for a night of sweet dreams, when I heard Paul come home. Suddenly, my hazy veil of repose was split in two by a barrage of cuss words, with Shaggy and God getting equal billing. I got out of bed, put on my glasses, and went to see what the fuss was about. Paul pointed to a large jelly glass that was resting upside down on the middle cushion of our couch. "Look what that damn dog did now!" There was a perfect two-inch border of chocolate milk seeping out from under the rim. When I went to bed, I had left half a glass of chocolate milk sitting on the end table instead of emptying it in the sink. According to Paul, our dog picked up the glass and carried it to the middle of the couch, then quickly turned it upside down, allowing the contents to ooze out. I couldn't even laugh at that ridiculous explanation; I was too tired. I shook my head, cleaned up the mess, and went back to bed.

By this time, Shag was full grown, but he was a medium-sized dog. His mouth wouldn't even open wide enough get around a glass that size. He would have had to walk to the middle of the couch on his back legs while carrying the large glass in his front paws. Then he'd be obliged to tip it over and clamp the rim to the cushion at lightning speed in order to keep the liquid inside. This was a trick that would have required the dexterity of a professional magician, so I would love to have seen Shag in action. Just for the heck of it, the next morning I tried to tip a half-full glass of water out on the lawn without spilling the contents. I tried three or four times, but I wasn't quick enough. The kids hadn't messed with it either. For one thing, they rarely woke up at night, and if either of them had found this tempting treat, they would have finished it. Shag might have knocked it over and lapped it up, but could he have performed that snazzy magic trick? I think not.

The Cat's Tale

Toward the end of our first summer in the house, we acquired a glossy black kitten named Pepper. He was my daughter's cat. Every morning before she went off to kindergarten, she kissed Pepper good-bye; however, on one morning she couldn't find him. He had been in the kitchen when I woke the kids, brought them downstairs, and got Krissy ready for school. I fed Pepper while the kids were eating breakfast. He was still hanging around before Kris left, because I remembered seeing him sitting by the stove and licking his whiskers.

Scott went off to play in the toy room after he finished his breakfast. When he heard his sister calling for Pepper, he came out to see what was going on. I said, "Oh, Pepper's around here somewhere. He'll turn up." My tearful daughter had to leave for the bus without kissing her kitten, and she wasn't very happy about it.

I got busy washing clothes in the basement and forgot about the whole thing until Scott started down the steps and called out, "Mama, I hear Pepper."

I quietly listened with him and heard the faint mews of the missing kitty as well. I took Scott's hand and we both hustled up the steps to find where Pepper was hiding. He wasn't in any of the rooms on the first floor. I went upstairs and looked all around. No Pepper up there either. I even put my fear on the back burner and steeled myself to check the storage area in front of that spooky cubbyhole. Nothing. I was praying the kitten hadn't somehow crawled into an air duct, because his cries sounded like they were coming from inside the furnace. Paul was asleep in our bedroom with the door shut. Even though I knew the cat couldn't be in there, I still quietly snooped around the room and under the bed. No Pepper. I was running out of places to look.

Scott squatted down on his haunches by the heat vent in the living room and kept insisting he heard Pepper inside of it. It didn't matter which heat vent we listened at, though; we could faintly hear the pathetic mews emanating from each one. I went back upstairs to check around one more time. Maybe Pepper had scampered under one of the beds and, since he was completely black, I had just missed seeing him when I'd looked under them. The kids had a few toys up in their bedroom. One of the items they had been playing with was an old metal suitcase that belonged to their dad. It was standing on its end, like a book, right next to the small heat vent up there. The suitcase was closed, but the snaps weren't locked. My intuition told me to check it out. I slowly opened the case, and out leaped a very grateful kitten.

How had Pepper gotten upstairs? For safety, that door was always kept closed after the kids came downstairs in the morning. When fully opened, it blocks the traffic flow between the kitchen and the living room, and when partially opened, there is the risk of someone running headlong into it. I can speak to that, because it happened to me once. After my unfortunate accident, no one ever forgot to close that door during the daytime. I knew Scott hadn't gone back up there to commit the mischievous deed, because he was a safety-conscious adult trapped in a three-year-old body, and since there was no handrail, he always waited for me to help him up and down those unstable steps.

While carrying the frisky kitty downstairs, I asked him to fill me in on his misadventure. I'm sure he did, but as I'm not fluent in the feline language, it will always remain a mystery. If Pepper had scampered upstairs before I shut the door earlier that morning, it was still unclear how he'd gotten inside the suitcase—unless he had help from our ghost. According to my husband, Pepper jumped inside the suitcase and then "somehow it closed." Mr. Logical! Where's the logic in that? If the suitcase had been lying flat on the floor and the top slammed down as the kitten jumped in, then it might have happened like that. But it was standing on its end like a book, for Pete's sake!

It Speaks

Another night, some months after we moved in, Paul was reading in the living room and Kristen and Scott were upstairs sound asleep. I was in bed drifting off to sleep when I heard a small child calling, "Mommy, Mommy," in my ear. I ignored it in my drowsy state, thinking it was Kris asking her daddy to bring her a glass of water, like she did almost every night when he got home from work. This was her way of connecting with a father who had worked nights since before she was born. But the little voice got louder and more insistent.

I finally opened my eyes, thinking one of the kids was standing next to the bed, but I was quite alone in the room. I couldn't stand it any longer, so I got up, walked into the living room, and asked, "Paul, why don't you bring Kris her glass of water? She's calling you."

He looked up from his book and said, "Kris hasn't called for me."

Although he sounded definite, I had to push it. "I heard her plain as day. She said, 'Mommy, Mommy.'" Remember, I was half-asleep!

He stared at me like I had two heads and asked, "Do I look like *Mommy* to you?"

I dashed upstairs to check on the kids. Both were sound asleep. I came back down and told Paul I must have been mistaken. Nevertheless, I heard, "Mommy, Mommy," till I finally stuck my fingers in my ears to keep out the plaintive little voice. At some point, I mercifully dozed off.

When morning came, I reviewed the incident from the previous night. In the clear light of day, I realized that neither of my children had ever called me "Mommy." A shiver ran down my spine. They called me "Mama" when they were small, and that changed to "Mom" when they became older. The term "Mommy" was never used by my children. Taking care of Kris and Scott was a full-time job for me; where the heck was it written that I had to raise a ghost child as well? Dr. Spock never covered this.

More Sounds in the Night

Friends of mine—those who weren't frantically checking to see if any mental hospitals had space for me—occasionally sent newspaper and magazine clippings on the subject of ghosts. They thought it might help explain what was happening around here. One afternoon, Martha brought over several newspaper articles featuring interviews with people in the Twin Cities area who were dealing with paranormal experiences. About the same time, my sister, Kathie, sent me a shipment from California of articles that she'd cut out of various magazines. A mother of two young children doesn't have much time to read during the day, so I stacked all the papers on the floor in a corner of my bedroom. To be completely truthful, my nerves were too jittery to read the articles at night, when I had some downtime, so for a long time they remained in the corner where I'd put them.

One night while trying to fall asleep, I heard what sounded like someone riffling through those clippings. I thought Pepper had gotten into the bedroom again. Since I had developed an allergy to him, he was kept out of our bedroom at night, much to his chagrin. I turned on the light and called his name but heard no sassy meow in reply. However, just to be sure, I looked under my bed, behind the dresser, and in the clothes basket. After all that, I heard him meowing on the other side of the door. I shook my head and turned off the light and tried once more to go to sleep. The mysterious rustling continued till Paul came home. He dumped his change on the dresser and went through his usual routine. He must have scared the paranormal pest away, because it was quiet the rest of the night. The next day, I quickly eyeballed a few of the articles and then burned them. It's a real shame that I was so afraid, because those articles might have been helpful to me. But a gal's gotta do what a gal's gotta do.

It Also Plays Tricks

One sneaky trick played on me by my little ghost involved my alarm clock. That particular evening, I set my clock for six a.m., as I did every school night. The alarm lever was pulled out and ready to go. After I climbed into bed, I heard Pepper nose his way in through the bedroom door, which I had accidentally left ajar. He jumped up on the dresser and began poking his nose into this and that, the stinker! I had enough noises in my life over which I had no control, but these, I did. I picked up the cat and deposited him back in the hall, closed the door tightly, and then went back to bed. It was one of the few nights I was permitted to fall asleep without hearing the sad little voice in my ear.

Next morning when the alarm rang, I jumped up, dashed into the bathroom, splashed cold water on my face, and then stumbled into the kitchen to start my coffee. I decided to drive Kris to school if it was storming when she left, because it looked really dark outside. I opened the back door to get the paper, but it hadn't come yet. Shoot! I loved to read the paper and have a cup of coffee before getting the kids up. The coffeepot was cheerfully perking away on the stove when I happened to glance at the clock in the family room. It was only three o'clock. What?! I took a flashlight and went back into my bedroom to check my clock. The family room clock was correct. Upon closer inspection, I found that the alarm hand had been moved back from six a.m. to three a.m. The night before, I thought I'd heard someone fooling with the clock when Pepper was on the dresser, but I had dismissed it as "curious kitten" noises. Well, Pepper couldn't have done this. I was furious that my ghost child would pull such a mean prank on a frazzled, worn-out mother. I turned the coffee off, reset the alarm, and crawled back into bed, hoping to resume the dream that had been interrupted by the ghost child's prank.

Paul and I moved our bedroom furniture upstairs at the end of September. This room would be too cold for the kids in the wintertime, because the heat vent is so small. They often kicked off their covers, so it only made sense that they should sleep in the warmer rooms. We'd planned on eventually giving the kids each their own rooms; it was just happening sooner rather than later. Kristen chose our room, and the toy room was claimed by Scott. The change in location didn't keep me from hearing that hollow-sounding voice crying, "Mommy" in my ear, however. That eerie disturbance continued for several years. On some nights, the voice was crystal clear, but on other nights, it sounded foggy, for lack of a better description. I can't count how many nights I raced out of bed and down those creaky steps, thinking one of the kids had thrown up. The voice didn't sound like it belonged to either of my children, but I never dared take the chance by ignoring it.

One January night early the next year, I heard another voice. This time, the small voice was sobbing desperately while I was hanging laundry in the basement. This was a chore I didn't appreciate for a couple of reasons: the basement had never felt welcoming to me, and I dearly wanted an automatic dryer. The hair on the back of my neck stood straight up as I listened to the disembodied voice for several seconds. The voice sounded hollow, distant, and mournful.

Maturity is highly overrated. I started up the stairs so fast that I slipped, and both my knees smashed against the edge of the second step. I was dazed for a time by the numbing, excruciating pain, and then I limped up the rest of the steps and looked in on the kids. They were both fast asleep.

The basket of wet laundry was left to its own devices. No way was I going back downstairs—not until morning. As I sat in the living room and rubbed my injured knees, I tried to summon all the logic I could muster to find an explanation. The couple in the next house over had just brought home a new baby, but I wouldn't be able to hear that baby crying in the dead of winter with both houses closed up. The crying didn't sound like an infant's anyway. Was my ghost child crying?

After that experience, I couldn't go into the basement at night for a long time. I was one terrified woman. I wondered if Agnes Miller had ever heard this child crying in the basement. That would certainly explain why her husband did the laundry. I doubted I'd be that lucky. Paul was a good man: he had a steady job and he didn't drink, gamble, or fool around. However, since he didn't buy the ghost theory, I couldn't see him offering to do the laundry for me.

During our first winter, amid the nightly light-dimming ritual, the noises in the cubbyhole, and the "Mommy" cries, one more ingredient was added to the psychic soup: loud, crashing noises. One night, as Paul and I were drifting off to sleep, there was a thunderous crash downstairs. I know he heard it, because he jumped, so I anxiously whispered, "What was that?"

"What was what?"

"That loud crash!"

"I didn't hear any crash."

That led to more inane babbling. He refused to go downstairs and look, and I refused to go downstairs and look. Our little kids were asleep on the level where the noise had originated, yet neither of us would venture down those steps to see if they were all right.

I finally said, "Sounds like the ironing board fell over in the family room."

He sleepily replied, "The ironing board couldn't fall over by itself. Go to sleep."

My maternal instincts didn't register any danger around the kids, so I said a special prayer asking the angels to watch over Kris and Scott till morning. Paul's remark upset me, but I was so worn out from weeks of trying to get my reluctant husband to buy into my ghost theory that I just rolled over and went to sleep.

When I woke up the following morning, the first thing I did was check the ironing board in the family room. It was right where I had left it, and nothing else was out of place either. It was enough to push me over the edge. Of course, Paul felt compelled to say, "See? I told you." The kids hadn't heard a loud crash either, but then small children usually sleep much more soundly than their adult counterparts—after all, they have very little to worry about. Life in this house made me feel like I was playing the Ingrid Bergman role in that disturbing old film *Gaslight* and, for reasons known only to him, Paul was trying to drive me insane. By this time, I was up to three packs of cigarettes a day, and I have no idea how many cups of black coffee.

A Noise from the Basement

Another evening while Paul was at work, I heard glass breaking in the basement. The commotion was so loud that it couldn't be ignored. Our basement was pretty empty still, except for a few unpacked boxes and the old piano the Millers had left behind. I nervously walked down the steps and found the laundry room door locked, so no one was hiding in there. Just the same, I had a bad feeling about it. I forced myself to go in and check it out.

There were no glass shards anywhere. Nothing was out of place. I even managed to scrape up enough nerve to walk back to Paul's workroom, but I found nothing out of place. If anything or anyone had been down there, the deafening sound of my throbbing heart would have sent the perpetrator flying up the steps and out the back door.

While writing this account decades later, I realize how stupid it was to go into the basement when I was home alone. Someone could have smashed a basement window to get in. But blaming the noises on a break-in was second nature to me, because it was logical. Paul couldn't dispute something like that.

More Basement Noises

One summer night a year or two later, I drifted off to sleep in the living room without first locking the back door. The distinct sound of someone rummaging around in the basement shattered my dreamy state of repose. After carefully listening for a second or two, I freaked out. I didn't know Earl's work schedule, but in a panic I ran to the kitchen and called Martha. As luck would have it, Earl was home that night. I could still hear the ruckus while I was on the phone, because I was only a couple of feet from the basement door. I asked if

Earl could come over and check out the noises while I stayed on the phone. He appeared at my back door seconds later. With a baseball bat in hand, he fearlessly ran down the steps.

I could hear him running around down there, into the laundry room and under the steps. He searched every possible area, then came back up five minutes later saying there was no one down there. Earl tried very hard to convince me I'd been dreaming, but I knew that wasn't the case. Those noises had woken me up in the first place. I thanked him for checking out the basement for me anyway. As Earl walked out the back door, he said to call him again if I needed him. Although I'd never felt quite comfortable around that man, I was grateful that he was home to help me out. Martha and I hung up after I thanked her for listening to my tale of woe.

Scott's Little Friend

My adult son once told me, in a disgusted voice, that he doesn't believe in ghosts. Like father, like son! But back when he was three years old, he played with an imaginary friend in the basement, next to the furnace. He actually conversed with this friend out loud. Since Scott jabbered incessantly from the day he learned to talk, I rarely paid attention to the conversations between him and his make-believe friend. That changed one night after I called him up the steps for supper. I heard him say, "I'll be back after I eat, Furnace Boy." I smiled at the name. When I was his age, I played with a family in the attic of the house that my parents rented. Their names were Mrs. Witch, Richard Witch (a teenager), and Baby Witch, so you can see I dared not laugh at the name he chose for his friend. I asked him about Furnace Boy.

"He's a little boy who lives by the furnace."

"What do you boys do down there?"

"We play with my cars and talk."

After supper, I asked Scott to draw a picture of Furnace Boy for me. He took a crayon and drew a figure with some odd-looking scribbling across its face.

"Hmm, I see the hair and the eyes and mouth, but what's this?" I pointed to the crooked lines on the drawing's face.

"Those are his glasses, Mama."

Neither of my children wore glasses at that time, and since none of their playmates wore them either, I was surprised to see Scott draw eyeglasses on the face of a child. That night, while waiting for the infamous light-dimming ritual, I called Martha and asked her to describe Johnny to me. Although I had seen a picture of him the day I looked at the house, I couldn't recall his appearance. Martha said, "He was blond, and thin. He also had asthma and spoke with a lisp." She paused for a second to think. "Let's see . . . oh yeah, he wore glasses."

My neck started tingling. When I told her about Scott's curious drawing, she uttered a loud gasp. Her response gave me full-blown heebie-jeebies. I expected her to say something like, "Oh, that's weird," but not gasp like that. As the years went by, Scott played with Furnace Boy less and less. Now it is just a funny reminder of when he was little. A couple of questions have always festered in my brain: Was Furnace Boy an imaginary friend, or did Scott play with our ghost child down there? If Scott had made this kid up, why did his imaginary friend wear glasses?

After that episode, I revisited my childhood interaction with the "Witch family" in 1944. Were they the psychic residue of a small family who had languished on this side of the veil after some terrible fate? Did they die in the attic of our rental house? They must have introduced themselves, because I couldn't have made up that strange name. I first learned of Halloween when I started school in 1947. Until then, I'd had no frame of reference for the word *witch*. Our family was not acquainted with anyone named Richard at that time either. Nor did I have any idea what a teenager was. My overprotective mother, who had lost her oldest child to a vicious murder a year earlier, had never allowed me to play outside without her, so I didn't even know the names of our neighbors.

I remembered that Mrs. Witch wore a small hat with a veil and a dark-colored cloth coat similar to the one worn by my mother.

Baby Witch was wrapped up in blankets, and Richard, the teenager, wore pants that ended at his knees. They sat quite closely together against one of the attic walls toward the front of the house. Now that I'm an adult, those attic visits hold a real fascination for me. The words *witch* and *teenager* reinforce the belief that this ghostly family communicated with me in some fashion.

I spent nearly every morning up in our attic visiting with the Witch family. When lunchtime came, my mother climbed halfway up the steps and called me down to eat. After lunch, I even brought the family food, when I could sneak it out of the kitchen. World War II was raging on two fronts, and like the rest of America, we had to make ends meet with ration coupons. There wasn't a lot of extra food for our family—and certainly none for an *imaginary* family—so my desire to share didn't make my mother happy. I also found out years later that my mom thought I was completely nuts when I was small. Ah, yes—misunderstood even then!

In recent years, a theory has popped up in the field of child psychology. After years of testing and interviews, the originator of the theory believes small children can see and speak to spirits up until the age of six or thereabouts. The special aptitude seems to disappear when young children start school, because by that time parents and other adults in the children's lives have convinced them that spirits are make-believe. In order to appease their elders, children quit "imagining" the things they see and hear, and within a short time, they forget they ever had that ability. It's relatively rare for children to continue this behavior after the ages of six or seven. That's why an extremely high percentage of the population brands those who still possess that ability as total nutcases.

If Scott's friend was imaginary, the coincidence of this make-believe playmate by the furnace would be nothing short of amazing, since that's where I heard the child crying the night I hurt my knees. I've never told Scott that Furnace Boy was a figment of his imagination. Maybe my son doesn't remember playing with his invisible friend; if he does, he's too embarrassed to admit it now that he's an adult.

Kristen's Bright Visitor

Kristen has been seeing things since she was two years old, so she's no stranger to paranormal phenomena. When she was two, she had an unusual experience in one of the many apartments we had called home prior to purchasing this house. Seven thirty was always a welcome time of night for me then, because that was the kids' bedtime. Some nights were easy; however, one particular evening Kris was giving me fits because she didn't want to go to bed yet. That night, after using all the child psychology I knew, I ended up chasing her around the apartment. While holding her baby brother in one arm, I managed to get a hold of her pajama top with my free hand and then tried to herd her into the bedroom. She zigged when I zagged, and then she pulled free. Before I could grab her again, she gave me the slip and ran straight through the swinging door that separated the dining room and kitchen. It sounded like she was talking up a storm to someone in there, but I couldn't make out what she was saying. The light was off in the kitchen, so I quickly put Scott in the crib and ran to see what was going on. Instead of finding a tearful child babbling to herself, she was all smiles when I turned on the light. I asked her if she was afraid of being in the dark all alone. She replied, "No, Mama, there was a bright lady talking to me."

I'll play along, I thought. "A bright lady, huh? What did she look like?"

"She was all white and shiny."

The back door was locked, so I knew no earthly individual had entered our apartment from outside. I had to pursue this further.

"What did she say, honey?"

"She said I could get the yo-yo I want." This yo-yo was advertised on *Lunch with Casey,* a favorite children's television show, and every preschool child in the viewing area of Channel 11 had lunch with Casey during the week. Krissy had had her eye on that yo-yo for weeks. It was not the usual yo-yo shape; this one was sort of a solid plastic ball, and we knew she couldn't handle it. Krissy didn't share our opinion, however. She begged for that yo-yo every time she saw it. At the age of two, she had the vocabulary of a second-grader, but her dexterity and judgment was still that of a two-year-old. Paul and I knew she'd end up injuring either herself or someone else, so we said no each time the question came up. But wasn't it clever of her to tie in the object of her desire with the bright lady? I gave her points for that.

We spoke no more about it until a week later. When I pulled out the living-room couch to vacuum behind it, I found myself staring at that orange yo-yo. It was not in its packaging either; it looked as if it were waiting for someone to pick it up and play with it. I asked Krissy where she got it. She proudly told me that the bright lady had given it to her. I was taken aback by her statement. I wondered if the bright lady also told Krissy to hide it from her parents. We had a bona fide mystery on our hands, because our family had had no visitors that entire week, and neither Paul nor I had bought it for her. I checked with the other parents in our building, and it didn't belong to their children either. Kris was never allowed outside alone, because the yard around that building was not fenced. Since logic cannot refute her story, I have to believe that the bright lady made good on her promise. Despite our daughter's ingenious method of obtaining this yo-yo, we ended up disposing of it before someone got hurt.

Scott's Sister Gets Another Turn

Kris had a visual encounter with our ghost child one night shortly after we moved in. She saw a little boy standing in the upstairs bedroom, staring at her when she woke up during the night. That shivered my timbers, so I danced around that one very carefully. I was a bundle of nerves, and I dared not let on to my children that I was frightened.

"Do you think you were dreaming, Krissy?"

"No, Mama. I saw him."

"What was he doing?"

"He was standing over by my dresser, just looking at me."

"I bet you were scared."

"Yes, I was."

"You let me know if you see him again." I never heard another word about it till she was an adult.

So, many years later, while chatting with Kristen on the phone, I was giving her the lowdown on some recent happenings at the house and wondered out loud if my ghost was back. She said, "Well, I'll never forget the night I saw him." I asked her what he looked like, just to see if it matched the description she had given me when she was five. She said, "All I remember is it looked horrible." Even though I asked her a couple of times to elaborate, that's all I could get out of her. Kris is a half-and-half combo of her father and me. She is open to ghosts, odd occurrences, and all things paranormal, but she tempers the supernatural with Paul's pragmatic, no-nonsense personality. She also tends to keep things locked inside, like Paul, which is very difficult for an "open book" like me to understand.

Kristen has since told her children that the ghost had brown hair, which puzzled me, because of Martha's description of Johnny as blond. But my daughter was only five years old when she saw the ghost child, and it was at night, so maybe she got it wrong.

Since Kris has paranormal occurrences at her current home, she believes in talking openly about them with her children. That's a bold step. I can see both good and bad in sharing that kind of information. While it's prudent to acknowledge what a child sees and hears, too much paranormal talk could result in very nervous children. I never told the kids what I was going through in this house, because I didn't want to scare them. Maybe confiding in them all those years ago would have given me the family support I dearly craved. But what if it had backfired? I didn't need any additional problems in those days.

Taps and Footsteps

When we moved upstairs, we placed our bed against the wall that separated the room from the scary cubbyhole. This arrangement has never made me happy, but it's about the only place the bed fits in that long, narrow room. Over the years, very light tapping noises have occurred above my side of the headboard. They seem to run back and forth for hours on end, but only on my side of the bed. Some nights they stop and tap directly above my head. Occasionally I'd be lulled into a false sense of security when they took a night or a week or a month off. Then the aggravating noises would burst back on the scene even stronger than before, which would scare the living daylights out of me.

One night I'd had enough, so I loudly yelled, "Knock it off!" And the noises stopped. Whoa! It seems I had a choice in whether I had to be serenaded by my little spirit. It hadn't even occurred to me that yelling at a ghost child might have the same effect as telling a human child to knock it off. This almost leveled the playing field, and I wished I would have known it years before.

The footsteps started up sometime back in 1968. I've heard very few in recent years. The very first night I heard them, I had gone to bed before eleven. I finished saying my prayers and was lying there with my eyes closed, hoping to go to sleep before the taps started dancing across the wall. Although I hadn't heard the back door open, I thought Paul had come home early when the footsteps started up the stairs. The quiet footfalls turned on the small landing and methodically continued up the two remaining steps. I waited for Paul to stop at the dresser and dump his keys and coins from his pockets and go back downstairs for a snack. Instead, the footsteps continued creaking across the hardwood floor, toward the bed. When they reached my side of the bed, they stopped. This was not Paul's normal routine. I wondered if something was wrong.

When I opened my eyes, my husband wasn't standing there. I sat up and looked over at his side of the bed, then suddenly felt cold when I realized there was no one in my bedroom but me. The ghost child had obviously come upstairs to visit. I could barely hear a thing over the pounding of my heart. I dived under the covers and stayed awake till Paul got home . . . till the footsteps coming up the stairs were really his.

After that night, this phenomenon occurred up to three times a week. I spent my nights shaking in my bed, waiting for the taps and the footsteps. The light-dimming ritual, which had tormented me for what seemed like a lifetime, had given way to these ghostly noises. If I'd had my druthers, I'd have opted for the dimming lights. Sometimes the footsteps were so loud I thought one of my kids had come upstairs; at other times, the steps sounded foggy, as though trapped in another dimension. How I gathered up enough courage to peer out from under the covers during those episodes, I'll never know. The mantle of motherhood weighed heavily on my shoulders, and although that responsibility was a burden at times like this, it also provided me the courage to function. If truth be told, snuggled deep inside that mantle was just a little girl who wanted to dive under the comforter and hide.

Occasionally, I heard those creepy footsteps behind me as I climbed the steps to bed. On those nights, I'd take a page out of my childhood playbook and quickly jump into my bed from a couple of feet away. Don't laugh. After all, with invisible footsteps on the stairs, God only knows what might have been lurking under the bed! Thankfully, the footsteps stop at the top of the stairs now. They haven't come up all the way back to my bed for a long time—knock on wood.

I Have a "Sighting"

I was afraid I'd see a ghost in this house ever since we moved in, and when I finally did, I didn't know what it was. Is that irony or what? The incident happened late one evening in 1969. I had made myself a snack and was on my way back to the living room to finish watching a movie. Out of habit, I glanced toward my kids' bedrooms. Their doors were open slightly, which cast a glow into the hallway. In the diffused light, I saw a figure about three feet tall, shaped like a classic cartoon ghost. It was grayish white and misty-looking. The figure didn't move. It only took me a couple of seconds to step from the kitchen into the hall, glance at this figure, and continue into the living room.

As soon as I was out of range, my heart skipped a beat. *What was that?* I instantly stepped backward into the hall to take another look at it, but it was gone. I had never seen it before and haven't seen it since.

If that figure was a trick of the light, as suggested by many skeptics, it wouldn't have vanished in a split second. In the years when our kids were small, they each had night-lights and slept with their doors ajar. If their night-lights had been responsible for producing the figure, it would have been visible all night and every night, now wouldn't it? I find it absurd that other people expect me to accept their explanation without giving mine any consideration.

Still Stuck in the Sixties

One night after taking my shower, I temporarily deposited my dirty clothes in the hallway instead of pitching them into the basement where they belonged. I plopped down on the couch to watch Johnny Carson—the other Johnny in my life back then. While laughing at a particularly funny monologue, something yellow caught my eye. It quickly glided into the bathroom. In the back of my mind, I thought Krissy had gotten up to go potty.

We were smack dab in the middle of Krissy's yellow period. Just about everything she owned was yellow, and on this particular night she was wearing one of her numerous nightgowns of that color. My little daughter had a habit of falling asleep on the toilet when she woke up in the middle of the night, so I listened for her familiar tinkle. Upon hearing nothing, I smiled, thinking, "She's fallen asleep in there again." I got up and walked into the bathroom to take her back to bed, but there was no sleeping child sitting on the toilet. Instead of my daughter, I found *my* yellow underpants in the middle of the bathroom floor. Is nothing sacred?

Around that same time of year, while curled up on the couch watching *The Tonight Show*, I caught another glimpse of something moving—this time it was over by the living-room heat vent. I found myself completely mesmerized as a pair of Barbie dresses slowly levitated a couple feet off the floor. I blinked—still there. Then, side by side, they deliberately turned over and gradually floated back down to the floor. I was fascinated. I crept on my hands and knees over to where they had landed. Had I imagined this? Nope! They had been facing front-side up earlier that evening, when I'd asked my daughter to put them away. Now those large snaps, which fastened the dresses in the back, were staring up at me. Apparently, our curious ghost child had picked them up, turned them over, and then put them back where he'd found them.

Even though I'd been reading countless books on hauntings and had the ability to be completely objective about other people's ghosts, mine scared the heck out of me. Since these unusual things were happening at random, he was probably hanging around me all the time. How often did he sit by me on the couch at night? Did he watch Paul and me make love? Was my bathroom time private, or was he sitting on the edge of the tub when I was on the throne or taking a shower? It was completely unnerving.

When I relayed these two incidents to Martha, my voice was trembling. She said, "You've got to get some help with this. I am more than happy to listen to the creepy stuff that goes on in your house, but you need more than a shoulder to cry on." I give her credit. At least she didn't call for the men in the white coats . . .

. . . But She Did Call in the Cavalry

I became more of a basket case while my scary days and nights dissolved into one another. Martha was truly worried about me. Heck, *I* was worried about me as well, but I had no idea how to make this activity stop. My neighbor heard about everything that went on around here, bless her heart. It always seemed like my personal panic subsided after I told her about each incident. But as time went by, the noises originating in the cubbyhole above the kitchen kept building in intensity. I heard them day and night. I realized that dumping my experiences on Martha's doorstep wasn't helping as much as it had at first. Now what would I do? I was right on the edge of a breakdown and couldn't stand it any longer.

One afternoon, as soon as Paul left for work, I called a woman I thought I knew fairly well. I told her I believed there was a ghost in my house. Why I said that, I'll never know. I had been rebuffed by so many friends already that maybe she was the only one left in my address book who hadn't slammed the receiver down on my ear. In a curt manner, she asked, "What are you talking about?"

Just as she uttered those words, several items simultaneously dropped on the cubbyhole floor above me, as if to corroborate my statement. I pleaded with her, "Can't you hear that? Can't you hear how loud those noises are?" My voice was trembling, and I was on the verge of tears.

At that point, she hollered into the phone, "Get help!" and slammed down the receiver. I never called her again. Who knows? If I were in her place, I might have done the same thing, although I've always been pretty open-minded. I doubt it's in my makeup to abandon a friend in that manner—even if, in my mind, she had become a raving lunatic.

Martha was afraid I'd have a nervous breakdown if something wasn't done soon. One evening, she casually mentioned Joan, a neighbor who lived directly behind me. Joan was a self-professed expert in all things spiritual; perhaps she could help me. Even though I was desperate, I was hesitant to involve more neighbors. Martha translated that wimpy excuse as a cry for help. She took the bull by the horns and arranged for Joan to come over the next day to figure out a plan to get rid of my ghost. So the die was cast.

Although I was terrified, the thought of waiting for my neighbors to come over to discuss a topic like that really embarrassed me. The following day, Paul left for work at three o'clock. Joan and Martha were at my back door two minutes later. It was too late to back out now.

Neither woman had been in my house since we'd moved in. Martha looked down at the step in the entryway leading into the kitchen and said, "Gee, they never fixed the tile that Johnny tried to pull off." My radar switched on: *Beep! Beep! Beep!* I asked her what she was talking about. She pointed to a half-tile with a jagged edge on the top riser. I saw that broken tile every time I mopped the steps, but until this moment, I hadn't paid any attention to it. I asked Martha to scratch that tile for me. She gave me a quizzical look and replied, "Okay," then bent down and scratched it.

"That's the noise I heard after we moved in. Remember the night I kicked the door shut? That was the same night I heard the sniffling on the steps, and there was no one there."

Martha said, "He is still messing around with it, huh?"

Apparently, she had shared that story with Joan, who volunteered, "Johnny had asthma and allergies. It must have been him you heard coming down the steps that night."

It was a ninety-degree afternoon, but I started shivering, wondering if it was possible for perspiration to freeze.

We nervously chatted at the table while sipping soft drinks and drawing up a plan of action. Our daughters played together quite often, but I didn't know Joan except to say hello over the back fence. What a unique way to meet your neighbors! Although the situation was awkward, we all knew we had a job to do. Joan was a woman of petite stature. She said she'd crawl into the cubbyhole to see if there were any items of Johnny's lying around up there.

"Just don't pass out. It's like an oven upstairs," I warned.

Joan downed her cold drink and then armed herself with a flashlight and some prayers. She boldly started upstairs, with Martha timidly following behind. I truly appreciated the role Martha was taking, because I knew how frightened she was about coming over here. My part in this drama was to stay in the kitchen to identify whatever Joan dropped on the floor, assuming she found something to drop. Just then, I heard her crawling around on the small floor above me. I had only seen that floor once—the day I first looked at the house. That awful cubbyhole door swung open whenever I walked by it, but I never looked in when I slammed it shut. I was afraid of what I might see. Joan's movements were much louder than the noises I usually heard up there. From time to time, I held my breath till my lungs hurt, because I wanted to be totally silent so as not to miss anything. It seemed like hours passed; then suddenly I heard that familiar sound of small articles falling on the floor. My stomach flip-

The Creepy Cubbyhole's Secret

Finally, the hostile feelings and mystifying noises coming from the cubbyhole above the stairway are solved when a neighbor explores its depths.

flopped; my heart skipped a beat. I ran to the steps and called out, "That's it! That's what I hear. What did you just do?"

Joan's voice was very faint, so Martha relayed the message from her position halfway up the steps. "She found some crayons . . . ," Martha said, ". . . a tiny metal car . . . a couple of jacks, a marble, and . . . the temple from a pair of eyeglasses. Then she dropped them on the floor."

My blood froze right then and there. A temple from his eyeglasses, oh my Lord!

The cubbyhole was an inferno for Joan, but being a woman of strong determination, she hunted around till she found an explanation for the noises that were driving me crazy. When my neighbors came back down the steps, Joan was triumphantly holding up the items she'd found. Martha remarked, "They must have fallen out of the boxes, because the Millers moved out of here awfully fast."

"Fallen out of the boxes, my ass," retorted Joan. "I found these items hidden underneath the insulation, out by the eaves. They weren't just sitting there in plain sight. That's what took me so darned long." She took a deep breath. "God, it's hot up there!" She wiped her dripping forehead with the back of her wrist and heaved a great sigh. In the back of my mind, I wondered what had inspired her to check under the insulation out by the eaves.

For a moment, we stared at each other in complete amazement. Johnny's family had abandoned him, so he was forced to amuse himself with possessions he'd hidden before they left. I know it sounds completely off the wall, but rational thinking hasn't produced anything better than our theory. Here's the kicker: *he put his toys away when he was done playing.* Otherwise, they would have been in plain sight when Joan opened the cubbyhole door. It gave the three of us a strange feeling to picture him carefully hiding each article until it was time to bring them out again.

Joan said, "God, I need a cigarette!" Martha and I nodded in agreement. I took three more sodas out of the fridge, and we parked our bodies around the table once again. We nervously lit up, laughing about "three on a match," and then sat in silence for several minutes. Once Joan had recuperated from her stifling ordeal, she spoke. "Want to hear something really strange?"

Martha and I nodded in unison like a couple of little children at story time.

"There weren't any cobwebs in that cubbyhole," she said. "It's clean as a whistle up there. Now why would a space that's had no human activity in it for several months have no cobwebs? I thought I'd be picking that stuff off me the whole time I was up there." Her question went unanswered as we three sat in silence, knowing full well the answer.

For those who think we are completely mad, consider this: why would the Miller family take the time to hide their dead child's toys under the insulation in the eaves of a house they were leaving—assuming they were the ones who hid them? Martha said they had left in a heck of a hurry, so it would have made more sense to either toss them into the boxes being pulled out of the cubbyhole or leave them where they fell. Surely the Millers wouldn't crawl around hiding toys up there, even if they were a bit eccentric. So the popular

theory among the three of us was this: Johnny hid some of his favorite belongings before his family moved. This explanation seemed to
fit the situation. But here's a more bizarre theory: the ghost child's
siblings hid his toys so he would have something to play with after
they left. Either way, we'll never know for sure.

After we recovered from our extraordinary adventure, Joan handed
me the fruits of her labor. "Here, take these out and burn them right
away!" It felt odd to hold Johnny's belongings. I rolled them around
in the palm of my hand, thinking how badly these items had frightened me. After all, they were ordinary little toys that belonged to an
ordinary little boy—a boy who just happened to be dead.

I wrapped them up in newspaper, and then the three of us walked
out to my burn barrel. I struck a farmer's match and watched as the
newspaper edge caught fire, then tossed in the bundle. "Should I
say a prayer or something?" I asked.

Neither woman answered. We quietly stood there watching the
flames envelop the newspaper. Then Joan broke the silence with these
reassuring words: "You shouldn't hear those noises any longer."

She also suggested that I burn the unsightly brown living-room
curtains that I had replaced but hadn't tossed out yet. "You'll have
to get rid of everything that was in this house when he was alive.
It's holding him here. He shouldn't be as likely to hang around if all
the familiar items from his past are gone."

Joan's words made sense. Heck, I was so desperate, I would have
swung a dead cat around my head thirteen times at the stroke of
midnight while standing stark naked under a full moon and reciting
"The Star-Spangled Banner" in French, if that would have done the
trick! That afternoon, we burned everything else that had belonged
to the Miller family that was still lying around. After the Big Burn,
things quieted down—but only for a while, because he started playing with other objects.

Items Start Disappearing

One early November evening in 1968, our family planned to visit some friends whom we'd met in our apartment building in Fridley. The kids and I had formed a close friendship with Cindy Johnson and her family, so when they moved, she gave me their new phone number and address. I'd memorized the phone number and written their address in my book. Our first visit to the Johnson home found Paul grumbling about having to go out on a cold Saturday night; he would have rather stayed home. The kids were in high gear, because they loved to go visiting, and I was really excited about seeing Cindy's new home.

When we were finally settled in the car, my perturbed husband asked, "Well, what's the address?"

Up until that moment, it hadn't dawned on me that I had no idea. I said, "I'm not sure. Let me go in and check it real quick." This was met with a loud sigh of exasperation. My husband was not exactly a social animal in those days.

After fumbling with my key in the back door, I quickly ran into the family room to grab the address book. It wasn't there! I cussed and ran into each of the kids' rooms, looking under the beds and rifling through the toy boxes. I frantically ran into the living room. *Honk, honk!* I was under the gun and running out of time, so after a quick look around the living room, I gave Cindy a call and got the address over the phone.

The next morning, I asked the kids if they had seen Mama's address book. It was bright red, and I could understand why it would be a tempting prize for a child. Neither Krissy nor Scott had seen it, though. The three of us searched every possible hiding place in the house but could not find the missing book. I finally ended up buying another. Fortunately, I have a talent for remembering phone numbers, but this bizarre disappearance meant I'd have to gather all those addresses again. What an inconvenience, I thought, especially with Christmas just around the corner.

Two weeks later, while watching *The Tonight Show*, I was craving a Diet Rite, so I bopped into the kitchen and grabbed a bottle out of the fridge. I opened it, tossed the bottle cap in the trash, and then turned to walk back into the living room. Whoa! On the white countertop was my red address book. I picked it up and muttered under my breath, "Thank you. It's about time." I put the book by the phone next to its replacement. I didn't tell Paul, because he would only have blamed the children, who had been asleep that evening since eight o'clock.

3: Settling In during the Seventies

I'm Home Alone . . . Well, Almost

We eventually had to give Pepper away because of my severe allergies, and Shag, the world's most neurotic dog, had somehow gotten away from us over a year before and disappeared. By the time Scott started kindergarten in 1970, I was all alone in the house after the kids left for school. Paul was always asleep upstairs till one p.m., but that didn't count.

My morning chores consisted of making the kids' beds, picking up their toys, and straightening up their rooms. From there, I moved into the living room. I vacuumed, dusted, put back whatever magazines were lying around, and picked up the newspaper that Paul had read the night before when he'd gotten home from work. Then I went to the bathroom and picked up towels, put the toothbrushes back, and straightened up after the morning rush. After the bathroom was picked up, I went into the kitchen to do up the breakfast dishes. My morning routine took a little over an hour.

If I had laundry—and with two little kids, who doesn't—I'd go down in the basement to start that job. We had an old-fashioned wringer washer and no dryer, so when I washed clothes, it was more of a time commitment than it was for the lucky women who had automatic appliances. Except in the winter or on rainy days, I hung my clothes outside. The outdoor air and sunshine made them smell fabulous, but I would have gladly exchanged that fresh, clean scent for the convenience of a dryer any day. The ironing board had been moved into the basement, a move I've often regretted. I've had many creepy experiences while ironing down there, which often felt like being watched by invisible eyes. Nothing is more uncomfortable than feeling like someone is standing at your elbow, silently watching the iron move back and forth. I never bothered to tell Paul why I only iron when a live person is within shouting distance, because he just doesn't get it.

With the ironing board in the basement, we needed to furnish the family room. Paul and I chose some inexpensive furniture and carpeting and gave the walls a new coat of paint. The room looked cozy enough; however, it always felt very cold. Paul explained that the floor was cold because there was no basement under this room. I thought it was because of the ghost. Regardless of why it was cold, we had to augment the furnace heat with an electric fireplace. We didn't use this room very often, but when we did, it would be comfortable now.

On this particular morning, while stuffing a load of clothes into that old wringer washer, I decided to face the inevitable and do a little ironing. I had to: my family was running out of things to wear. Suddenly, from the bedroom above me came the sound of faint, creaking footsteps. I had heard footsteps in the upstairs bedroom, but never on the main floor. My neck began tingling. I calmed my fear by saying, "Paul must have come downstairs to use the bathroom." I waited to hear the toilet flush, but it never did. As soon as I finished the jeans on the ironing board, I quickly gathered up the fruits of my labor and dashed up the basement steps, two at a time.

I knew Paul could not have gone back up to bed, because in this house you can hear every footstep in every room, human or not. I looked in the bathroom. It was empty. Then I opened the upstairs door and heard him snoring, loud and clear. I peeked into Scott's room and didn't notice anything out of place at first glance. Next, I checked Kris's room. It was spotless, just as I'd left it. Then I stuck my head in the living room.

Aha! There, in the swivel rocker, sat Scott's pride and joy—his Lego version of the Starship Enterprise, along with two small Klingon vessels. Scott was a devoted Trekkie, so he combined his love of Legos and his favorite television show and built these models. I had just put these same toys on his play table not more than an hour before. No human child had wandered into the house since then without my knowledge, but to satisfy my curiosity, I checked the front door anyway. Just as I thought, it was locked. As I picked up the toys to put them back in Scott's room, I yelled into the empty living room, "Damn you! Quit doing this to me. Just stop it!"

But He Kept Pushing My Buttons

A few days later, I was sitting at my desk in the family room and telling our good friend in Omaha about the Lego episode. During a lull in my typing, I heard those same faint footsteps again. What a coincidence: here I was bringing my friend up to speed on the most recent incident while another was taking place. This time I knew my husband hadn't come downstairs, because I could see the door. Besides that, the footsteps were too muffled to be an adult's. As I sat at my typewriter and strained to hear more footsteps, I heard the rustling of paper coming from the living room. I quietly tiptoed into the room, hoping to catch whatever was making the sounds. Lying in the middle of the couch was a *Life* magazine with a single page standing straight up in mid-air! My mouth dropped open as I watched the page lazily turn over as if someone was thoughtfully looking at it. I had just put that magazine on the bottom shelf of the TV stand when I'd straightened up the room less than an hour before. I reacted the only way I knew how: I pleaded at the top of my lungs. "Please stop doing this. Why don't you just leave me alone?" Then I got angry. I stomped my foot and hollered, "Just get the hell out of here!" Once more, my words were swallowed up into thin air.

My behavior may have been peculiar, but I felt like a crazy woman anyway, so why not act like one? It's a good thing my skeptical friends weren't around to witness my outrageous performance. They already thought I was certifiable. They might have been right, because here I was yelling at an invisible ghost child like a true lunatic. The tension was getting to me, and I couldn't help myself at that point. Maybe I subconsciously wanted Paul to hear me and come downstairs to ask what was wrong. No such luck; he sleeps like the dead. (Now there's an unfortunate choice of words!) If he heard my frustrated cry for help, he ignored it. So I returned to the letter I was writing and added one more incident to the list.

A Rough Patch for Kristen

Kris's godmother, Jeri, died tragically in an auto accident in August 1970. She was my husband's only sister, and her death sent shockwaves throughout his entire family. Krissy and Jeri had had a special bond, and I wondered how Jeri's death would affect my little daughter.

A few weeks later, the school year began, along with Krissy's odd behavior. One Monday morning, she woke up in tears. When I came downstairs, she was sitting on the edge of her bed, sobbing her little heart out. Since Jeri's accident was all too fresh in everyone's mind, I figured Kris was grieving for her aunt. It had to be either that or something was bothering her in school. When I asked her what was wrong, she cried all the harder, so I dropped it. By the time she left to catch the school bus, she had forgotten about whatever had upset her. Or so I thought.

The same thing happened on Tuesday morning as well. My daughter wouldn't or couldn't tell me the reason she was sobbing so hard.

On Wednesday, it happened again; however, this time Krissy was standing in the hallway and looking into the living room. I pleaded with her, "Can't you tell me why you're crying?"

She sobbed out the words, "That rocking chair keeps squeaking, and it wakes me up. There's nobody in it, and it keeps rocking and rocking."

I felt goose bumps on my neck and all down my arms. "Do you think you could have dreamed it?" I asked. You can't blame me for hoping!

"No, it rocks every morning."

Against my better judgment, I had to tell Paul about this when he woke up. He said Krissy was imagining the whole thing. "We can't have her crying every morning," I said. "We have to do something about that chair." He looked at me like I was nuts.

He wasn't having a very good time of it either. He had taken the untimely death of his beautiful twenty-three-year-old sister very hard. They'd had a close bond too, and he was so proud of her. He probably blamed himself for her death, because a few weeks before the accident, she had purchased a new car and drove it out to show us. She couldn't get the seat belt adjusted snugly, and Paul said he'd fix it. That night, he couldn't get that belt adjusted properly. He worked on it for a long time, but for some reason, it just didn't fit securely against her tiny frame. When she left, he told her to have the dealer take a look at that belt. She promised she would, then smiled and waved good-bye as she pulled out of the driveway. That was the last time we saw her alive.

When we heard the details of the accident, how her car had gone off the road and rolled, we immediately wondered if she was wearing her seat belt. Several months went by before we found out she had been wearing it when the accident occurred. Knowing that didn't take away the hurt, but it was helpful to know just the same. Paul missed Jeri terribly, and although I didn't want to push him with this rocking-chair business, I knew some action had to be taken so Kris wouldn't have to wake up crying every morning. I couldn't haul that chair downstairs by myself, or I would have already done it.

One question buzzed around in my mind like a pesky insect: was the rocking chair occupant our resident ghost child, or Paul's sister? I knew Jeri's spirit was around here, because one evening a week before school started, I accidentally fell asleep in that same chair while smoking a cigarette. During that drowsy state when I was more asleep than awake, I heard Jeri call my name: "Marlene." She had a soft, distinctive voice, and I immediately knew it was her. I opened my eyes just a slit, thinking I was dreaming. We had just attended her funeral, and although common sense told me it couldn't be her voice, hearing it didn't seem all that unusual. In fact, it was comforting. I heard it a second time but dozed off again. By the third time she called my name, she was very insistent and very loud. "Marlene, wake up!"

That got my attention. All of a sudden, I realized my cigarette was missing. I panicked and dropped to my knees, feeling around to see if it had rolled under the chair. It wasn't there, so I started fishing down in the insides of the rocker and under the cushion. Hello! My fingers ran headlong into the smoldering ash. If the rocker had burst into flame during the night, our little family might have perished. I thanked Jeri for saving our lives. Now this same chair was rocking every morning. Was she still keeping watch? If it was Jeri, why would she frighten her little goddaughter so badly?

On Thursday, not only was my crying daughter standing next to the chair when I came downstairs, but her little brother was standing in the hallway right behind her.

I asked Scott, "What is going on?"

"Mama, this squeaky chair rocks every morning just before you get up. It quits when you come down the steps." He wasn't crying or scared. He was a card-carrying pragmatist even back then. My little five-year-old was standing there in his pajamas and bare feet, giving me a blow-by-blow account of the whole thing. This rocking chair had frightened Kris to the point of hysterics while Scott remained unruffled. At least he didn't share his father's outlook by vehemently denying that something was happening with the chair. I admired him for that.

Kris sobbed, "It always stops when it hears you." Scott nodded in agreement. I promised them I would set my alarm five minutes earlier Friday morning so I could see it rock too. They were okay with that suggestion.

The next morning, I woke up ten minutes earlier and crept down the steps as gingerly as possible. I steeled myself for whatever was waiting for me; then I gently turned the doorknob and opened the door. Kris and Scott were already in the living room. Scott looked up at me and said, "I guess you can't fool it, Mama. It stopped rocking when you started coming down the steps."

"Daddy will put the chair in the basement on Saturday so you won't hear it rock anymore," I promised. "It can make all the noise it wants to down there. Is that okay with you two?" They nodded in unison. I'm sure Paul thought I had gone off the deep end, but thankfully he didn't argue. He carried the rickety chair down into the basement the following day. Eventually, that old chair was thrown out, because it had already seen its better days.

Even though the chair was gone, questions still begged to be answered. Was Jeri sitting up all night to keep watch over her older brother's home and family? Did she vanish in the morning until her shift began again? It seemed like a logical explanation in some odd way. If it wasn't Jeri, it must have been our regular ghost child. But if it was him, why would he suddenly decide to rock in the chair every morning before we got up? We'd had that creaky chair *and* the little ghost ever since we'd moved in. Maybe he just wanted something new to entertain himself. If that was the case, my kids and I were not amused!

More Occurrences from the Stormy Seventies

One steamy summer evening, we had a torrential downpour, the likes of which I hadn't seen for a long time. The lightning and thunder were horrific. It was the kind of "dark and stormy night" they write ghost stories about—the kind of night when you keep candles burning just in case you suddenly find yourself sitting in the dark.

I was pounding on my old manual typewriter next to an open window in the family room in the hopes of catching a breeze or two. The rain was coming straight down, so thankfully the window could remain open. While working on a letter, I heard a female voice humming a beautiful melody. I listened carefully as I glanced slowly around the room to determine its origin. Strangely enough, it sounded like it was coming from outside. But who in their right mind would be standing outside a window and humming in a deluge such as this? For some ridiculous reason, I had to know, so I opened the back door to check it out. Of course, there was no one there, and my curiosity got me soaked. That was the only time I have ever heard humming in this house.

Some weeks later, closer to autumn, a to-die-for fragrance wafted through the family room while I was typing away. The scent was so heavenly that it actually defied explanation. It must have been created in one of the best Parisian perfumeries. Flowers might be a reasonable explanation, except I didn't have flowers planted in my yard at that time, so it had to have been coming from inside the room. I caught a whiff of that beautiful fragrance a couple more times, then never again. Oh well, what's one more mystery?

Play Ball!

Kris didn't like the basement when she was a child, and she rarely went down there by herself. One late afternoon while I was trying to catch a little catnap before starting dinner, she and her brother decided to start fighting. After ignoring the scuffling for as long as I could, I finally yelled at them to cut it out. Scott went to his room. Kris went into her room as well, or so I thought. The next thing I knew, I was aware of someone bumping the couch. When I opened my eyes, I found Kristen sitting on the floor next to my arm. She was trembling and holding a rubber ball about the size of softball. I asked her what was going on.

Her quavering voice replied, "This ball came back to me in the basement."

I shook the cobwebs out of my head and put my glasses on. "What?"

Kris told me she had been sitting on the cement floor in the area that had been the Millers' family room. She found a ball and decided to roll it through the open door into the laundry room, just for the heck of it. Talk about the epitome of boredom! After she rolled it in, it came rolling back to her. Of course, this startled her, but being a curious kid, she rolled it in a second time to see what would happen. It came rolling out again. Then she threw it once more, as hard as she could. This time it didn't come back. She waited a few seconds, then got scared and started for the steps. At that point, the ball flew out of the dark laundry room right at her.

"It just flew out and rolled across the floor," she said with a shaky voice.

The first couple of times the ball rolled out, Kris thought the floor slanted toward her. The last time, she thought it had gotten stuck under the laundry tubs—until it flew at her. My daughter's experience freaked me out as well, but I didn't share that with her at the time. That floor slants *into* the laundry room, toward the drain, so if gravity had been her playmate, the ball wouldn't have rolled back to her at all. Interestingly enough, the laundry tubs are only a couple of feet away from the furnace. Was Furnace Boy playing ball with her? After that evening, she never went back into the basement alone again until she was a teenager. This happened in 1972, when she was nine, and even today she doesn't go down in our basement unless it is absolutely necessary.

Here's a curious thought: I didn't recall ever seeing that particular ball in the house before either, so where did it come from? Don't tell me; I really don't want to know.

I Become a Casualty

Up until this time, nothing dangerous had happened to us in this house—only vaporous voices, paranormal pranks, and supernatural silliness. We had been here five years and we weren't moving, so I was glad we only had to contend with pranks. However, that was about to change in a rather dramatic way.

One morning in 1973, I woke up with a sore neck. It didn't feel like I'd slept on it wrong; it just hurt like crazy. I bustled around, got the kids off to school, made coffee, and read the paper. When I went to take my shower, I saw a shocking sight in the mirror. There were four angry scratches etched across my throat. They were quite deep. I couldn't believe my eyes. My first thought was that a small animal had scratched me. We have tons of squirrels in our yard, but to my knowledge there were no openings where they could have gotten inside the house.

I called the clinic in Fridley and told them I'd woken up with these deep scratches on my neck. The triage nurse asked, "When was your last tetanus shot?" I had no idea, so she told me I had to come in for a booster shot that morning. I showered, dressed, and went in to face the needle.

No fewer than five nurses looked at my neck. None of them could determine what had made the bloody wounds. They called in a doctor for his opinion, but he was as stumped as they were. The nurses fired their questions at me, and I patiently answered them.

"Do you have a pet cat?"

"No, we gave our cat away some time ago."

"Did your husband do this to you?"

"Of course not."

"Has this happened to you before?"

"No, and I hope it doesn't happen again."

"Where did this happen?"

"While I was in bed, sleeping."

"Are you sure?"

"Yes. When I went to bed, I didn't have these scratches, and when I woke up, I did."

I finally told them I had no idea what had happened, because that was far safer than telling them what might have done it and risking ending up in a rubber room. It was easy to see these medical people were at their collective wits' end. I had the shot and went home, leaving the good nurses to ponder my mysterious marks. My neck was probably the subject of a few coffee breaks at the clinic for a day or so.

This event totally unnerved me. I couldn't help but wonder if this attack was a one-time occurrence or the beginning of a whole new phase of our haunting. The dimming-light phenomena had finally quit. The sound of toys dropping in the cubbyhole had stopped as well. If scratches were the newest weapon in our ghost child's arsenal, God help us all! Was it going to be mutilation from now on?

The scratches on my neck were as fine as those of a newborn kitten. Yet each scratch was at least a half-inch away from the previous mark, and they didn't line up uniformly like animal scratches would. No creature, to my knowledge, could make uneven slashes that thin with a paw span that wide. It made absolutely no sense. The two middle scratches were so deep that they bled. Three days later, they became infected. Another call to the clinic resulted in a prescription for an antibiotic salve. In addition to the glaring neck wounds, there was also a deep, V-shaped scratch on the inside of my right forearm, about three inches up from my wrist. The nurses didn't see this one. I often sleep with my right arm above my head so that the underside is exposed, making my wrist an easy target. I began covering the infected wounds on my neck when I left the house, because of the stares that came my way out in public. Someone even teased me about being bitten by a vampire. If they only knew! Now I was worried about my kids getting scratched also.

Later that week, my husband and I made plans to go to a movie. Betze, our neighbor from across the street, offered to babysit for us. We rarely go to a movie, so this was a real treat. When we returned, Betze noticed my neck. She was shocked when I told her that I'd woken up with the scratches several days earlier and that no one, not even the doctor at the clinic, could explain what kind of scratches they were.

Betze is a very logical woman—certainly not given to flights of fancy of any type. Yet out of the blue she asked, "Is your house haunted?" I started to speak, but Paul jumped in and quickly changed the subject. I will always wonder if she heard noises she could not explain while our kids were sound asleep. There had to be a good reason for her to step out of character like that. Some years later, I asked her about the incident, but she couldn't recall what had prompted her question. By the way, Paul had no idea what had made the scratches either, but you could tell he was concerned. It took a couple of weeks for the wounds to start healing over, but the deeper scars lasted for nearly four years.

About a week later, I was in bed reading when an idea popped into my head. These scratches were the size of a fine pinpoint, even finer than a stickpin. I checked my bedside table and, sure enough, there was a teeny brass safety pin lying there—and it was open! Then it hit me. Whatever scratched me made four separate slices across my throat and my wrist with this pin. A couple of these cuts were so deep they had caused bleeding and infection—and yet I hadn't felt a thing. My only memory of that night was the sensation of being smothered. I remember pushing the bedclothes off me because I couldn't catch my breath. At the time, I thought the blankets were cutting off my air supply, but that sensation could have been caused by *whatever* was cutting my throat. What a terrible thought! I slept with something wrapped around my neck every night for no less than five years after that incident.

I had finally kicked my two- to three-pack-a-day cigarette habit a few months earlier. Boy, could I have used a cigarette to calm my nerves then. The thought of waking up in the morning with new injuries was more stress than I could handle, and the paranormal activity was escalating. Someone wanted my attention quite badly; however, I was not equipped to deal with it. What if this entity was demonic? I'd read books about demon spirits and knew they are next to impossible to banish. I nervously kicked that idea out of my mind while I tried to remember if there were any cigarettes hidden around the house—there weren't!

A couple of years before, I had begun augmenting my smoking habit with some heavy-duty snacking to soothe my jangled nerves. Eventually, this led to my joining a weight-loss program. Now my most recent Pap test had revealed pre-cancerous cells, forcing me to consider a hysterectomy at the ripe old age of thirty-two. How many more stressors could I possibly fit into my life?

In January of 1974, I had the hysterectomy. I was hospitalized a total of nine days. Those were the good old days when hospitals kept patients till they were well enough to come home. During that time, Paul slept on the couch. Why would he leave the comfort of a nice, empty double bed and bunk in the living room on a lumpy narrow couch? It made no sense to me. When I asked him, he replied, "No special reason. I just felt like it." Ha! He'd never admit it to anyone, but I bet our ghost bothered him. The kids were at my parents' house, so who else did it have to torment?

Sometimes I Just Know

On October 19, 1976, my psychic ability prepared me for my father's death. I started feeling uneasy at about nine o'clock in the morning and began to fill up with unbearable sadness. I knew something was wrong with my father, because I sensed he wasn't in his house. Perhaps he was back in the hospital, because his emphysema had been bothering him again. I didn't phone my parents' home at that time, because I *knew* no one was there to take the call. The sorrowful feeling became more profound as the day wore on. About five p.m., my mother called me. She started saying, "Marlene . . ."

Words burst out of my mouth: "Daddy's dead, isn't he?"

She paused for a moment, then asked, "How did you know?"

I replied, "I just knew."

Mom began softly sobbing. "He died between eight thirty and nine this morning, right after I left for work. I found him when I returned this afternoon. The coroner just left."

Bingo!

The Case of the Missing Plumber's Friend

The last significant incident from this decade happened in 1977. The morning started out like any other. My kids left for school after the normal morning bedlam, and I ate my breakfast and read the paper. Then it was laundry time.

Laundry was no longer a drag, however, because now I had a nice, new automatic washer and a dryer. They had shown up in the basement when I'd returned home from the hospital three years before. Guess Paul didn't appreciate the amount of work involved in using the old equipment during my absence. *Wink, wink!*

After completing that task, I came back up and got busy with another project. When the washer started to empty, it sounded way too watery. I ran down the stairs and found a lake one inch deep at the bottom of the steps. I looked around for the plunger. "Hmm, it's not down here." I dashed up the stairs, through the kitchen, and into the bathroom for it. Why I thought I could stop this flood with a simple plunger, I can't say. That's just the way I am. But the plunger wasn't in the bathroom either. "Damn it!" It must have been in the basement after all and, in my panic, escaped my anxious gaze.

I turned on my heel and ran back through the kitchen and down the steps. I looked all over the basement. Ugh! I even waded through the dirty water and found no trace of our plumber's friend. This was very puzzling, because it's always in one of the two places. Maybe I had looked too quickly in our tiny bathroom, so I ran back up the steps and started through the kitchen once more. This time, smack dab in the middle of the kitchen floor—in front of God and everybody—stood our plunger. I grabbed it, yelled, "Thank you!" over my shoulder, and hurried back down the basement steps. I plunged for all I was worth, but to no avail. This was a job for the professionals. The sewer backup was not rooted in the paranormal, although the problem did have something to do with roots. Our weeping willow had infiltrated the sewer line, and we had no alternative but to have the graceful tree removed.

There was no "normal" explanation as to how I had missed seeing the plunger as I ran through the kitchen three separate times in a traffic path that is only thirty-six inches wide. Come to think of it, what would it have been doing there in the first place? I didn't share this inexplicable incident with Paul until our vacation in 1993. I was so tired of him pooh-poohing these paranormal incidents that I had quit telling him things back in the early seventies. We were walking on the windy moors of Cornwall, England, when I gave him the lowdown on that plunger episode. He didn't say much about it. I think he realized that his wife was never going to quit talking about the ghost.

Intermission and Admission (Of Sorts)

I remember very few curious happenings between 1978 and 1982. The stress of living in this haunted house, among other personal reasons, was making for a very shaky marriage. If any strange events occurred, I blotted them out of my mind. Oh, there were the usual taps and ghostly footsteps, as well as the new noises that sounded like things falling over in the kitchen, but nothing out of the ordinary for this house. Thank heaven that terrifying neck-scratching event was a one-time thing. And better yet, Paul and our children had never been never harmed.

In September of 1979, two important things happened in my life. First, my husband and I decided to divorce. Things were getting to be too much to handle, and we just couldn't hang in there any longer. One upsetting night on the eve of our seventeenth wedding anniversary, we had a blustery, soul-searching dialogue upstairs in bed. This was not a quiet little tête-à-tête. It was four solid hours of clearing the air of everything we'd lived through in the past seventeen years.

I don't remember much of what was said, but one thing I vividly recall: this was the first time the two of us actually talked about the ghost. That momentous exchange began with Paul accusing me of being unreasonable about something or other, and me retaliating with, "I wouldn't be so unreasonable if you were more supportive." Then the dam burst. Out poured story after story about my early experiences, along with all the pent-up tears of frustration that I had been holding back since we'd moved in. I chastised him royally for not believing me.

He finally admitted he knew there was something here. I cried out at the top of my lungs, "You *knew*? You always knew and you let me think I was going crazy all that time?" I could not believe what I was hearing. The neighborhood folks probably couldn't believe what they were hearing either, but I didn't care. How could he have let me suffer all that time when he knew there was something in this house?

He replied, "I was afraid if I admitted it, you'd want to move, and we couldn't afford it. I always knew it wouldn't hurt us." Wouldn't hurt us? Apparently he hadn't noticed the three packs of cigarettes I'd smoked each day during the first few years we'd lived here. And what about the constant stress I suffered on a daily basis? How could he ignore my infected neck? I bore the physical scars of that psychic attack for years before they completely faded. Also, what about the night I heard that ghostly crying in the basement and fell on both knees trying to run up the steps? My knees were so damaged by that fall that they became painfully arthritic.

I didn't mention any of this stuff to him, however. That would have put him on the defensive, quite possibly prolonging the juicy argument we already had going. I never liked to fight. I had been raised in a home in which my parents argued every day, usually at mealtime and often quite loudly. Although I love my parents, I didn't want to model my life after theirs. But my aversion to conflict resulted in a severe lack of self-esteem, which in turn destroyed my ability to stand up for what I want or need—and my marriage suffered for it. (By the way, Paul and I weathered that storm and stayed together, and we're still living in this house.)

Several months after our impromptu spat, while watching the beginning of a television show about ghosts, Paul admitted that he believes in the supernatural but, because it scares him, he chooses not to discuss it. Then he got up and left the living room. Aha, the old "If you don't acknowledge it, it doesn't exist" gambit. Now I respect his point of view and defend to the death his right to it, except that it does not support me in any way. The spiritual activity has recently returned with gusto. And here I am, alone once more, unable to share my experiences with my mate. I could just as well be a divorcee, or a widow. I've always said that if Paul dies before I do, I'm outta here. I will not spend one night alone in this house ever again.

I did once. Paul was on a fishing trip, my son was at camp, and my daughter was spending the night at a friend's house. Try as I might to put on a brave face that evening, I was terrified. Even though the television was cranked up as loudly as it could go without bringing the police to my back door, I still heard muffled noises in the family room and basement, not to mention the same old stuff in the kitchen. My poor nervous system went into overload.

About ten thirty, I couldn't stand it any longer. I called Maynard, our neighbor across the street. He was on his own for the summer months. I kept him on the phone until almost two in the morning, yakking about absolutely nothing. He finally said, "I hate to mention this, but I have to get up for work in three hours, so I really must get some sleep." He is a true friend for putting up with me. I knew it was terribly selfish to keep him talking that night, but boy, did I appreciate hearing a voice on the other end of that line. Of course, we didn't discuss the real reason I had called him, because he might not have understood. Our families were very close friends. Our kids and their kids ran around together. We went to the same church and did many recreational things as a group. I couldn't risk all that because I was afraid of a spirit.

After Maynard's early-morning announcement, I reluctantly hung up. At his suggestion, I located a big flashlight and radio to keep me company. I lay awake on the couch until my eyes would no longer stay open. The noises continued in the family room until I fell asleep, but by that time I was too exhausted to care. Even if the denizens of Hell showed up to carry me off, I wouldn't have cared. I haven't stayed alone for an entire night in the house since.

The second big event of September 1979 was my re-entry into the workplace. I hadn't worked since Kristen was four months old. But on September 17, thinking I was facing an impending divorce, I returned to the job market. Working outside the home could account for why I wasn't experiencing as many paranormal incidents. I was gone all day and dead tired at night. When I got home, there was dinner to make and then the cleanup afterward. The biggest headache was finding something to wear the following day. By the time I fell into bed, I was exhausted. The next morning, I would get up and do it all over again. I eventually assigned chores to Paul and the kids, but it was still tough getting used to working outside the home. For several years, I had been quite a night owl, and getting up early was a huge change for me. The days and nights seemed to blur, and weeks became months and months became years.

Scott and Kristen were growing up, and so was I. The positive part of working outside the home was that it was teaching me a sense of self-esteem and self-worth. I was broadening my horizons, building confidence, and becoming a more interesting person. I even bought my first car—at the ripe old age of forty-six. Things in general were looking pretty darn good. Paul and I began taking real vacations. In regards to the ghost around here, I had trained myself, as best I could, to ignore the taps on the wall. I no longer heard the child's voice in my ear but decided if it started up again, I'd wear earplugs this time around. I couldn't have done that when the kids were small, in case they needed me. Household items continued to walk away; only now that I had the money, I no longer turned the house upside down looking for them. I simply whipped out my checkbook and replaced them. The noises in the kitchen still bothered me regularly, but when that happened, I would hit the remote and turn up the volume on the television. I had finally adapted in some fashion to the ghost that shares our house and had learned not to let it disturb me quite so much—at least for the time being. Even with this uneasy alliance, I couldn't completely relax, because I never knew when the ghost would strike again with something worse than I'd experienced in the past. Living in this house was very much like hearing the *Jaws* theme playing over and over in my head.

One downside to my new beginning was this: After my husband's startling revelation, he went back to his old behavior pattern and avoided any mention of our resident ghost. Here I thought we had finally overcome that hurdle and opened up a channel of communication, but it slammed shut right in my face.

4: Eek-ing through the Eighties

A Swan Song for Kristen

In 1980, Kris graduated and moved out of the house to find her way in the big, wide world. She had one last ghostly encounter before she left. When she was ten years old, her father had brought her home a cable-car music box that he'd purchased in San Francisco during a tour of duty with the Air National Guard. It played Tony Bennett's signature song—what else? The mechanism broke shortly after he brought it home, so it had not been wound or played for several years. Kris just kept it around as a memento.

Sometime during the night, after she fell asleep, Kris heard the music box start playing. She thought she was dreaming at first, because although she was sleeping, she was well aware that the mechanism was broken. The music continued until she opened her eyes and sat up in bed, as if the little music box wanted her full attention.

A minute later, it abruptly stopped. She told me about it the next day and said, "Let Dad explain how the wind turned this broken switch on." He irritates her too, with his pat answers that explain absolutely nothing. By the way, when we tried to start the music box up that morning, it didn't work.

I Shed Tears of Joy!

In the summer of 1981, something occurred that would give me the validation I so desperately craved regarding my house, but I didn't find out about it till my sister's youngest daughter called one night in 1990, nine years after the incident occurred.

"So, Auntie M, have you seen your ghost lately?" she teased.

I was somewhat taken aback but replied, "Well, some stuff still happens occasionally."

"You lie!"

"What?"

"Geez, that time when Danielle and I were staying at your house, I thought for sure we killed it."

I could not speak for several seconds. This was the first time someone other than my children had admitted to witnessing a paranormal event in this house. When I regained my composure, I demanded to know what she was talking about.

My sister's girls had spent a couple of days with us that summer before going to my hometown to stay with my mother. However, while this visit didn't last very long, a memorable experience made up for it. (It's true: sometimes less is more!) Kristen had taken her belongings when she'd moved into an apartment; therefore, her room had no furniture in it. So, on the girls' first night here, I made up beds for them on the two couches in the living room. I had to go to work the next day, so when I turned in for the night, I told them to shut off the television and get some sleep. The scamps promised they would, but after I went upstairs, they decided to stay up and sample the late-night television programming in the Minneapolis market.

While watching my old buddy Johnny Carson, they noticed a light suddenly come on in the kitchen. Scott hadn't left his room, so they knew it wasn't him. The light stayed on, so they decided to investigate. According to Erika, they walked out to the kitchen with palpable apprehension. They knew Auntie M had a ghost in her house, and although they were scared, curiosity got the better of them.

Out in the kitchen, they saw the refrigerator door standing wide open. Danielle told her younger sister to slam it shut. Erika replied, "No way!" For several seconds, they stood there temporarily paralyzed by fear. Then Danielle took the door and gave it a good, hard push. According to Erika, "When the fridge door was about a foot away from closing, it bounced off something invisible. Then it shot back open with such a force that it bumped against the stove." The girls freaked out. Out of sheer reflex, Erika grabbed the door and slammed it shut again. They both raced back to the living room, jumped under the covers, and didn't stick their heads out till morning.

When my nieces returned home to Denver, they told their mom and dad about their scary night. When Kathie and I visited on the phone, the subject never came up, because she thought her girls had already told me about their brush with the ghost. I guess the girls had expected their mother to relay their story to me. Therefore, the confirmation I so desperately needed tumbled through the cracks—until Erika's call. She ended her story with, "It's the only true ghost story we know, and all our friends in Denver know about your house."

I recently asked her older sister, Danielle, what she remembers from that visit. She gave me a couple of incidents. Danielle recalled sitting on the family room couch, reading a book, when she began hearing noises in the basement. The kitchen door was open, so she could hear the racket very clearly. When she looked downstairs, she noticed the light was on. Even though there was no one in the basement, there was definitely movement down there. This scared her, but she returned to her book and ignored the noises. (While this was a separate experience from the refrigerator incident, it confirms all the nights I heard noises down there.)

She also remembers the refrigerator story, but in her recollection, it happened in the morning, while they were making breakfast. Their mom thinks Erika's version is the closest to the story they told back in 1981 when they returned from their exciting visit to Minnesota. Even though my nieces recall their spooky experiences differently, I have no doubt in my mind that they most definitely met up with our ghost on two separate occasions.

When Erika hung up, I was shaken and in tears, because someone outside my immediate family could finally corroborate my stories. And, even better, contribute one of their own. The relief and vindication I felt at that moment was indescribable. I only wish Paul had been on the extension instead of snoring upstairs.

A Dog Named Pete

Paul began working days in 1980, after eighteen years on the night shift. Boy, did our routines change around here! At first it was almost like having a stranger living with us during the week; however, we made it through the adjustment period. Paul went up to bed early from that time on, because getting up early required extra sleep. Pete, my neighbors' white terri-poo puppy, entered my life in July of 1979. This little guy would eventually become my Knight Protector, vowing an oath to keep me company throughout my scary evenings. We called him our foster dog, because he wasn't really ours but only lived with us on a temporary basis—at first.

It was love at first sight for both Pete and me. I believe we were soul mates from the day we first set eyes on each other. My receptionist job had turned me into a desk potato, so I began walking Pete every night in the fall of 1979 to provide the exercise my body was craving. During the summer of 1982, I started bringing him over to our house for weekend visits. It was so pleasant to have a friend to talk to, even if he had four legs and canine intellect. One thing bothered me, though: Pete never really seemed comfortable when he stayed here overnight. He would often stand in the kitchen and gaze into the family room for several seconds. He'd cock his head and stare intently. Eventually, he'd back out of the room, stand at the door, and wait to go home. His posture would become that of a beaten dog.

He moved in permanently during the winter of 1986 with permission from the owners' son. Thankfully, his parents agreed with him. Across the street, Pete had lived in an unheated garage, slept in a box full of quilts, and held down the job of guard dog, but over here he had a real bed and central heat and lived like a king. Guard dog or king? It was a no-brainer. He eventually settled in and learned to coexist what whatever frightened him.

Most evenings, Pete would stretch out in the hall, where he could keep a watchful eye in the living room and still conduct his surveillance of the dark kitchen. We'd hear the frightening sounds of objects falling out there all the time. Some nights, when the noises were fairly loud, they'd really scare him. I'd whisper, "Pete, what's that?" He wouldn't budge. Then I'd say, "You big baby. Come here and sit by me," and before I finished my sentence, he'd be up on the couch with his head in my lap.

Occasionally, the kitchen noises sounded threatening, like they were daring us to investigate. It sounded like items falling on the floor, cupboard doors clicking open—that sort of thing. On the nights the sounds were exceptionally loud, the atmosphere set my nerves on edge, and Pete was uneasy as well. At other times, when we felt quite bold, we'd just laugh. What do you mean, dogs don't laugh? This one did. And for the record, Pete really hated the basement. Enough said.

In February of 1988, I also took in a stray cat, whom I dubbed Murr the Purr. Murray was a gorgeous reddish orange tabby who had been abandoned. I carefully watched our new pet to see if he noticed the unseen guest in his new digs. But Murr never acknowledged anything ghostly in the family room—or any other room, for that matter. His reaction to the loud noises in the kitchen was a mere flick of the ear. He may have grown up with stuff like this, and it was old hat to him, or maybe he was the only cat on the planet who wasn't psychic.

The Next Generation

Scott graduated from high school in 1982, but he remained in our home till 1996. What's my best explanation for this? He's a Taurus.

According to the horoscope devotees, Taureans are believed to be home-loving people. I think I can corroborate that statement: my son, the Bull, overshot his April due date by ten agonizing days. Then, to build on that theme, when I reached the delivery room, he was stuck in the birth canal. Even forceps couldn't dislodge him. He was finally brought into this world with the skilled hands of my doctor, which slowly and gently guided him out. I think it's safe to say that once he puts down roots, he seems to have no desire to leave womb or room.

With all the activity that goes on around here, I was torn between wanting him out on his own, which would be good for him, and letting him remain here, which was good for me. It was very comforting to have another night owl around, even though he's a very private person. He was a semi-serious little boy who became a reclusive teen. He eventually turned into an intense young man who preferred to share only selected parts of his life with us. His friends were privileged to know his fun-loving side, and I thought that perhaps when he got older we'd see more of him. I missed my sweet, talkative Scott from years ago.

As Kristen and Scott grew out of their teen years, our house got fairly quiet. Except for the nuisance noises in the kitchen, the ever-present eerie feeling in the basement, and the tapping above my headboard in the bedroom, I felt almost ghost-free. Believe me, I wasn't complaining. And neither was Pete.

Kristen got married in 1985, and in 1987, John-Paul arrived on the scene. Our first grandchild! He was a quiet, smiling baby who would turn into a boisterous, inquisitive child. In 1989, Kari-Lynn came along. After a noisy bout with colic for the first five or six months of her life, she became very soft spoken and turned into a shy little girl. What a little doll!

Since the heaviest activity had taken place in this house when my kids were small, Kristen and I often discussed the possibility of the activity picking up again when her kids became old enough to spend the night.

5: A Rough Start to the Nineties

This Decade Is Not Starting Out Well at All

At the office, things were getting complicated. Corporate politics can knock a company on its rear. The tension in my department had been building for a couple of years, but it came to a head for me one week in February. First, I was taken to lunch and told how valuable I was to the team, how my excellent work habits, phone skills, and problem-solving talents were instrumental to our department's success. And I got a raise! I was on cloud nine. The following week, my manager placed me on probation. I'd been with the company for twelve years— eight with him. He must have had a reason, but he revealed it to no one. Our human resources division even wondered about the action, as my performance reviews had always been fantastic. The charges were bogus, but no one wanted to challenge a vice-president, so I was screwed. I showed up every day and handled all the tasks assigned to me, even though my hair was falling out from stress and I wasn't sleeping. To make matters worse, our daughter was pregnant with her third child and was contemplating divorce. My health deteriorated, as did my self-esteem during this awful time. That manager finally moved on; however, the damage was done.

Amid all the unhappy stuff that swirled around our family in 1990, at least I had my grandchildren—the bright spot in my life. In October, Camden appeared on the scene. He was a wonderful, content baby who turned into a very vocal toddler. I often babysat the kids, so they felt like my own. The grandchildren were a pleasant diversion from the corporate turmoil that took up much of my day and the paranormal noises that bombarded my evenings. But I held fast to the job I hated, because I was helping support these little buggers. I hoped and prayed for a better year when January rolled around.

Things Are Looking Up

I acquired a new manager in 1991 who was a real peach. It took a while for him and me to learn to work together, but after we clicked, my job became a lot less stressful. In fact, going to work was a joy most of the time. Kristen was still having problems, which worried me, but with one area of my life on an even keel, I was able to concentrate on helping her out. Paul and I were doing well on a personal level, so the only stresses I had to deal with were the noises in the house. But Pete and I had everything under control in that department . . . until December, that is.

On a cold Thursday evening in 1991, two days after Christmas, my beloved Pete died, leaving me to face my scary evenings alone. He was nearly thirteen years old at the time of his death and had been my furry protector for far too short a time. I missed him so very much. Paul had a private cremation for him, and I still have his ashes in my office.

One *happy* paranormal incident involving Pete occurred immediately after that agonizing weekend. When I opened the kitchen door to leave for work on Monday morning, I was still aching inside from losing my furry friend. Suddenly, I heard the familiar jingling of his ID tags and the clicking of his toenails walking across the kitchen floor. I turned around, smiled, and said, "Bye, Pete!" For years I'd heard those sounds each morning when he gave me one of his famous "See ya later" nose bumps on the back of my leg. His dog tags jingled a couple more times after his death—then nothing more was heard. I think he was just saying, "I love you. Thank you for loving me. Good-bye." Remember the comparisons I made to Jan Bryant Bartell's life in the beginning of this book? She also lost a beloved pet during her years in the haunted apartment, and her dog's name also began with the letter P.

Kari-Lynn and the Television

In 1992, Kristen went through a divorce. For over three years afterward, she cleaned my house once or twice a week to earn extra money. I would gladly have given her the cash, no strings attached, but she insisted on doing something to earn it. In the summer, she would bring all three children along with her. However, during the school year, when John-Paul was in class, Kristen would occasionally leave either Kari-Lynn or Camden with a friend. This arrangement gave her the opportunity to spend some quality time with her favorite kid *du jour*. On the morning in question, she brought Kari-Lynn, age three. The kids loved watching television at our house, because we had cable. Kris found a show for her little daughter to watch while she did dishes, dusted, and vacuumed. When it was time to go, Kari-Lynn's program wasn't over yet. Kris took the remote and clicked off the television, saying, "Come on, Kari-Lynn, we have to get going."

The princess protested in a royal style. There were no two ways about it; she wanted to watch the rest of her show. Even though Kari-Lynn is the quietest child of the three, she let out one heck of a holler, according to her mother. And suddenly, the television came back on! Kris looked at the TV set, pointed the remote, and clicked it off a second time. Kari-Lynn objected loudly once again. A few seconds later, as Kris was gathering the unhappy child off the couch, the television popped back on—a second time.

At that point, Kris just sat down with the remote in her hand and watched the show with her little daughter till it was over. She later told me, "I knew better than to argue with your ghost."

A Real Fish Story

Although the spooky incidents were fewer in number for several years, my ghostly drought ended with a bang—quite literally—in the autumn of 1994. This event ushered in a whole new wave of happenings, which prompted me to write this book.

One morning around six, I was getting dressed for work in the living room. I avoided my bedroom upstairs as much as possible. It's horribly cold in the winter and insufferably hot in the summer, with noises and scary experiences thrown in free of charge. It's never been much of a room, if you ask me. Over the years, I've tried my best to decorate it and give it a friendly atmosphere, but I've always fallen short of the mark. We've carpeted the floor, and the walls have been painted and papered several times. I've also purchased many sets of coordinating bedding and curtains, but it just never became the cozy room I had hoped when I'd first I laid eyes on it. Paul has never mentioned the unfriendly atmosphere up there, but then I doubt he'd ever make an unfavorable comment about the vibes of the room, since his pride would never allow it. On the flip side, though, it's possible he feels nothing up there. Lucky him!

While I was sitting on the couch that September morning pulling on my pantyhose, I heard a loud metallic clunk in the vicinity of the recliner. I looked over at the end table and in the soft glow of the television noticed that a heavy brass dolphin had tipped over on its side. My heart started to pound in my chest, and the back of my neck began to tingle. Scott had brought this souvenir back from Hawaii a couple years ago, and I hadn't known this knickknack to fall over until just that very minute. How odd!

The dolphin was about eight inches long and cast in such a way as to balance by its nose and wide tail fin. Placed low on either side of the body were two side fins. These fins did not touch the table surface; however, they stopped it from tipping completely over if jarred. This morning, something had bumped it with enough force to knock it over, because it had landed on its side with a bang. I righted the little dolphin, then hit the table with my hand to try to make it fall over again. After several failed attempts to tip the dolphin on its side, I finally picked it up and dropped it. Aha! It was the same loud sound I'd heard a few minutes before. Looks like someone is *baa-aack!*

While I drove to the park-and-ride, a thought struck me funny. Most of the other women catching the bus were thinking about their daycare providers or wondering whether they could get by with meatloaf again for dinner tonight. As I climbed aboard the bus, I wondered what kind of ghostly shenanigans to expect this time around. However, after the dolphin incident, I heard nothing more for weeks.

The Spirit of Christmas

A couple of months later, in December 1994, my ghost let its presence be known again. I love decorating for Christmas. On this day, I filled the bay window area with my quaint little village and several candles. I taped up colored lights and cards around the windows, and then I started working on the tree. It was mid-afternoon when I finally finished draping the few remaining pieces of tinsel on the branches. I made myself a cup of tea and then sat down to admire my handiwork.

A series of soft clicking sounds around the bay window drew my attention away from the tree. I looked over my shoulder to see if a card or Christmas light had wiggled loose, but nothing was askew as far as I could tell. We have some shrubs growing next to the house, and I thought perhaps they had brushed against the window at the bidding of the wind. I turned back to admire my masterpiece. While deciding whether a few more ornaments were needed, I observed an unbelievable sight. A solitary icicle slowly began to curve up and form the shape of a backward letter J. Wow! This was incredible.

I was far too captivated to be frightened. How was this possible? I couldn't take my eyes off that branch. The icicle remained in that position for only a couple of seconds. Then, while my eyes were locked on the curious sight, the silvery decoration slowly returned to its vertical position—without shimmering, without fanfare, without any visible help. The other pieces on that branch remained motionless. The composition of icicles is such that the very slightest puff of air can start them dancing. Therefore, it was physically impossible for this single icicle to move without disturbing the others. I had witnessed a feat that truly defied physics.

I sat there completely captivated for a few seconds before trying to reproduce that motion by gently blowing on the tree. My attempt to re-create the trick made all the icicles shimmer in the late afternoon sun. I moved closer to the tree and took that same piece between my thumb and index finger, slowly turning it up till it formed the backward J, then carefully let it go. The icicle promptly returned to its vertical position, then shimmered and squiggled along with the rest of its neighbors.

I should have called Paul in there to witness the phenomenon, because it would surely have proven to him that something paranormal was living with us. It's just as well I didn't, though. The whole incident happened so fast that he might not have made it into the room quickly enough, giving him one more reason to think I'd lost my mind. It was my secret: my Ghost of Christmas Past had announced its presence to me alone. After that bit of Christmas magic, the house quieted down once more.

My Journal of a Haunting

6: Afloat on a Psychic Sea—1995

What Will This Year Bring?

Over the years, many things had disappeared from our house. Sometimes these items had reappeared in the same place after a period of time. Sometimes they hadn't. Even though this routine was annoying and often expensive, it usually wasn't frightening—until the following happened, that is.

I have always prided myself on having enough guts to climb those creaky steps and take that long walk to bed in the dark. Over the years, a few improvements were made to this area, so at least it was not as frightening now as it was when we moved in. Paul installed a lock on the creaky cubbyhole door so it couldn't swing open and scare me. Good dog, Paul! After he replaced the damaged treads, we put new carpeting on the stairs, which was a vast improvement over the original covering. He also put up a wall lamp just inside the door, which is helpful, but only if one is coming back down. There is no way to turn the lamp off once the stairs have been climbed, so we still have to negotiate them in the dark when we go to bed.

Paul began working days in 1982. He hits the hay hours before I do, so for many years my journey to dreamland was done in the dark to keep from disturbing his sleep. I managed to do this successfully until an event in 1995 wrenched my security blanket off me, leaving my shattered nerve ends exposed and shivering. Now I go nowhere in this house at night, especially upstairs, without a flashlight somewhere on my person, be it in my pocket, under my arm, in my hand, or between my teeth—yes, between my teeth, if I need both hands to carry other items.

On the night in question, I bravely padded up the pitch-black stairway around half past eleven and headed for the bed, on the far side of the room. As I shuffled by the area where the closet is located, I felt my husband standing there. He often gets horrible leg cramps at night, and the only way he can work them out is to get up and walk around for a while. As I brushed past him, I remarked, "Another cramp, huh?" I received no answer, but he wears earplugs to bed, so I thought nothing of it. Secure in the knowledge that Paul wouldn't be disturbed, I allowed myself the luxury of bouncing into bed and rooting around to find a comfortable spot—an activity usually done as carefully as possible. A low, snorting sigh arose next to me. My heart stopped for a split second. *Paul was in bed!*

Oh . . . dear . . . God, then who or what was standing over there? I had felt or sensed someone not more than a hair's breadth from my right arm only moments ago.

I have walked up those steps to bed, in the dark, every night since September 1968. I've heard footsteps follow me to my bed, tapping noises race back and forth across the wall above my head, a child's voice repeatedly cry "Mommy" in my ear, and the cubbyhole door creak open every time I walk by it. However, none of those incidents had ever frightened me as much as this.

Later, in the spring and summer of 1995, I had a rash of umbrella abductions. Since I have an aversion to getting rained on, each time

A Hair's Breadth from . . . Who?
It's a chilling sensation to walk by your bedroom closet door and sense your husband standing there, then climb in bed to find him deeply asleep.

an umbrella disappeared, I immediately bought another. All the umbrellas disappeared from my briefcase. After the first disappearance, I thought I'd left the missing item at work, but that wasn't the case. As each subsequent umbrella disappeared, I realized my ghost had something to do with it. Eventually, they all turned up in odd places, for example, back inside my briefcase, inside the deacon's bench that sits in the kitchen, and on a shelf in the family room. Suddenly, I had five umbrellas. Except for the three that eventually broke over the years, I still have the others I bought that summer.

Although my briefcase was only a supporting player in the Great Umbrella Caper, it played a starring role in a vignette that took place a few weeks later. That evening, while sitting in the family room and attempting to cut an outline for this story, I heard a startling crash behind me. This in itself was not unusual, because over the years I've had the bejesus scared out of me in that room. The usual noises consisted of taps, scratching noises, and sounds of items falling. Each time I heard these noises, the location was the same. They always originated from one of the corners of the room, usually at night and always behind me.

Some nights while working on my writing projects, I would feel *someone* standing directly behind me, staring at the back of my neck. I've heard of a ghost writer, but a ghost reader? Come on! I never turned around to see what it was. I know, I know. What a chicken!

My father died from a massive heart attack. I'm convinced I will, at some point, go that same way, but I didn't want to hasten that final experience. For that selfish reason, I made a practice of ignoring the areas that produced the startling sounds. If that makes me look like a paranoid fool, I'll humbly accept the title.

This bold noise was much too deliberate to be ignored, however. Immediately after the commotion, I got up and looked behind me. My briefcase, which had been resting against the back of the sleeper sofa, was lying on the floor about two and a half feet in front of it. This was interesting, because it hadn't moved since I'd arrived home from work three hours ago. My soft-sided nylon briefcase had a ton of stuff in the top compartment, so it must have become unbalanced and rolled down from its own weight. To test my theory, I picked it up and put it back where it had been sitting, then gave it a little push. It flopped over and landed flat on the sofa cushion. So I experimented further, pushing it harder and harder till it landed on the floor. At no time did it end up where I'd first found it. It was tossed—that was the only conclusion I could reach. Whenever anything spooky happens in this room, I abandon my writing, and that night was no exception. It was just too creepy to sit there any longer.

Meanwhile, the mysterious tapping noises that had announced the icicle trick became a regular feature in the house. They were more hit-or-miss than the dimming lights that had plagued me every evening several years ago. Since I'd always heard the taps in the living room, I decided to check the front of my house as soon as the snow melted. I was positive that the evergreen branches were the source of the noise. Imagine my surprise when I saw that the shrubs were three feet away from the house and another couple of feet below the bay window. I fear another ghostly actor has joined the cast. Now what?

I heard nothing more till summer. The next time the annoying taps entered my comfort zone, I was sitting in the recliner reading the latest issue of *FATE* magazine. It was a warm summer night in July, around eleven thirty, and this time the sound was coming from the lamp. A bug must have gotten inside the lampshade, I thought, and was tapping against the bulb, frantically trying to find its way out. I ignored the noise as long as I could, but eventually ran out of patience. Finally, I peered up into the light but couldn't see any bug. I shook the lamp shade. Nothing flew out. It pains me to report that those noises have become my constant companion ever since that night, and they do their thing wherever I sit.

Rest in Peace, My Friend—Please!

My former neighbor, Martha, died of cancer this summer. She and Earl divorced many years ago, and she moved out of that destructive household and remarried. Although I saw her from time to time in the shopping centers near me, I'd had no idea she was ill. She had been a real lifesaver the first ten years we lived here. I'm sorry to say I didn't attend her funeral. I'd never felt comfortable around Earl, and I knew he'd be in attendance. Even though I dearly wanted to pay my respects to Martha, I couldn't face her ex-husband, because I blamed him for making her years with him so unhappy. Kristen didn't go to the funeral either. Later I found that many of the neighbors did not attend, and it seems each of us stayed away because of Earl.

A few days after the funeral, I heard another strange noise in my family room. It was coming from the northeast corner of the room and sounded like the frenzied scratching of a large rodent trapped in a paper bag. Get this: there was no paper bag in the room, and there wasn't so much as a stick of furniture in that corner. For a second, I considered mice inside the walls, but this noise was much louder. It definitely was originating from inside the room, and only a few feet from me. My logical mind was screaming, "Who is doing this?" I left the room at once, because I couldn't sit there and listen to that. Stress was burning me out. Without Pete as my buffer, I was having trouble coping.

I called Kristen later that evening. She said, "Martha is probably upset with you for not going to her funeral." What a kid I raised! She wanted to know if I asked who was trying to contact me. To be perfectly honest, if I had asked and *someone* had actually answered, I would have died from shock, giving our neighborhood another funeral to ponder. Kristen called me a chicken, and I did the chicken thing and clucked at her.

Bathtub Tales

Every spring, my son spends his two-week vacation filming tornadoes in Texas, Oklahoma, and Kansas. The rest of the year, when he's home, he is my security blanket of sorts. He wakes up about the time I leave for work. If I have car trouble, I can count on him to drive me to the park-and-ride. If I should become seriously ill, he's there. If something scares me, he might not give a damn, but it's still a comfort having him in the house.

At least once during my son's vacation, I will hear footsteps walking around the house while I'm taking a bath. It's a common phenomenon to hear noises while bathing, and everyone on the planet has probably had that experience at one time or another. Research might yield a scientific, textbook explanation for these sounds, but here's mine: our brains feel compelled to mess around with our senses while we're at our most vulnerable—*stark naked and dripping wet!* With everything that has occurred over the years, my bathroom was just about the only place in this house where I felt safe. Oh, there was the yellow panties episode years ago, but I wasn't in the room when they flew in, so that doesn't count.

The first time I heard someone open the kitchen door while I was getting ready to take my shower, I thought Paul had forgotten something when he left for work. But it wasn't him. This was just a new twist in the plot cooked up by my ghostly nemesis. When the episodes became more frequent, I began to chain-lock the kitchen door before getting into the shower. I knew a mere chain lock wouldn't stop *it*, but doing this seemed to give me some peace of mind.

One experience turned out to involve a little more than unexplained noises. I heard what sounded like the back door opening and someone walking through the kitchen and into my son's bedroom. That was something new. Scott was on one of his storm-chasing trips and wasn't due home for a week. However, if/when the weather pattern turns sour, he sometimes comes home early. I put on my robe and cautiously opened the bathroom door and called out his name. He didn't answer. Scott's bedroom door was shut, so I knocked on it—again, no answer. I looked out the kitchen window for his green Honda, but there was no car in the driveway. The chain lock was still in place. So why, with those obvious clues beating me over the head, would I still walk back to Scott's room and open the door? It always amazes me why my brain keeps searching for logical explanations when I know none exist.

Of course, things have also happened when my son was home. One morning, I experienced something very odd while taking my shower. I was rinsing my hair by slowly turning my head from side to side under the warm, relaxing spray. My right hand grasped the shower rod while I extended my elbow for balance. This pushed the shower curtain out into the room. My morning shower was the perfect time to plan my work day, because I was totally alone and totally relaxed. Or was I? All of a sudden, *something* gave my elbow a sharp jab. Then a firm, mysterious pressure actually forced my arm down about four inches. I cautiously pulled the curtain aside and peered out into the steam. There was no one there, and the bathroom door was still locked. Here we go again. I stepped out of the tub, forced my wet body into my robe, and foolishly walked into the kitchen to check the kitchen door. The chain lock was still in place.

That sharp jab shouldn't have surprised me at all. I've experienced pokes of one kind or another ever since we moved into this house, most of them taking place while I was asleep. I've been poked in the back while lying in bed and facing my husband, knowing therefore that he wasn't responsible. I've been poked while taking a catnap on the couch after the kids left for school. Many a delicious dream

has been interrupted by a well-timed poke announcing an impending phone call. One night, I was even poked in the butt through the
slats of a rocking chair while watching a television show. I thought
the chair had shifted on the carpeting and that I had rocked myself
into the corner of the end table. However, my chair was a good foot
and a half away from, it so I muttered, "Stop that," under my breath.
There's never been a rational explanation for any of these occurrences,
so I always did my best to ignore them. But this was the first time I'd
been poked in the shower. All I can say is . . . how bloody *rude!*

A Friend Lends a Helping Hand

A haunting is one topic a person wouldn't want zipping around the
office grapevine, but I had to trust someone. I began sharing my
experiences with Nancy L., a longtime office friend of mine. I don't
recall the first time I told Nancy about my house, but something
about her let me know I could take her into my confidence. During
our lunchtime chats, I found out that she also believes in earth-
bound spirits and odd occurrences. She's a treasure. She has never
told me I'm nuts, nor has she ever doubted me. Nancy always listens
attentively, and her interest has kept me sane. For years I wanted to
find a professional to sweep the psychic dust from my house, but I
always worried about what Paul would say. At lunch one day, Nancy
finally convinced me that it was none of Paul's business, since he
wasn't the one having problems with ghostly occurrences—I was.
Last year, fired up by Nancy's assertive support, I drafted a long
letter to Echo Bodine, a Minneapolis psychic and author who has
achieved both local and national recognition for her work in ridding
places of unwanted spirits. My letter outlined several of the more
dramatic experiences I've had over the years. I waited for a week or
two but heard nothing back from Ms. Bodine. I didn't have the guts
to follow up with a phone call. When I told Nancy about it, she took
over. Without my knowledge, she called Echo's office and left my
name and phone number on the answering machine. "Hey, what are
friends for?" she teased when she told me what she did.

A few days later, on a lazy Sunday afternoon, Echo's secretary called. Now there was a call I wasn't expecting! With Paul reading the paper only a few feet away from me, though, I didn't feel relaxed enough to open up to her. I ended up taking the phone into the family room for some privacy, but unfortunately I choked. When asked what was currently happening in my house, I said, "Not much." My mind went completely blank. I can't believe words failed me after all the years I'd suffered with my supernatural pest. I told her what I really wanted was to have a psychic verify that there had been paranormal happenings here—for my peace of mind. She said Ms. Bodine was in such demand that unless something really traumatic was occurring at the moment, the popular ghost buster wasn't accepting any new assignments. Then the young woman asked if there was any new activity. If so, was it violent? Was it continuous? Did I feel myself threatened by it in any way?

My ill-thought-out answers to those questions were "Not that I can think of at the moment," "No," "Not any longer," and "Not really." Wait a minute! Did I just dismiss the stress I'd suffered over the years with those stupid, noncommittal answers? Somebody shoot me.

Out of embarrassment, I changed the subject. I asked if Echo had received my letter. I had sent it in a distinctive envelope to make it easy to spot. The secretary said she was not aware of any letter but that, due to Ms. Bodine's schedule, she doubted the letter had been read; she said it might be in a huge stack of mail somewhere in her office. Then she suggested I call someone else, whose name and phone number I later lost. This substitute was a former student of Ms. Bodine's and was reputed to be every bit as good. My cry for help was wimpy at best, and all I had to show for it was utter disappointment.

Nancy was even more disappointed than I was. On our next standing lunch date, she blurted out, "Are you aware that you have not been able to relax in that house for twenty-seven years? Do you want this to continue? It's ruining your health and your life."

As always, she was right. When we moved in, I was a healthy twenty-seven-year-old woman. Over the years, I have developed (not necessarily in this order) allergies, depression, paranoia, irritability, extreme nervousness, asthma, irregular heartbeats, panic attacks, intestinal problems, arthritis, severe headaches, and chronic lung problems from years of heavy smoking. In addition to all those conditions, I suffer from persistent insomnia, which has exacerbated my fibromyalgia; I never sleep deeply enough or long enough to heal the damaged tissues. I've also managed to gain a considerable amount of weight due to nervous eating late at night, resulting in a bad back and even more painful arthritic knees. Now, God help me, I am a borderline diabetic. I'm not saying the ghostly activity caused all this, per se. But I am suggesting that the stress generated by living with these paranormal events day after day—without knowing how to cope and without the emotional support I need—could very well be the culprit. You know what a killer stress can be.

I always wished I could handle the scary occurrences in a blasé manner. You know, just blow it off, ignore it. In the stacks of library books I've devoured over the years, I've discovered that some families pack up the kids, the dog, and Grandma and move out at the first sign of something paranormal in their home, while others seem to take pride in their ghosts. For example:

Houseguest: "I say, what was that noise?"

Homeowner: "Oh, that's just our ghost, Old Benjamin. He's harmless. We think of him as one of the family. He's quite amusing to have around."

Yeah, right! If only it were that easy for me. These families present a united front against whatever haunts their homes, unlike in my house, where it's just me, myself, and I—and none of us are emotionally equipped to handle it.

Why couldn't I shrug off these ghostly events? I was angry with myself for not being able to ignore the pranks and noises. I was angry for not being strong enough to stand my ground. Years before, I should have given Paul an ultimatum: "Either you start giving me some support around here or we pack up and move." But I could never find that voice inside me, and that made me angrier. Anger causes stress, and stress will eat you alive. It also ruins relationships. I had very little self-esteem when we moved here, and what I had continued to erode over the years. I couldn't stand my ground back then, and I was just starting to learn that skill in my fifties.

Trying to find a ghost buster forty years ago was akin to getting a back-alley abortion. Those services weren't listed in the phone book. Of course, one could call a Catholic diocese to see if they would send someone out to exorcise the house. Not being Catholic, I honestly didn't think that option was available for me. In the enlightened nineties, it was easier to find someone to come in and do some psychic housecleaning. I was sorry Ms. Bodine's schedule was so full, because she was reputed to be one of the best around here. Guess I was back to square one. The Minneapolis Yellow Pages had several listings for psychics. Nancy didn't agree that I should look elsewhere for help, though. She still thought we should keep pressing Echo to come out. Nancy's persistence was amazing, and her friendship a blessing. She was the life jacket that kept me afloat on a psychic sea that kept trying to pull me under.

7: Ninety-six Brings More Tricks—1996

Flashlights I Have Known

Nineteen ninety-six would become a year of paranormal events, only I didn't know it yet. It began in January with the innocent disappearance of my flashlight. It had been about a year since I had been scared into carrying a flashlight to bed every night. I admit to being a disorganized person, and my flashlight stays wherever I toss it during my manic morning rush. However, I always find it by eleven p.m., so it's no big deal. I panicked the first night I couldn't find it, because I absolutely knew I'd left it on an end table in the living room that morning. A frantic search ensued. I looked in drawers, under the couch, under the love seat, under the recliner, in the bathroom, in the kitchen—in every conceivable place one could put a flashlight. Granted, my house has that lived-in look, so it really could have been anywhere—but it was nowhere to be found. I ran into my husband's office and grabbed his large emergency flashlight, because this situation definitely met the criteria.

The following evening, after dinner, I bought another small flashlight. Within two weeks, that one went missing too. By April, I had gone through seven flashlights! One Saturday while doing my weekly vacuuming in the living room, I noticed that one of the missing items had turned up under the recliner. Aha! One prodigal had returned. However, within a short period, that flashlight went missing for a second time. I never found any of the others. Even in the messiest of homes, seven flashlights can't hide indefinitely, so I have no recourse but to believe they are in another dimension or up in that creepy cubbyhole on the farthest end. I finally bought a small flashlight with a rubber wrist strap and wore that to bed each night. It stayed with me for several years. Since we moved into this house, numerous objects have disappeared. Some of them turned up at a later date; others, like these flashlights, have yet to return.

It Wasn't the Kids

Our grandchildren stay overnight from time to time, as a package deal or separately—their choice. While the three together are a little more challenging for us, we manage to live through it. In July 1996, we had the trio of mischief-makers while my daughter had major surgery. Kristen missed her kids so much during her hospital stay that she wanted them back the day she arrived home. They stayed with us less than a week; then the activity began again. My new iron was discovered on the basement floor, tipped on its side with the temperature-control plate several inches away from it. I had purchased that iron only a couple of weeks before the kids' visit, so I was just sick thinking it was broken. Thankfully, it still worked.

When I asked Scott if he had done any laundry or ironing or if he had noticed the iron on the floor, he replied, "Don't you think I'd notice if I knocked an iron on the floor?" It wasn't my intent to accuse him, although in retrospect it probably sounded that way. I was just trying to determine when the iron fell. I explained to him that odd things had been happening for as long as we'd lived in this house, and this incident was just one more to add to the list. He emphatically stated, "Look, I don't believe in ghosts!" I hadn't used the word *ghosts*, so this abrupt declaration intrigued me. He refused to believe that anything paranormal happened in the basement. He simply tied it in with the little kids' visit. He's entitled to his own opinion, but I beg to differ.

The portion of the basement that houses the laundry facilities is closed off in the summer. We only dehumidify the laundry area, not the entire basement, due to the cost. It's doubtful that the two youngest kids could have reached the hook-and-eye contraption near the top of the door. It's possible that their older brother might have stood on the basement steps and reached it by balancing precariously on his tiptoes. However, that kind of operation would have attracted my attention. I honestly didn't think the little kids had anything to do with this iron ending up on the floor. Anyone who has taken care of young siblings knows that if one of them gets into serious mischief, the others can't wait to tattle. Also, in my grandkids' defense, they rarely play in the basement, because they simply do not like going down there.

I told Scott that a million strange things had happened in this house, especially when he and his sister were small. His reply was straightforward and to the point: "Kids in the house—things happen!" Okay, point taken! Even though I could tell he was finished with this conversation, I wasn't. I went on to say how odd occurrences had continued to happen even after he and his sister grew older, and even after Kristen moved out. I added, "There were no small children in the house before the grandkids were born and still mysterious things happened, so a child's physical presence in the house isn't necessary." He didn't agree with me. Now there's a real surprise!

I believe the spirit (or spirits) that abides in this house feeds off the exuberant energy of children as well as the emotional turmoil of adults. There was a lot of that going on in our house right then. Our son was moving away from home for the first time, and he was uncertain as to what to expect from living on his own. Since he was under a lot of stress, I believe his energy contributed to our supernatural activity in some way. Day-to-day relationships within a family are tough enough to maintain when there is no paranormal force to jam up the works. So it's safe to say that this house, at any given time, was a veritable powder keg on many levels.

More Iron Tales from the Basement

Most of my stress comes from being treated as though I imagine things. I am an intelligent woman. How bright would it be of me to keep insisting there is paranormal activity in my house all these years if it weren't true? Even a spoiled five-year-old stops holding her breath when she realizes that turning blue isn't getting her anywhere. If only the men in my life would say, "I don't believe in the supernatural, but since you do, I'll listen to what you have to say." But the only thing I get is ignored and put down. Here are a few more examples.

September 1, 1994: While I was ironing in the basement, the light went on and off twice in rapid succession. This family signal has been used over the years to (1) check if the light was left on by mistake or (2) let whoever's down there know they are needed upstairs (e.g., phone call). When the light is flashed, the person in the basement loudly responds, "I'm down here!" The light is turned off if there is no answer. At the first flick of the light, I loudly yelled, "I'm down here!" The light went on and off one more time a few seconds later. I called out even louder this time, "I'm down here! What do you want?" No one replied.

I finished ironing my shirt and ran upstairs. I asked my son if he given me the basement signal. From behind his bedroom door, I heard, "No. Why would I do that?"

I then asked my husband, who was reading the paper in the living room; he, too, denied giving the signal. I said, "Well, it just went on and off—twice." Paul again confirmed that he didn't do it. I stood my ground and reconfirmed that someone had. Paul replied, "Did you ask Scott?" Augh! No stress in my life.

Wait a minute. I hadn't heard any footsteps above me before the light's mysterious performance. Whoever had fiddled with the light switch knew the family signal and would have had to walk through the kitchen or enter through the back door to accomplish it. Footsteps, even ghostly ones, can be heard when one is quietly ironing in the basement.

Another perfect example took place in July of 1996. I noticed the basement light was on late in the afternoon. I asked Paul if he was finished ironing in the basement. He said he was but he'd probably forgotten to turn the light off, so I took care of it when I went outside to turn our hamburgers on the grill. Seconds later, when I walked back into the house, the light switch was flipped back on. I immediately asked both Paul and Scott if they had just turned it on. "No" from the father and "No" from his son, so it must have been the ghost again, that rascal!

The next afternoon, I found my iron on the basement floor about two feet away from the ironing board. This time, it was sitting on its heel, as if someone had set it down to reposition an item of clothing. I asked my men if they knew anything about it. I couldn't wait to see what kind of lame reasons they'd invent this time. Again I was met with guarded irritation. "It must have fallen off. The ironing board is shaky and the dryer vibrations made it fall off." The dryer vibrations? I just shook my head. The ironing board sits at least two feet away from the dryer. Granted, our old dryer is a real monstrosity. To be fair, items *have* vibrated or slid off the top of it while it was running—but I will never be convinced that the dryer was responsible for placing my iron ever so carefully on the floor.

The amazing thing about this peculiar experience was the identical replies. I got the same story from both Paul and Scott—almost word for word—even though I asked them at separate times that afternoon. They each said, to the syllable, "Why don't you put the iron on a separate table? Then it won't fall off." I replied to each in turn, "I've had the *same* ironing board and the *same* dryer for twenty years. Why would the iron fall off now, twice in one month?"

They couldn't explain it, so they handed me feeble excuses. Men! The excuse that wins the award for being the most creative is, "It vibrated off the ironing board because of the home-remodeling job going on next door." I won't tell you which one said that. I'm too embarrassed.

You know me: I had to test their theory. The iron didn't topple over until I gave the board a rather decent push. It tipped over on its side, on the ironing board surface. If the iron had fallen to the floor, what are the odds of it landing straight up? Later in the week, I found an old, wobbly TV tray placed adjacent to the dryer (actually *touching* it), with my iron parked on top. Am I the only one who appreciates the *irony* in this situation?

The Prodigal Scissors

The first year we lived in this house, many pairs of scissors disappeared, one after the other. Within a six-month time frame, I purchased as many as nine replacement pairs after diligently searching for each of their predecessors. Back in the sixties and seventies, the only scissors I could afford were the knockoffs that resembled the big-name originals with the orange handles. I abhor the color orange, but it was the only color available. Thankfully, the eighties ushered in the Southwestern desert colors; oddly enough, none of the later pairs disappeared.

There hadn't been any orange-handled scissors in this house for two decades until one Sunday afternoon, when a pair appeared quite suddenly on my counter. Now, I can't swear that an invisible magician uttered *"voila,"* causing the pair of scissors to appear out of thin air, but when I walked through the kitchen to bring up a load of clothes from the basement, they weren't there. When I returned, they were. It made the hair on the back of my neck stand up.

Of course, you know the drill: "Paul, did you put these scissors here?" "No!" "Scott, did you put these scissors here?" "No!" "Okay, since I didn't put them on the counter either, where did they come from?" My words had once again run headlong into the wall of silence that went up whenever I implied that something supernatural had taken place. It's the kind of silence that begs, "Please don't bring that subject up again. Please!" Maybe I should have felt sorry for those two. Perhaps they were simply incapable of dipping their toes into the waters of the paranormal. The sad reality is, I'd put up with their absurd opinions for far too long to be that charitable toward them. I said no more about it and put the scissors in a safe place . . . for old time's sake.

August 1996—A Hat Trick

When my back is bothering me, I often bunk in the living room on the couch or the recliner to keep from disturbing Paul's sleep. One evening while I was getting my bed made up, I turned the fan on the low setting and pointed it away from the couch to avoid waking up stiffer than a corpse. While tucking a sheet under the cushions, I felt an aggressive stream of air hitting the back of my legs. At the same time, the whirring noise of the fan became noticeably louder. I turned around to see what was going on. The control knob had returned to the medium setting, and the fan was back in its previous position, blowing directly on the couch. This happened only a few seconds after I first adjusted it. I twisted the knob back to the low setting and repositioned the fan the way I wanted it. Then I gave it a good scolding. That always makes me feel better.

Five minutes later, I was in the bathroom, getting ready for bed. I noticed the toilet paper had run out, so I slipped on a new roll. This roller is tricky, and if you don't get it squarely in place, it shoots out the next time someone uses it. There's nothing worse than hearing that *ping* at three o'clock in the morning. It can stop your heart! I grabbed the roll and gave it a good tug just to make sure it was tightly secured, and then I began brushing my teeth. Seconds later,

I heard a very loud *ping* coming from the dispenser, as if it had expelled the roll. I pulled on it again. It was secure! There was no conventional reason for that noise. Quite frankly, I was not amused; although I was terribly grateful it happened then rather than in the middle of the night.

A few minutes later, I threw my laundry down the basement steps. The little bundle consisted of a white shirt and a pair of dark pantyhose rolled up inside a skirt. After executing this maneuver, I checked the landing to see if anything had fallen where it shouldn't have on its flight down the stairs. There was nothing on the steps or entryway. Then, I went to sleep.

The next morning, I woke up after Paul left for work. Before I took my shower, I brought in the morning paper. When I stepped down onto the entryway landing to open the back door, there was something dark on the floor. Flipping on the overhead light, I found myself standing on top of my pantyhose. My neck tingled. I had tossed them downstairs at midnight. It was now five thirty. First the fan, then the toilet-paper roller, and now this—all in less than a six-hour period. *Someone* was getting very bold.

That afternoon when I returned from work, I asked Paul if he had seen my pantyhose on the landing, on the off chance I had missed them the night before. I braced myself for his lecture about leaving things on the steps, but to my surprise, he replied, "I don't remember seeing anything there when I left." Yikes, that nailed it. The hose must have been tossed back up the stairs that morning after Paul left. I didn't bother to ask my sleeping son about this one.

Another Goal Scored

One Saturday in September, while dusting my angel collection, I placed a couple of figurines on the electric fireplace in the family room. The larger of the two is a white ceramic angel that is kneeling in prayer, and the other is an old blue "kissing angel" keepsake that lost its wings years ago. I arranged the figurines to face into the room. Later that day, when I walked in the room to get my asthma medication, I noticed the little blue angel had been turned a full ninety degrees and was now staring at the white one. The men in this house don't even take notice of my knickknacks, let alone take the time to reposition them.

As long as I didn't mention our psychic pest to Paul or Scott, our day-to-day existence was as smooth as glass. If I went so far as to hint that something out of the ordinary had happened, however, Paul stiffened up, and his speech became guarded. Scott just got upset. On days when things didn't bother me (and there were a few), I laughed at Paul and Scott's reactions—to myself, of course. It was rather amusing, in a pathetic sort of way. Here was a fifty-eight-year-old man who would rather say perfectly absurd things than admit that a paranormal event was happening under his very nose. And it appeared that our son was following in his dad's footsteps. I yearned for the old days, when Scott was small—and he still had an open mind.

An Empty Nest at Long Last

This trio of tales will seem unrelated at first glance, but hang in there. I promise they all tie in together.

- On October 4, 1996, our son moved into his own apartment. Paul and I had not lived alone for thirty-three years, so we were more than ready to experience the empty-nest syndrome. Scott was eager to have his own place, and I was looking forward to having an office: someplace with a door where I could pursue my passion for creative writing. It was a win-win situation all the way around, even though it meant I'd be on my own at night.

The morning he moved, Scott left behind a brown paper grocery bag with some small items in it, as well as a pair of black loafers and several pieces of poster board that he said he'd pick up later. I stacked them neatly on the floor of his closet . . . uh, make that *my* closet!

• Scott's departure gave us the feeling of a new beginning. I suggested we celebrate by purchasing new living-room furniture, which we sorely needed. I had always wanted a sectional. Paul and I sprang into action the morning our son left. We knew that in that small living room a sectional would be a tight fit, so we grabbed the tape measure and took off for the furniture store. When we found the perfect piece, I took its measurements. Back at the house, we arranged our couch and love seat in a somewhat curved shape to approximate those specifications. For a better visual idea of how a sectional would look, I placed some drapery fabric over the furniture to give it the look of one unified piece.

• The next component in this story actually took place a few weeks earlier. In 1962, we'd received a beautiful punch bowl for a wedding gift, and I just love it. The bowl had been camping out in a storage area of the entertainment center for years, however, because I had lost track of the box containing the matching glass cups. Since I use plastic punch cups, the missing box was no pressing concern of mine. I figured one day I'd find them and the set would be reunited.

One weekend in September, while cleaning out a closet, I found the original box and cups. With Thanksgiving around the corner, I could finally use the entire set this year. I placed the bowl upside down in the box, tucked the ladle in next to it, overlapped the flaps, and pushed it under an end table by the couch. I'd find a convenient place to store it later.

That Saturday morning, after moving the living-room furniture this way and that and carefully measuring the clearance on all sides of our mock sectional, we sadly realized the piece we'd looked at wouldn't fit, no matter what we did. I pulled the fabric off the furniture and carelessly tossed it over some boxes. One of them happened to be the punch-bowl box, which had been pulled out from under the end table when we'd first moved the furniture around. Paul and I ended up trying a different layout for our old furniture, since we were stuck with it for the time being. I shoved the punch-bowl box off to one side so no one would fall over it, then left the room to make a phone call.

In the meantime, Paul went across the street to get our neighbor, Maynard, to help move the entertainment center. With that heavy piece of furniture safely in its new spot, Maynard went back to his own Saturday chores.

After making my call, I returned to see how everything looked. While leaning on a fabric-covered carton that was sitting on an end table, my hand suddenly slipped down inside it. I moved the fabric and saw it was the punch-bowl box—but the bowl was missing. Wait a minute! I was taken aback by this unusual sight. "Where is my punch bowl, Paul? I just put it in here a couple of weeks ago."

My husband replied, "It's in the entertainment center, where you always keep it."

"Did you put it back in there?"

"I haven't touched it. When we moved the entertainment center, Maynard wondered why you carelessly threw that beautiful old bowl into the storage compartment like that, and I didn't know what to tell him."

I whipped open the storage compartment door, and there was my bowl, pitched on its side and sitting atop of a jumble of books. I put it back in its box and decided to store it in my newly acquired closet.

When I opened the door to put the box up on the shelf, I noticed that Scott's shoes, poster board, and grocery bag had been flung around on the small closet floor. Aha, our ghost had struck again, the stinker. I tried to visualize it tossing the shoes around the closet. I would have loved to have caught it in the act of removing the punch bowl from the box and placing it in the entertainment center. Do you suppose the bowl floated through the air like in a scene from a horror film? And when, pray tell, did our ghost perform this trick? I'd caught it in the act of making the Barbie dresses float in the air several years ago, and that was a riveting sight—but a punch bowl floating through the air would have been truly awesome to see.

It's Teasing Me

On the first Saturday in November, I did my pre-vacation housecleaning. We were getting ready to leave in a couple of days, and although I wanted to come home to a spotless house, my ulterior motive was to see if my ghost would mess anything up while we were gone.

I began by vacuuming out a cold-air-return vent in the family room. It had been hidden for a decade by my computer desk and two bookshelves, which now resided in my new office. While sitting on the floor to remove the stubborn screws from the grate, I noticed a curved piece of wicker on the carpet. It must have broken off a basket that had sat there for years, I thought. I carelessly tossed the wicker piece over my shoulder and heard it hit something. I turned around and spied it under the dining table. Back to my cleaning, I shifted my position on the floor and felt something stick me. I reached under my right cheek and picked up another piece of wicker. I tossed that one behind me as well, uttering a very bad word. Being overweight and over fifty makes sitting on the floor tough enough without having to be jabbed by sharp objects.

I finally removed the stubborn grate, evicted a large cache of dust, and began replacing the screws. I was miserable by this time. The dust was raising havoc with my asthma, and I was getting stiff and sore. Now what? There was something under my left leg. Good God, not another one! I squirmed around and picked up one more piece of wicker. "Okay, that's the last straw," I thought. I painfully pulled myself up. When I bent over to pick up the other two wicker pieces that had landed under the table, there were no other pieces in the room—only the one in my hand! Apparently my little buddy had been having some fun with me again. That wicker piece will never divulge its part in this supernatural drama, but I ended up saving it anyway. It could keep the orange-handled scissors company; they could compare stories. Wouldn't it be smashing if a paranormal forensic team could dust these pieces for ghostly fingerprints? A hauntee can dream, can't she?

During our vacation, nothing happened. Darn! I'd always held out hope that something dramatic would occur while the house was closed up, like it had that night in 1968. I felt my argument would be won hands-down with no son and no dog in residence now. But no luck there. Apparently, my ghostly actor only wishes to play to an audience of one—that being me . . . lucky, lucky me.

Why Do I Even Bother?

On Thanksgiving Day, my mother, son, daughter, and grandkids were here for dinner. It was an enjoyable, albeit exhausting, day. After dinner, Scott and Kristen packed up some leftovers and returned to their respective homes. My mother and youngest grandson would be spending the night with us, however, so I made up the pull-out sofa bed in the family room for them. Paul went upstairs to bed at seven o'clock, as he does every night, and I plopped down on the couch to enjoy the peace and quiet. My eyelids felt heavy, and even though it was only nine thirty, I was seriously thinking about turning in as well.

While relaxing on the couch and watching television, that irritating tapping started up again. Curses! The spring before, I'd replaced my badly worn fabric lampshades with a molded vinyl pair, and I had regretted it ever since. The solid shades make the taps much easier to hear. They mimic the sound of fingernails drumming on a plastic tray, and they usually occur whenever I'm sitting by one of the living-room lamps.

The taps were quite faint at first but, as is their custom, grew louder and louder. Our couch and end table are in a direct line with a living-room heat vent, and I wondered if the heat was causing some sort of reaction with the cold surface of the shade. Yes, I'm ashamed to admit, I allowed my mind to wander down the Garden Path of Logic once again. Why do I even bother? Several minutes after the tapping began, the heat suddenly came on with a bang. It was winter, and there were no bugs flying against the light bulb. The lamp wasn't even switched on, so the heat in the light bulb wasn't teasing the molecules in the cold vinyl shade. I realized it was my paranormal pest and I was stuck with it. And while I knew I might have to accept that explanation, I didn't have to like it.

I sat there quietly for a moment, letting the spirit have its way, and then firmly said, "Look, I don't want you to bother my mother. I don't want you to bother my grandson. I don't want you to bother me. Get the hell out of here and go to the Light!"

I had seen Echo Bodine use that technique on television many times and decided to give it a try myself. Maybe the pest would actually leave. Of course, Echo is a true professional. She omits the curse words and the snippy attitude. I would have as well, but on that night I was really tired. I always throw myself into cooking holiday dinners, and after the day is over, my whole nervous system craves total peace and quiet. Too much commotion irritates me. I just want to be left alone. After my outburst, the noises abruptly stopped, and nothing happened for a couple of weeks.

Saturday, December 7, 1996—A Month of Surprises Begins

This morning after I got dressed, I placed two large rolls of transparent tape on the kitchen counter to be used later, when I would attach Christmas lights to my office window. They say men can't live without their duct tape. I can't speak for all women, but my world revolves around transparent packing tape. I use it for everything from repairing a hem to hanging Christmas decorations. Nearly every window decoration in my house has sticky tape underneath it. Paul was upstairs getting dressed to go to a ham radio fest in Wisconsin, and I was eating breakfast in the family room. Around eight thirty, I heard a loud metallic crash in the kitchen. Of all the noises I've heard in that room over the years, nothing had ever sounded like that. I had to check it out. One roll of tape had flown off the counter and landed on the floor in front of the stove. Whoa!

Around ten o'clock, while washing up the breakfast dishes, I heard a muffled sound, like something soft had fallen onto the floor. I peered around the counter and discovered that a stack of paper plates had taken a nosedive off a small shelf. Hmm, a second visit from my little ghost.

Vibrations had not caused either of these incidents. That's Paul's favorite rationale for anything strange that happens around here. This morning, I blew it. When the tape flew off the counter, I should have yelled up the steps, "Did you hear that?" The stairway door was open, so he couldn't have helped but hear the noise. I missed the perfect chance to tell him what had just happened; I simply put the roll of tape back on the counter and returned to my cereal and toast. I'm so conditioned to taking these things in stride and keeping my mouth shut that bringing them to Paul's attention doesn't even occur to me. It was the best chance I've ever had to prove my point. Paul wasn't even home when the paper plates fell—not that it would have mattered.

Sunday, December 8, 1996

While relaxing in the recliner this evening, an abrasive scratching noise came from behind the Christmas tree. It sounded like someone was rubbing a piece of heavyweight butcher paper against the wall. Strange! There was absolutely nothing behind the tree, because all the gifts were in the family room, waiting to be wrapped. My thoughts drifted back to the mysterious icicle that formed a backward J last year. That visual was amazing to see; however, noises are a different breed of animal altogether. Sounds scare me!

Saturday, December 14, 1996

We had homemade vegetable beef soup tonight. I made way too much for the two of us, so I called my son to see if he wanted to stop by tomorrow and pick some up. He said he'd come over on Monday evening. It's Paul's favorite homemade soup, and since he always pigs out when we have it, I decided to put some aside tonight just in case Paul couldn't stop himself.

I took the kettle of soup out of the refrigerator and placed it on the counter to the left of the sink; then I realized I didn't have any containers for Scott's portion. After rummaging through the recycling bag, I found an applesauce jar and washed it up, and then went back to find the lid. No luck there, so that jar went back in the sack. I recalled seeing three pint jars with covers in the laundry room and went down to grab a couple of them. I rarely go down there at night; to be honest, I hate to go down there at all unless Paul is awake.

As I began washing the jars, I noticed that one contained a hardened transparent substance on the bottom of it. Curses! I was forced to go back downstairs again. The third jar was perfect, so I washed and rinsed the containers. As I reached for a dishtowel, those irritating taps began knocking on the kitchen door, which I had just closed. They were really loud; in fact, they were downright impertinent. It was disturbing to hear them clicking on the door—and even more so when they began their irritating cadence from *inside* the recycling bag, several feet away. The hair on the back of my neck stood straight up. I wanted to flee the kitchen, but tonight I refused to be bullied. I took a deep breath and finished drying the jars.

When I turned to dish up the soup, I stopped dead in my tracks. Right next to the soup kettle stood a sticky plastic syrup bottle— the same bottle that I'd tossed in the recycling bag after breakfast, twelve hours ago. I just shook my head and picked it up. I managed to say, with a good deal of conviction, "You are not helping me one bit. This has got to stop." I whaled the syrup bottle back into the bag with a vengeance and heard no more taps that night. Oddly enough, only a half-hour earlier I had foolishly thought to myself, "What a peaceful weekend." That'll teach me.

Saturday, December 21, 1996

Kari-Lynn is spending the weekend with us. She's a delightful child. The kids have grown into great little personalities, and Paul and I enjoy each of them equally. When all three are here, however, it's pandemonium, so we're trying out this one-kid-at-a-time schedule. It's working very well. Each child gets to feel special, because they don't have to compete with the other two for our attention.

This morning, we were going to do some last-minute power shopping. Kari-Lynn had just gotten out of the shower and was checking in with her mom on the living-room phone. Paul was in his office. I was in the family room, writing out a schedule for today. With way too much to do and an extra passenger with me, I'd have to make every minute count. I could not find Kari-Lynn's medication, so I asked her to check with Kris to see if we had left it at their house last night. Kari-Lynn said, "Mom says you have it. You put it in your fanny pack." When I checked, it was in there all right. Where was my brain? I zipped the bag shut, left it on the kitchen counter, and returned to my schedule in the family room.

Several minutes later, while Kari-Lynn was still chatting on the phone, I walked back into the kitchen to get a tissue. My ghost was showing off now. My sunglasses had been removed from the little bag and were sitting out on the other counter, next to the tissue box.

When Kari-Lynn hung up the phone, I asked her if she had taken my sunglasses out. She looked very puzzled. "What sunglasses, Grandma?" I knew she hadn't, because she'd been in the living room the entire time she was on the phone; Paul hadn't even been in the kitchen. Why do I always play twenty questions? Because it's a hard habit to break, that's why. I hoped this would be the ghost's one and only performance today, because I really didn't have time for these antics.

This evening, after trying to decide where to sleep, Kari-Lynn chose to bunk down on the inflatable bed in the living room. I had already made up the family-room sofa bed for the two of us, so against my better judgment, I decided to sleep in there tonight by myself. Around eight o'clock, while working in my office, I heard a loud crash in the kitchen. Kari-Lynn was giggling at a video in the living room. Paul was asleep upstairs. Although I immediately felt goose bumps on my arms and the familiar tingling on the back of my neck, a good twenty minutes elapsed before I left my writing project to check it out.

I've never gotten used to the crashing, scraping, bumping, clicking, and thumping noises in the kitchen, and I probably never will.

It isn't easy for me to describe what I hear. The noises mimic the click of cupboard doors opening or the soft thud of a bag of sugar falling on the counter. Sometimes I hear the kitchen floor creaking or the sound of a door opening or softly closing. This time, as always, nothing was out of place. I checked in the family room. Everything was in tiptop shape in there as well. I turned on the television for a welcome diversion and then decided to wrap a few small gifts as long as I was in there. I have been very lax about wrapping Christmas gifts this year because of the arthritis in my hands and fingers. Wrestling with tape and wrapping paper just hasn't been high on my list of things to do. While assembling the items needed to wrap a gift, I heard a familiar sound behind me, next to the microwave cart. It was the distinct sound of heavyweight paper being dragged across the wall, the same sound I'd heard in the living room a couple of nights ago. This occurred in the area where we store newspapers for recycling. I quickly turned around but saw nothing moving. I picked up the sack of papers and shook it just in case this time it *was* a mouse—a mouse with a large piece of butcher paper in its wee mouth! We haven't had mice for years, but hope springs eternal. Nothing moved in the sack, so I returned to my wrapping.

The scratchy noise started up again the minute my back was turned. That did it! I knew I couldn't sleep in the family room tonight, so I folded up the sofa bed while cussing at my tormentor. The living-room couch is old and not the most comfortable place to sleep any longer. As I surveyed the cramped situation, I cursed under my breath. With the inflatable bed butted up against the recliner, it would be impossible to extend the footrest without disturbing Kari-Lynn, who was sound asleep by this time. I guess it's the couch for me tonight, if I can reach it without tripping over something. I know I could go upstairs, but it's always been my policy to sleep down here whenever one of the kids is visiting, in case they get scared or need something. I am not happy.

Later in the evening, when I finally got settled on the couch, a couple of teasing taps broke the silence of the room. My warning worked quite well at Thanksgiving, so why not try it again? With my sleeping granddaughter a foot away from me, I quietly said, "I don't want you to bother me or my granddaughter tonight. Do you understand?" A series of loud taps burst forth near the small living-room window behind the recliner. From the window, the noises moved next to my head, causing my nerves to snap—then, delicious silence. For a second, I wondered if this ghost speaks in Morse code. I don't know Morse code, except for SOS—which is quite appropriate, come to think of it. Then I fell into a fitful sleep.

Monday, December 23, 1996

During lunch today, I told Nancy about my weekend. She scolded, "I told you to get a ghost buster out there. The sooner, the better." I promised to think about it before spring comes. Daytime noises don't even bother me anymore, unless they are extremely loud, but nocturnal outbursts affect me deeply. I'm developing frequent chest pains and palpitations from stress. It has to stop.

Nancy agreed. She pointed out that it was ruining my health. As usual, she was right.

A Christmas Eve to End All Christmas Eves

Christmas is a magical time of year, when children and adults alike look forward to opening the beautiful packages under the tree. Each year, we spend Christmas Day with my mom; however, Christmas Eve belongs to Paul's family in South Minneapolis. On this frigid night, we carpooled, so Kristen and her husband rode with Scott, and our grandchildren rode with us. The kids were having a serious discussion about what Santa Claus was going to bring them. Paul and I nearly burst from holding in our laughter while we eavesdropped on their conversation. Occasionally, the kids would sing along with the Christmas carols softly playing on the radio. Kari-Lynn decided to help the Muppets belt out "The Twelve Days of Christmas." Kari-Lynn has always had expensive tastes, so it was no surprise when she customized the lyrics a little. Instead of "Five go-oold rings," we heard "Five dia-mond rings" coming from the back seat. She was flanked on either side by John-Paul and Camden. Each time she messed up the lyrics, they both turned to her and, in one loud voice, said, "It's five *gold* rings, Kari-Lynn . . . five *gold* rings." Laughter erupted in the front seat. We could no longer contain it. It was such a bright spot to have the kids riding with us. It helped lighten the evening, because Paul's mother was terminally ill, and although laughter and good times would ring throughout her home tonight, the inevitable would be on everyone's mind.

When we arrived, we marveled at how she had managed to put together a dinner with all the traditional dishes and cookies she always makes for the holiday. Everything was set out on her lovely dining-room table, complete with candles, china, and flatware. Dora's strong personality keeps her bravely hanging on, never complaining about the pain that is wreaking havoc with her frail body.

A few weeks ago, Dora sent out an announcement insisting that *all* her children come to Christmas Eve dinner and be there at four thirty sharp. All but two sons showed up. One lived on the West Coast and, since he had been back to see her at Thanksgiving, was not planning to come for Christmas this year. The other, who lived a few blocks away, decided to stay home with his wife, who is recovering from surgery. They planned to spend Christmas Day with Dora, when the house is less noisy.

The sons who came for dinner were out running errands before the big meal. Her oldest went to pick up her favorite German bread. We knew he wouldn't find that bakery open, but he went anyway to see what he could find. Tradition means a lot to Dora, and she has always served this bread on Christmas Eve. Somehow amid the hustle and bustle of Christmas preparations, it had fallen through the cracks. Dora was upset about her missing bread, because she wanted everything to be perfect. A record snowfall had inundated our area a couple of days earlier, leaving the driveways and streets full of deep icy ruts, so Paul volunteered to pick up his brother Barry, who was stuck in his driveway at home.

While we waited for the guys to return, Dora asked Kristen to help her from the kitchen table to her favorite chair by the fireplace in the living room. I sat down in a chair a few feet away from Dora. Her daughter-in-law Abby and Kristen were sitting across the room from us, along with Kari-Lynn, Camden, Abby's little daughter, and my nephew's wife. We were all waiting patiently for the guys to come back so we could eat.

I asked Dora if she needed anything but didn't get a reply. I smiled and thought to myself, "She's dozed off," because she had leaned her head over to one side, facing the fireplace. Immediately after I spoke to my mother-in-law, Abby and Kristen noticed that she wasn't breathing. While Abby grabbed Dora, Kristen hustled the little kids off to join the others in the den, and then she hurried back. The two young women tried to rouse her, but Dora had already left us. The 911 call was placed, and the house was in an uproar from that moment on. Our never-to-be-forgotten Christmas had begun.

Unfortunately, Dora had neglected to sign the "Do Not Resuscitate" form. As a result of that oversight, a series of paramedics, firemen, and police invaded both her home and her body on this, her favorite holiday. As each son returned from his errand, he was met outside by emergency response vehicles and inside by the surreal sight of paramedics pumping up and down on his mother's naked chest. Without a signed DNR form, her lifeless body was forced to endure aggressive CPR for twenty agonizing minutes before she could be officially pronounced dead. The paramedics apologized to the family, because although they found no vital signs, their hands were tied. Rules are rules. It was especially painful for Abby, who had carefully cared for her mother-in-law for the past several years. I overheard her sob to her husband, Barry, "I heard a snap. I think they broke her ribs."

Talk about a silent night of contradictions! Inside the warm house, the police were asking tough questions of family members to rule out foul play while the paramedics whose heroic efforts could not bring Dora back tenderly consoled those same family members. Outside in the bitter cold, the piercing lights on the emergency vehicles loudly screamed, "Warning: There's trouble in this house!" while the soft Christmas lights that adorned the other neighborhood homes gently whispered, "Peace on Earth, goodwill to men." Dora released her spirit on that cold winter night, leaving dinner on the table, gifts unopened, and her family—both old and young—in a state of shock, confusion, and sadness. Sincere condolences, and Merry Christmas to all!

Dora's death brought back a painful memory of her husband, who had passed away a few years earlier. One Saturday morning, eight months prior to his death, he telephoned our home and said some appalling things to me. He spent close to a half-hour berating me, saying that of all his daughters-in-law, I was the absolute worst. He was in extreme pain from cancer and was probably intoxicated that morning as well. Although I was aware of that, I was being treated for depression at the time, and his tirade upset me to the point where I could not bring myself to answer my home phone till after he died. Even though I've never been fond of answering machines, I gladly allowed ours to screen our calls during this disturbing period of time.

Since my mother-in-law had never seemed too fond of me, I couldn't help but wonder what I was in for now that she had crossed over. Raging paranoia, perhaps. Don't judge me till you've walked a mile in my moccasins or survived ten thousand evenings in my home. My daughter teased me that Grandma's ghost would come back and nag me about my messy housekeeping. Dora kept an immaculate house, but I don't always achieve that goal. She often pointed that out to me in not-so-subtle ways, and I always resented it. Enough said.

Now, here's the most peculiar thing. The ghostly activity that has escalated in the past few months has suddenly stopped. There was no explanation for this, unless the ghost was leaving me alone out of respect for the dead. Only time will tell if anything starts up again, but in the interim I'm going to enjoy this quiet period of mourning. I'll put this journal away for now but will start it again if anything else happens. Since *it* has come and gone in the past, it'll more than likely return.

During this introspective time, I am doing some serious soul searching. It seems when the ghostly activity is bugging me, I absolutely hate it. My personality can't deal with it. I can't sleep. The stress causes me to eat way too much. I jump at the slightest sound. And boy, am I crabby! That's no way to live. But now, with my house so quiet, I actually miss it. Have I become so conditioned to those ghostly happenings that my life is empty without them? That's pathetic. The annoying mischief that takes place around here must keep me company in some perverse way. But please don't get me wrong: I'd much rather have a dog for company at night. To be more specific, a dog who doesn't know how to tap on lampshades, or mess around with lights, or hide things!

8: New Visitors, New Light—1997

January 1997—What Will the New Year Bring?
A scant couple of anemic taps have danced back into my life. But at this point, there is nothing worth writing about.

February 2, 1997—Well, That Didn't Last Very Long
The noises have returned, bolder than ever. In fact, while working on this project today, the tapping sounds literally walked into my office. I first heard them by the door. Then they proceeded across the office walls, and they now appear to be hovering on the oppo-site side of the room, next to my PC. This winter has been so severe that many people are having leakage problems in their homes, so out of habit, I checked for dripping water. Just as I thought, our house has no visible drips—only an invisible pest.

Earlier this evening, while we were eating dinner in the living room, a weird noise came from the kitchen. Paul probably thought it was the oven cooling off, but I know every sound in this house, and it wasn't the oven. You see, I'm not upstairs every night at seven o'clock drifting off to sleep, like he is. I'm fully awake till past midnight, and I have heard it all. The noise came from over by the refrigerator, and it wasn't the sound of the compressor turning on and off either. It sounded more like something had fallen off of it onto the floor. I didn't say anything to Paul, because we were having a pleasant evening and I didn't feel like stressing myself out over a silly argument. I scrapped the idea of hiring a ghost buster last month, because nothing was happening. Now *it* has returned, and even though I've been quite assertive with my ghost in recent weeks, my assertiveness doesn't work as well as it did a couple of months ago.

Living with paranormal activity is a taxing experience. Years ago, my neighbor predicted that my sense of humor would keep me sane. Sense of humor or not, I guess I've hung in there longer than most people would under these circumstances. Having someone or something to keep me company at night would certainly help. Unfortunately, I cannot go to sleep as early as Paul does, and my allergies and asthma have made it nearly impossible to get another pet. My doctors have probably posted my mug shot over every cash register in every pet shop in the Western Hemisphere with this warning: *Do Not Sell to This Woman.* If I really wanted one, I'd buy one, but knowing the impact a pet would have on me, it's my decision to remain without a furry buddy.

February 13, 1997—Do You Hear What I Hear?

Some evening I should invite a trusted neighbor over after Paul goes to bed. Last night, immediately after he went upstairs, the tapping noises began in the bay window area. I'd love to find out if others can hear them. My entire nervous system is highly sensitive to these anomalies, which is why I have heard them from the day we moved in. It would be an interesting experiment to see if someone else—

someone who knows nothing about my house—can. If they hear the taps, I'll have the confirmation I need. However, I have to face the possibility they would hear nothing, since my ghost seems to target me alone.

Lonely (adverb): isolated; longing for company

Paul and I seem to live a very isolated life. In the years since the kids grew up, our only visitors are family members and one or two really good friends. As a couple, we have practically no social life. Since Paul goes upstairs to bed early on weekdays and weekends alike, there isn't much time for any home entertaining, and we rarely go out for a night on the town. However, I could certainly have visitors on my own or go out with friends. Sitting here alone is my choice, and the ball is in my court.

My unique lifestyle is rooted in my troubled childhood. My parents were very poor and could not afford to do much entertaining. My mother went into a severe depression and suffered a nervous breakdown after my older brother's murder. She may have been a little more outgoing prior to that day, but I can vouch for the fact that she shut herself away after that terrible tragedy. Back in the forties, if you were committed for any type of mental health problem, you were subjected to electric-shock therapy or worse. I can understand why my mother hid out on her brother's farm till she felt well enough to face the world again. Would any of us have done it differently? However, while hiding from the world, she forced me into exile as well. My dad worked in town and stayed at our apartment during the week; he drove out to see us on the weekends. I had no idea my reclusive role models would shape my future life.

The relatives and friends who visited our home when I was young were almost too few to mention. Other than our yearly visits from Dad's sisters from Illinois and the occasional visit from his brother's family from Seattle, our home had no out-of-town company. We kids eagerly looked forward to those visits. Occasionally, aunts and uncles who lived in nearby communities would come to see us. They did so to help my mother out of her malaise, not because they were invited. I sometimes think she resented their intrusion.

Even though I am responsible for my own life now, I can't help but wonder how much those early years shaped my personality. My mom hid because of her sorrow; I hide because of my ghost. I don't feel comfortable in my own house, so I'm positive others won't either. Martha's words still ring in my ears: "Everyone knew your house was haunted." That's why I don't invite neighbors over for coffee, nor accept invitations to their homes. I have no idea whether their interest lies in getting to know me or getting inside my house because of the ghost. Every neighborhood needs an enigma. It's not a bad thing, just a sad thing.

When our children were small, our house was a magnet for all the kids in the neighborhood. During those years, not a day went by when we didn't have neighbor kids in here doing crafts, playing games, jumping on beds, sleeping over, yelling, fighting, making peanut-butter sandwiches, spilling drinks, and so much more. Although my house was noisy and messy, I didn't mind, because I always knew where my kids were. I took on the task of guiding twelve little Bluebirds through their weekly meetings so Kristen could join the group. Before I knew it, I became a Campfire leader. After that group disbanded, I volunteered to take over for Scott's den mother when she went into labor. These activities took my mind off my little ghost, at least during the daytime hours.

When our children became teenagers, their pool of friends dwindled to two or three really good ones. Even after Scott became an adult, his pals would sit in his room and visit with him, so there was at least some social activity going on. Maybe I should start inviting people over just to visit with me, because the annoying taps aren't very good company. It would be a nice change of pace, even if I have a hidden agenda.

February 19, 1997—Somebody Pinch Me

The other night, while Paul and I were eating dinner in the living room, he began staring at the bay window. He actually got up from his recliner and started listening intently over by the curtains. Then he began running his hands along the paneling and the windows. *Now this is an interesting turn of events*, I thought.

He said, "Something must be dripping somewhere. I keep hearing tapping noises."

I was so shocked I almost choked on my food. "Nothing is dripping, Paul." I tried to sound rational for his benefit, yet mysterious enough so he would elaborate a little more on this noise. Now my heart was pounding in the back of my throat.

"Maybe it's the house settling."

"The house isn't settling, Paul." I punched each word. My inner voice pleaded with him to argue with me, but he paid no attention. He returned to his dinner, pausing a couple more times to glance in the direction of the windows. After their dinnertime appearance, the taps laid low for the rest of the evening.

The next day at lunch, I filled Nancy in on the previous evening. Her eyes lit up, and she pounced on that piece of information. "Did you finally discuss the noises with Paul, since he was the one who brought them up?"

I explained to her that we had been eating dinner. I didn't want to pick a topic of conversation that I knew would end in an argument, especially when Paul and I only have a short time to spend with each other after work. She didn't understand my reasoning, so I explained that I'd hoped my guarded replies would force him to ask me what I thought it was, but that didn't happen. "Nancy, he knows what I think it is. I know he knows what I think it is. It's gotten to be a game with us, and I just dropped it." Nancy shook her head out of sheer frustration, even though she probably wanted to shake *me* instead. I can't fault her. I wish I had her assertive personality, but I don't. I'll have to bide my time till this whole thing plays itself out.

Here's an interesting note worth mentioning: clicking and tapping furnace noises have occurred ever since we bought the house, so it seems odd that Paul would suddenly mention them after all these years. We've often heard curious noises around the bay window when the furnace was running. There is a vent on that wall, and I'm sure that's what my husband heard the other night at supper. What surprised me was the fact that he actually admitted to hearing a noise. I wonder if he's heard taps in that area before and had no explanation for them. The mini-blinds are nowhere near that vent, but he still placed a throw pillow against them so they couldn't wiggle in those imaginary air currents of his. That's what he decided was making the noise. It must be nice living in his world.

For those who might not know this, when heated air flows through cold furnace ducts, it can cause anything from little clicking sounds to sharp knocks. It's pure science—all about the cold metal being expanded by the heated air. The taps I hear vary their level of intensity as well. However, they also vary their location, and they do so all year long—not just during the months when we run the furnace.

A Whiff of Nocturnal Mischief

While drifting off to sleep a couple of nights later, the oppressive odors of cigarettes and whiskey enveloped my entire body for several minutes. Just as I was about to choke, they left as abruptly as they had come. Paul and I haven't smoked for over twenty-five years. We haven't had alcohol in the house for ages, and I can't remember us ever buying whiskey, since neither of us like it. There is only one explanation for these specific smells to materialize in a closed house in the middle of winter: my father-in-law's spirit dropped in to annoy me. Having my father-in-law's spirit hanging around, especially after our last conversation, is not a comforting thought. Even though we'd always been friends and I adored him, his last phone call was loaded with negative energy that caused me great anxiety for months afterward.

Beware the Ides of March

The year is well on its way. Nancy keeps asking me when I'm inviting Echo Bodine out here. I keep wondering why I don't. That's a lie—I know why I don't. The ghost buster may come up empty, leaving me no recourse but to check into the nearest mental health facility. That is the moment of truth I cannot face. After all the mental suffering I've endured, I think it would destroy me if my home were found to be spirit-free.

There is new "stuff" happening these days, but I can't deal with it. I have surpassed the status of borderline diabetic and now need pills to control my blood sugar. My whole life is out of whack. As I'm writing this, those damn taps are inching along the walls of my office near the ceiling, and a truly disagreeable odor, which I will explain later, is hanging in the air. I'll get back to this journal when I get all my doctors' appointments squared away. I promise.

April 1997—The Saga of the Chair Begins

Three months ago, my brother-in-law, Barry, insisted that Paul and I and our children take some of Dora's belongings. In accordance with her last will and testament, Barry and his wife were left with an entire household to dispose of, and they pleaded with all the family members to take something. Paul had already told his brother several times over the phone that we didn't want anything; however, Barry kept asking us to reconsider, because everyone else had already gone through the house and taken what they wanted. Against our better judgment, Paul, Scott, Kristen, and I drove three vehicles to South Minneapolis one frosty Saturday morning to check out the leftovers.

When we arrived, Dora's well-ordered home resembled a picked-over garage sale. Odds and ends were piled on the beautiful dining-room table and matching sideboard. Dora had always kept a spotless house, so the disarray in front of our eyes was totally out of character for her. I couldn't imagine what she'd be thinking if her spirit were hovering somewhere close by. All the really good items had already been claimed by family members who were more enthusiastic about this process than we were. Those items had "Taken" signs taped to them.

Scott looked around but took nothing. He'd had the same type of relationship with his grandmother as I had. For some reason known only to Dora, neither of us had ever bonded with her. Kristen found a few things that she wanted as keepsakes. Paul took nothing for himself. I found a new earthenware bowl and pitcher set still in its original box on a shelf in a bedroom closet. There was no name on it, so I claimed it. I could always give it as a gift. After spending a half-hour in the house, I noticed there were no names on the two small chairs in the living room. For years now, I've wanted a comfortable chair for my office, so I considered choosing one of them. Paul didn't look very thrilled when I told him. The oatmeal-colored tweed fabric on both chairs was in wonderful condition, though, so it was tempting. The chairs were small in scale, too, and compatible with my office's color scheme. Now for the bad news: Dora died in one of them! After I made my final decision to take a chair, Paul and I spoke as one: "We don't want the chair she died in." Everyone in the room that morning was there on Christmas Eve, so we all knew that the death chair had been sitting next to the fireplace. I chose the one I had been sitting in that fateful evening.

Paul, Scott, and our nephew hauled the little swivel rocker, some folding chairs, a cedar chest, and many mismatched plates, cups, and flatware out to our vehicles, and we were off. I really didn't feel right taking anything from Dora's estate. We had never been friends. Paul and I had talked about this for days and felt that, due to the circumstances, taking any of her belongings made us no better than the tacky scavengers who raided Scrooge's rooms while the old curmudgeon was out doing the town with the Ghost of Christmas Yet-to-Be. The scene where the filthy old charwoman brags about her ill-gotten booty to the shifty-eyed broker is one of my favorites. I love it when she tells him, "Aye took down 'is bed curtains—rings and awl. 'E shan't be needin' them anymoah, now will 'e, deh-rie?" (My 'umble apologies to Mr. Dickens.)

The chair sat in our family room for a week. The following Saturday, I decided to haul it into my office, because I was tired of waiting for my husband to do it. Paul reminds me a little of that old film character, Pat Kettle: "I gotta do that one of these days." This was a feat of physical endurance, logistics, and sheer determination. I struggled to pull the chair across the carpeting into our small kitchen. The swivel-rocker design made it awkward to handle. The chair was much too wide to fit through the eighteen-inch opening that led into the hall, and too heavy for me to lift it up and over that opening. I solved that problem by pushing the rocker up onto the counter, sliding it across, and then lowering it on the other side and pulling it into the hall. Piece of cake! Although it kept getting hung up on the hall carpeting, I managed to coax it into my office. Once in place, I immediately plopped down into the chair, because although I felt a tremendous sense of accomplishment, I also felt a familiar pain in my chest.

The Sweet Smell of Spring Is in the Air (But Not in My Office)

The chair gave my office some class, and I quickly forgot the misgivings I'd had about bringing it home. All was right in my world—that is, until the room began to smell. The chair hadn't smelled the entire week it had sat in the family room, so I was puzzled by this turn of events. The sickening odor was faint at first but soon became intolerable. It wasn't body odor or urine, but an icky combination of both. My office had not smelled before I'd brought the chair in, so it didn't take a member of Mensa to figure out the origin of the sickening stench.

Had Paul's mother died in this chair? No, she was sitting in the other chair; I was sitting in this swivel rocker. Did someone switch the cushions? We told them when we walked into the house that we didn't want anything, and we were going to stick to our guns. So *no one* knew I was going to take that chair until the very second I made the decision—not even me.

I remember glancing at the chair when we walked in that morning. Although the two chairs were similar in size and shape, the only thing identical about them was the fabric. The cushion didn't fit quite right on the swivel rocker, but I didn't give it a second thought, since I didn't want it. The family was right there in the living room when I decided to take the chair, so when did the switcheroo take place? Before we arrived, perhaps? But why bother? Someone had probably wanted the nicer chair but not the cushion on it, so whoever had ended up with this little rocker got more than they'd bargained for. Hello . . . that would be me!

Hindsight being twenty-twenty, I should have brought the ill-fitting cushion to everyone's attention as soon as I noticed it. At least then I could have exchanged it. Unfortunately, that didn't happen. With the death theory already formed in my mind, I had no recourse but to cautiously lift the cushion to see what it looked like underneath. Ugh! There was the death stain, all right. A brownish discoloration covered over half of the reverse side. I sniffed it: it had a faint odor of urine. I dropped the disgusting item to the floor. My heart sank. That very moment I knew I couldn't keep the chair. That woman had disliked me from the day we met and had never run out of ways to show it. Now the cushion she died on is mine. It's the ultimate insult.

I called my daughter and told her all about it. She started laughing and said, "They stuck you with the death chair? I wouldn't want that chair in my house." I was sitting in *that* chair when Kristen uttered those words. From directly behind me came a dull thump, as if the wall had just been struck with the palm of an invisible hand. I wasn't rocking at the time, so the chair hadn't bumped the wall. I quickly sat upright, as rigid as a statue, and told Kris what had just happened. The back of my neck was tingling. She said, "I'm glad it's in your house and not mine." Gee, thanks a lot, kiddo!

She promised that the next time they came over, she'd check it out. Her chance came two weeks later. Kristen walked into my office, and three feet into the room she said, "Whew, this room smells like a nursing home. I can smell BO and urine and God knows what else." The smell grew stronger the closer she got to the chair. She lifted the cushion and sniffed it. "Yup, it's coming from right here."

I said, "Check the rest of the chair. You don't smell a thing."

She said, "I'd throw it out if I were you, unless you want to write your book in a nursing home."

I whined back, "If Grandma is haunting me now, what will she do if I throw her chair out into the snow?" Kris shrugged her shoulders. I knew she empathized with me, but there was nothing she could do.

I had been complaining to Paul about the odor in my room for some time now and how I thought it might be coming from the chair. He'd told me to get rid of it, but I was dragging my feet because I still wanted a comfortable chair. My checkbook looked pretty bleak, so I made the decision to hang on to the offensive item till spring, then clean and thoroughly air out the cushion. But when I told him about the stain, he said, "That does it. Out it goes."

On a cold, sunny Saturday in March, my husband hauled the stinky chair out the front door and perched it on a high snowbank next to the mailbox. Since it was in such good shape, he left the cushion standing with the stain side up so an unsuspecting rummager wouldn't pick it up by mistake. We had a good laugh over what the neighbors would think about that big ol' urine stain. They were probably taking bets on which one of us did it.

Coincidentally, soon after this happened, a famous German car company came out with a commercial about two young men driving along in their cute little hatchback. They spy a rocker almost identical to this one sitting on the curb by someone's trash. They grab it for their apartment and continue on their way, smiling and feeling good about the free chair they've found. Moments later, it begins to give off a disagreeable odor. They sniff the air and make terrible faces at each other. Ah, art imitating life. The difference here is they had the presence of mind to immediately drop the chair off and proceed on their way. Of course, they had writers!

But wait, there's more. The garbage people hauled the chair away over a week ago, yet for some reason, the odor remained behind. I have no rational explanation for this unpleasant development. It's too cold to air out the room yet, so I have been forced to spray air freshener—heavily and repeatedly—to clear out that smell. It works . . . for about five minutes, and then the odor triumphantly returns. It smelled even stronger than before we tossed out the chair. How could that be? Kristen was as puzzled as I was. We tried to figure out how to clean air that refused to be cleaned. I've dealt with spirits in this house from the day we moved in, and I'm not ready to accept another—especially this one.

Since I didn't want to admit that it might be Dora's spirit, I fanatically immersed myself in finding another source for the odor. I checked every inch of the carpeting by crawling on my hands and knees. I sniffed the padding on my desk chair, I sniffed the drapes, and I sniffed every cloth item in that room, including the clothes inside the closet. I became a human bloodhound. The result of this humiliating exercise was disturbing, because *nothing else smelled*— only the air. My mother-in-law's spirit was probably laughing quite loudly at my expense on the other side of the veil.

Sometime in April, the temperature rose to fifty fantastic degrees, and I cracked each window a couple of inches. The fresh air smelled so good. I left for work on that first warm morning expecting to come home to a clean-smelling office. However, when I returned, I walked into the same pungent mixture of body odor and urine that had saturated the air in my office for the past couple months. As the outdoor temperature became warmer, I opened the windows wider. Each afternoon when I returned from work, the room smelled the same as it had in the dead of winter when the house had been sealed.

Now I'm really worried. She's never going to leave. Paul doesn't come into my office much, and his sense of smell is not good; therefore, he hasn't gotten a whiff of the stubborn odor yet. He'd never believe my theory anyway, so it's just as well.

One night, while trying to drift off to sleep with the ever-present taps dancing on the lampshade, that god-awful urine odor smothered my face for just an instant. The sickening smell was intense, and it made me nauseous. For a moment, I wondered if the odor had gotten so strong that it was invading other rooms in the house. But in the blink of an eye, it vanished. Had she drifted into the living room to taunt me before I dropped off to sleep? Why that night? Why didn't she float upstairs and haunt her son for a while? I wouldn't mind. Since it would be too difficult to explain to Paul how I could still smell that chair weeks after it was gone, I opted to tell my support buddies, just to unburden myself.

The Merry Month of May

Spring continues to be very unsettled this year. A few pleasant days in the sixties are repeatedly replaced with daytime highs hovering around the freezing mark. I have been keeping my windows open nearly the entire time, regardless. The odor stubbornly remains in my office and doesn't appear to change in intensity whether the windows are open or not. I guess you can't air out a spirit—especially this one. It's so stubborn that it won't allow fresh air into the room at all. What can I do?

At lunch one day, I confided this aberration to Lu, a very good friend. "How long can this odor linger in my office?" I asked. "It defies all logic." Lu just shook her head. She is very much like my husband: sensible and never given to flights of fancy. When she can't logically explain something, it bothers her. The only difference is, she doesn't make up goofy theories when she's stumped. While we munched on our sandwiches, I offered Lu my theory.

I truly believe my mother-in-law's spirit is haunting me. That's as rational as I can get about this dilemma. I know my dear friend has trouble buying into my explanation one hundred percent, but at the same time, she can't disprove it. She's probably thankful it does not inhabit her house, and I'm thankful she hasn't suggested I check into the local loony bin. But despite all this thankfulness, the air in my office still smells, and there's no apparent way to get rid of it.

May 11, 1997—When Did It Leave?

I was waiting for the weekend to roll around, so I could shampoo the carpet, rub down the walls with panel cleaner, and wash the curtains. That vile odor had to go, one way or another. If fresh air didn't take care of it, maybe overpowering it with cleaning products was the only option I had. It would be nice, I thought, if Dora noticed the effort I was making and just up and left.

On Thursday evening, Kris called and asked what we were going to do for Mother's Day. Oh, brother. I'd been so preoccupied with this mess that I'd completely forgot it was Mother's Day weekend. On Friday night, my mother called and said she was driving down Saturday morning, so I decided to postpone my cleaning effort till next week. What was another week at this point? Gag!

When my daughter and her family arrived for dinner on Sunday, she headed straight for my office. Kris said she couldn't smell a thing. At that point, neither could I. That odor was such a part of my life that I had no idea when it disappeared. This inexplicable—yet welcome—turn of events couldn't have come at a better time, however, because I was at the end of my rope. I wonder if my mother's presence scared my mother-in-law's presence away. Gee, if that's all it took, I should have had my mom down here months ago!

A Summer of Opposites

June of 1997 was an extremely dry month in our neck of the woods. I had to water my flower garden every other day to keep my plants alive. How I wished the annoying taps would dry up and blow away with the hot, arid wind that was whipping around outside.

As dry as June had been, July set a record for the most rainfall in one month since back in the late 1800s. The floods were raging up in the Red River Valley. Paul and I watched the news each evening, along with the rest of the country, as the network anchors announced catastrophe after catastrophe. Just think of the massive cleanup and moldy smells the residents will deal with when they move back into their homes—if they have homes after the water recedes. My haunted little house didn't look so bad to me when compared with other people's problems. There's nothing like a natural calamity to take one's mind off a supernatural pest—for a while, that is. Although this sounds petty, those unfortunate people can clean up, rebuild, or move elsewhere and start their lives over in a new house, but I'll be stuck here forever.

September 15, 1997—Are You Ready for This?

Echo Bodine called today and left a long, apologetic message on my voice mail at work. Hallelujah! This is what I have been waiting for since 1994. I sat there in shock while she complimented me on the well-written letter I sent her. Then she asked if she could use that letter in a book she's planning to write on the subject of home buyers who find they've purchased a haunted house. Apparently, the book will contain tips on how to deal with these unwanted spirits. She felt my letter contained some very good examples of what unsuspecting homeowners go through when they share their new home with some old residents.

I must admit I am very flattered; however, I cannot call her from the office. Some privacy is needed for this conversation. I hurried to call Nancy, but she was at lunch. I was crushed. I had to share this wonderful news with someone, so I took a couple of minutes and called my daughter. I can't believe Echo finally called. I got a hold of Nancy after lunch, and she was pumped. We discussed how I should handle the call.

September 17, 1997—I'm Dragging My Feet

I still hadn't returned Ms. Bodine's phone call, because I was unsure of what to say. I am writing my own book and am planning to use all the examples I sent her. Ellen, another friend who believes in ghosts, brought up the possible legalities that might arise if we both use the same information. I hadn't thought about that. I didn't know if I should give Echo permission to use my letter or not. She left me another voice mail today. She sure seemed eager to talk about my house. I decided I'd call her tonight, after I had more time to think about it.

In the evening, after Paul went up to bed, I sat on the couch for over an hour, mustering up some courage and deciding what I would say when I called her. As I reached for the phone, it chirped. That rearranged my heartbeat into a lovely, syncopated rhythm. It was my friend Dave S., calling to see how I was doing. We hadn't chatted for a while, so I filled him in on Echo's phone message. He was very happy and said, "Go for it." He's been another anchor in my life over the past few years. We gabbed a while longer, and then I told him I had to make my call. He wished me luck. My stomach was in knots, but I couldn't put it off any longer. *Here it goes.*

If discussing ghosts with a friend is awkward, think what a daunting task it becomes when your conversation partner is a total stranger. I admit I was nervous the minute she said hello. Fortunately, Echo is such a warm personality that she immediately put me at ease. In fact, we were on the phone for nearly an hour. She asked if things were still happening in my house. I told her the truth—they were still going on but weren't as frequent or dramatic as they were years ago.

We discussed the fact that I was writing a book about my experiences and would be using the same material I sent her. She assured me that would not present a problem. Believe it or not, she actually sounded pleased that I was writing about my ghost. During our conversation, I casually mentioned I wanted to get rid of the pest because I was tired of living with it. Although I wasn't hinting that she should take on the task, it must have sounded that way to her. She told me she wasn't doing that any longer, so I asked if she would recommend someone reputable. After a long pause, she replied, "I'll do it. I'll come out."

I was speechless. I didn't expect that response at all. She wanted to come out next week already. I told her it would be impossible to get time off until my manager leaves for his yearly planning session in October. A lot of preparation goes into those planning sessions, and I'd be too swamped at the office to take a vacation day. However,

I could get in touch with her as soon as I could swing it. I added that my daughter and my friend Nancy were going to be out here the day she and her editor come out. Echo replied, "We'll make it a fun day—just us girls."

And the ghost, I thought to myself. *Don't forget the ghost.*

I could hardly wait till the next morning to tell Nancy about the phone call. "Hey, lady," I said, "I used your negotiating techniques, and Echo decided she'd do her ghost-busting thing in exchange for the use of my letter."

Nancy crowed, "What did I tell you?" Nancy had spent quite a long time convincing me to use that negotiating technique, and I kept making excuses: "I know it won't work," "I don't want to do it," "I'm not comfortable saying those things" . . . blah, blah, blah. When I finally took her advice, we got the outcome we wanted. Nancy is literally dancing with joy. In some ways, she is more excited about Echo's visit than I am. But then she doesn't have to face the possibility that the ghost buster will find nothing paranormal in her house. Be that as it may, I'm still thrilled to death that Echo is coming out.

September 19, 1997—A Doubt Is Overcome

Lately, I have been reading several spiritual books about angels and how to pray for a protection when the need arises, so I've been doing just that. My evenings have become quiet and uneventful. Now I fear my prayers have squelched the persistent ghostly tricks of recent years. Are they just a thing of the past now that I've finally arranged for a ghost buster to come out? Don't get me wrong: I appreciate the peace and quiet, but what incredibly bad timing.

One evening, Kristen verbalized what I have feared all along. She asked, "What if *it* isn't there any longer?"

"I told Echo that things have quieted down a lot," I replied, "But she still wants to come out with her editor, so the editor can watch her in action. It's her choice whether it's here or not, I guess." I hung up the phone with Kristen's question rattling around in my head. What if the little ghost child isn't here any longer? I got the chills for just a second.

I didn't have to wait very long for the answer to my daughter's disturbing question. Around eleven o'clock, I was in the bathroom getting ready for bed when I heard a suspicious creak in the kitchen. That sound is only audible when someone is standing in one particular spot in front of the base cupboard a few feet from the bathroom door. I figured my sleepy husband had come downstairs to use the facilities and was patiently waiting for me to vacate the bathroom. I was in the process of rushing through my moisturizing regimen when I heard it a second time. It was a loud, distinct creak, as if someone standing in that squeaky spot was shifting from one foot to the other and back again. I called out from behind the bathroom door, "Hang on. I'll be out in a jiffy."

I quickly wiped my hands on a towel, and as I opened the door, another loud creak came from the kitchen. I expected to see my husband standing in the hall with squinty eyes, waiting to rush past me, but there was no one standing there. That puzzled me. Then I assumed he'd walked into the family room to wait, but he wasn't in there either. Out of habit, I checked his office and the living room and my office. Okay, this was weird. Then I realized I hadn't heard Paul coming down the steps, so I opened the upstairs door and heard him snoring quite loudly. The hair on the back of my neck stood up, and chills rushed down my spine. The impatient creaks weren't my husband's after all. I guess this answers Kristen's question: *it* is still here!

September 21, 1997—I Call Out the Ghost

The smells, sounds, and colors of autumn are definitely in the air. The subdued season of autumn is so much more interesting than its boisterous, fun-loving summer cousin. As a child, I loved dressing in warm clothes and taking quiet walks while the chilly wind wrapped itself around me, or going for a drive with my family to admire the scarlet, gold, and orange leaves making their final appearance of the year. Those are cherished memories. I still love autumn, and today is a perfect example of the days I enjoyed so long ago.

Autumn has also been my most haunted time of year. Before we bought this house, I could count on at least one uncanny experience happening each October, often around Halloween. Although living here has managed to stretch my "most haunted time" across all twelve months, my radar still seems to be more active in the autumn.

I have been working outside the home now for many years and have become a real convenience-food freak. I rarely serve good, home-cooked meals any longer, so I decided to forgo our usual weekend takeout and make something warm and satisfying for dinner tonight. My comfort food of choice is a robust beef stroganoff. It's one dish that I do really well. It simmered most of the day, giving us "the slobbers," as Paul so aptly puts it. To accompany the beef dish, I made a crunchy coleslaw, then decided to round the meal off with some baking-powder biscuits. To be truthful, I've never liked baking-powder biscuits, but today, for some strange reason, I was craving them. My husband was running errands this afternoon, so I was as alone as one can be in this house. While kneading the sticky white dough, I decided to find out if my ghost would communicate with me. I was feeling very strong; after all, a ghost buster would be here any day now. I knew I could handle it.

"Are you still here? If you are, please show me."

I waited for something to happen. When nothing did, I tried once more: "Are you still here? If you are, please show me."

Again, nothing happened. The magic number is three, so for the last time I asked, "Are you still here? If you are, please show me." I raised the volume of my voice each time, hoping to irritate the ghost a little bit.

Nothing! Nada! Zip! *Okay, enough of this silly stuff,* I thought. I had better things to do with my time than talk to spirits, anyway. I glanced at the clock. Paul said he'd be home by quarter to five, so he'd be pulling into the driveway any minute. I popped the biscuits into the oven and set the timer. The noodles were already cooked, so as soon as the buzzer rang, I'd reheat them and dinner would be ready.

In the living room, I picked up the cookbooks and catalogs that I had been looking at earlier this afternoon. While bending over the couch, I noticed a white object on the carpet. It looked like a chunky grub worm, only whiter. I quickly snapped it up in my fingers and tossed it into the wastebasket. The instant I touched it, it felt soft and puffy, sending my senses into overload. What was that, for cryin' out loud? I knew the minute it dropped into the basket that it was no grub worm, because they feel hard and rubbery. I fished around in the basket contents till I found it, then squished it between my fingers. It was a piece of dough about one inch long, left over from my biscuit cuttings. I smiled and tossed the spectral evidence in the kitchen trash. When did my ghost sneak this dough off the counter? It doesn't matter, because my question was answered in a rather theatrical way. *It* is still here.

September 22, 1997—Where Are You, Echo?

On September 19, I faxed Echo the dates Nancy and I would be available. Patience has never been one of my virtues, but I waited as patiently as possible for three whole days. When I received no reply from the ghost buster, I started getting a little nervous. A week ago, I told her the last thing I needed to finish my book was her visit. Until she shows up at my house, I'll just bide my time by reporting any further happenings.

In the past week or two, the taps have been getting persistent again. Hearing them reminded me of my Aunt Nora, God rest her soul. She used to hear three loud thumps in her upstairs storeroom whenever a friend or relative passed away.

The evening she first heard the mysterious thumps, she was home alone. Her husband was out of town on a buying trip. Aunt Nora was a bit apprehensive about seeking out the source of the noise, but it had to be done. My aunt was an organized woman who lived by the old adage "A place for everything and everything in its place," so she set out to find what had fallen over. After a thorough assessment of the storeroom, she found nothing out of place, so she went back downstairs. Within a matter of minutes, another thump occurred on the second floor. She climbed the stairs again and again found nothing out of place. When my aunt came downstairs after the third trip up there, her phone rang, announcing a death. The next time this phenomenon happened, she just waited by the phone till she heard the third thump, and then took the call.

I overheard her telling my mother about it when I was twelve years old. I thought it was kind of cool. I had already had many psychic experiences in my young life, and I just figured it was a talent my mother hadn't inherited but her oldest sister had. Apparently, my mother hadn't inherited a tolerance for such things either. After listening to my aunt's storeroom tale, Mom was appalled. I vividly recall her words: "Don't tell this to anyone else, Lenora. People will think you are crazy." I wonder what my mom would think about the ghostly activity that I've witnessed in my house or the experiences her granddaughter, grandson, and great-grandchildren have had. After the stern warning she gave Aunt Nora all those years ago, I kept my supernatural experiences to myself, because I knew she'd never understand.

On the other hand, my dad believed in strange happenings. I found this out when I was a young teen. Once, while sitting at the kitchen table doing my homework, I overheard a conversation between my parents, who were reading the paper in the living room. They were quietly discussing my older brother, who had been murdered eleven years earlier. I overheard my dad say, "We've sure had bad luck in our lives. It must be the Cook Curse." That caused my little ears to twitch! I called out, "What curse is that, Dad?" As soon as he started talking about the curse that someone had put on his family a few generations before him, my mother put a quick stop to "all that nonsense." In a warning tone, she exclaimed, "Don't you ever talk about that stupid curse again—ever!" That really upset me, because to keep peace between them, my father never brought it up again, not even to me when we were alone. By the time I was grown up and married with children, the memory of that night had slipped my mind, and I never found out what he meant. My dad and all his siblings have all crossed over now. Even if my mother could remember that conversation, she would never speak about it, so the Cook Curse is lost in history.

Oddly enough, when Mom comes to visit us, she never stays more than one night. Ever since my father died, she doesn't care to be away from her house for more than twenty-four hours at a time, because she thinks someone will break in and damage her home. At least that's what she tells us. My sister and I, as well as our daughters, have other ideas.

September 26, 1997—A Prank and a Nocturnal Voice

During the last couple of years, my arthritic back rarely affords me the luxury of sleeping upstairs in my bed. I need the subtle curve of the recliner to wake up as pain-free as possible. One drawback to this method of repose is the feeling of being on display in front of God and everybody. When I don't get as much sleep as I need, it's difficult to maintain a cheerful attitude. Anyone who has slept in a living room for any length of time knows there is no real "bed" time connected with it. This partially explains why I don't turn in at a decent hour, nor experience deep, restful sleep. There is no freedom to toss and turn; you can't snuggle up to your partner when you hear mysterious noises; and, as irritating as those disgusting taps are early in the evening, they take on a more hostile tone as midnight draws near.

But bad back or not, I'm sleeping upstairs tonight, because a most bizarre experience has left me quite shaken. While I was dozing off, I heard a voice—either next to my ear or inside my head—speak a thought that wasn't my own. To add to the fright, it was a menacing male voice. That does it. The voice and the taps can keep each other company tonight—I'm outta here! I put my glasses and slippers on, grabbed my glass of water and flashlight, and dragged myself upstairs to sleep. Better to have a backache in the morning than listen to that disembodied voice down here.

Earlier this evening, while on the Internet, I saw what looked like a flashbulb go off in the hallway. The kitchen was dark and so was the bathroom, which made the flash all the more impressive. I thought at first it might have been lightning, although it is rare to see lightning this time of year. Come to think of it, I can't ever remember seeing lightning flash in our hallway, even in the worst summer storms. I stared at the spot for a couple more seconds and then went back to the instant message I was sending my sister in Denver.

Later, when I took a bathroom break, I found the toothpaste and the nail brush smack dab in the middle of the sink. They had been on the vanity earlier that evening. *Aha, that's what the flash was.* This did not frighten me. I just put the articles back where they belonged. Over the years, audio events have frightened me much more than their visual sidekicks. I find visuals fascinating and take them in stride; however, one ill-timed noise in the dead of night can send my nervous system into panic mode.

When I returned to my office and told Kathie about it, she said, "Gee, I wish I could be there for your de-ghosting ceremony." I wish she could too. Over the years, I've kept my sister and her two daughters up to date on all the ghostly happenings in this house. I'm so lucky to have a sister who understands. I tried telling my brother and his wife about my frightening experiences when we first moved in, and he made some comment about my imagination working overtime. I was such a bundle of nerves in those days that I didn't present my case in a meaningful way. I knew I probably sounded like a total lunatic, so I dropped it. My brother probably inherited our mother's aversion to the paranormal. I didn't try too hard to convince him, because there were enough disbelievers in my life at the time as it was.

A Rite of Passage (Of Sorts)

I paid dearly for sleeping upstairs last night. My back felt like it had been put in a crooked cast, and I could barely get out of bed, let alone walk down the steps this morning. I spent a half-hour on my heated massage mat to take care of the pain and stiffness, then went on to have a very productive day. Tonight I will drift off to dreamland in the recliner so I'll be assured of being able to walk tomorrow. I better not hear that voice again, or else! There is a 1-800 number for almost any emergency or service known to man—would it be so hard to set up a paranormal hot line?

While thumbing through some catalogs this evening, I heard those pesky taps once more. They started up around eleven fifteen. Until now, these noises have always caused me to look in the direction of their origin. As they grew louder and more insistent, I decided not to play that game tonight. I'm going to ignore them. I know this goofy ghost just wants me to look. The taps remind me of a small child begging for his mom's attention, but now she is purposely turning a deaf ear. Of course, this causes the child to whine even louder. I ignored the child and kept paging through my catalog. Finally, in a last-ditch attempt to get my undivided attention, the lamp went out. To be fair, this lamp has a short in it, so that might be the reason I'm sitting here in semi-darkness. But it doesn't matter, because damn it, I looked—the whiny kid won.

The darkened room was bathed in the glow of the television. I addressed the ghost in a clear voice, with just enough authority to let it know I meant business. "Sorry, that doesn't impress me any longer. You'll have to do better than that." Moments later, I started laughing at the absurdity of my remarks and turned the lamp back on. Ah, the switch had been turned off, so it wasn't a short after all. After that incident, the noises stopped. Apparently, my admonition had hit a nerve, because it was as if the little stinker had been completely humiliated and bugged out of here.

Years ago when the lights would blink or go off completely, I became a basket case. I couldn't eat or sleep. My legs turned to jelly. I smoked a whole pack of cigarettes after the kids went to bed. I had to be on the phone with someone every night around 11:20 just so I could make it through. My nerves were completely shot. Tonight, here I am laughing at the ghost's feeble attempt to get my attention. I've come a long way, baby!

Furnace Boy (Reprise)

Ever since we moved into this house, there have been "basement days" and "non-basement days," so for years I've done the laundry or ironed only when someone else was home. On non-basement days, I couldn't make myself walk down those steps, because my radar told me to stay upstairs. The most frightening times down there occurred when it felt like I was being watched. The hairs on my neck would tingle till I got the shivers. I have fled the basement countless times when I felt *someone* at my elbow or standing behind me while I ironed. Occasionally, *it* followed me to the bottom of the steps while I made an uneasy departure. My laundry often waited till the air cleared so I could return to it.

Paul was home today while I was doing laundry, but that aside, I was feeling sure of myself. The knowledge that Echo would arrive in a few days gave me the confidence I needed. I pulled one of my T-shirts out of the dryer and snapped it in the air to straighten out the wrinkles before folding it. A split second later, I heard what sounded like someone bumping into the furnace. The sound was muffled but quite real. Did the snap of the shirt startle my little pal? I pulled out the next shirt and snapped it even harder to see if that noise would happen again. Nothing happened this time, but the atmosphere started feeling heavy, like *it* was gearing up to produce a more significant event. I quickly pulled the rest of the load out of the dryer, stuffed it into a basket, and hauled it upstairs to fold. At that moment, I knew I'd better get the hell outta Dodge. There went my newfound bravado.

I'll often chain-lock the kitchen door when I'm frightened during the nighttime hours, like I was tonight. There have been many mornings when Paul got the shock of his life trying to open the door when he left for work—*bam!* Funny thing is, he has never asked me why I lock it. Apparently, he thinks I have a good reason—or he doesn't really want to know.

October 2, 1997—We're Getting Closer

On Tuesday, Echo called to say she and her editor will be out on October 8. Apprehension is attacking me from all sides. Every time I think about that day, extra-large butterflies begin to flutter around in my stomach. This is one adventure few people experience, and those who do rarely ever talk about it. Ghosts rank right up there as one of the top ten topics people seldom share with anyone for fear of being shunned. It has taken years, but I have finally found friends who are open to hearing about my experiences without making me feel rejected. Bless their hearts.

One of those indispensable friends is Melissa. She grew up with supernatural occurrences and has been advising me on how to deal with mine. She is a "person of spirit" who has met Echo Bodine. Missy assured me, "Echo is one powerful woman. If she tells a spirit to go to the light, it will go to the light." I want to believe her, yet the idea of confronting the supernatural has started to worry me. I don't feel as confident about the idea of having a ghost buster out to my house as I did a few weeks ago. I'm getting cold feet while worrying whether Echo will finish her spiritual house cleaning before Paul arrives home from work. He has avoided this topic for nearly thirty years, and I don't know how he'll take it if he arrives home before she is finished. Echo knows that he is not open to this kind of thing. During our phone conversations, I told her two or more times that Paul would be home at three o'clock on the dot. She cheerfully replied, "Oh, we'll be done long before that. Don't worry, sweetie."

I'm also apprehensive because even though I had planned to, I still haven't told Paul about the ghost buster coming out to the house. Today at lunch, Nancy and I were chatting about Echo's upcoming visit. I launched into a barrage of questions and answers: "Should I tell him? What will happen if I don't tell him? What will he do if he knows about it ahead of time—tell me I can't have Echo over here? What will he do if he hears about it afterward—make a big stink over it? Nancy, I just don't know what to do. He's not a violent man—please don't get that idea—but he might be very upset.

What would you do if you were in my place? Would your husband understand?"

My buddy sat across the table from me, grinning like the Cheshire cat. She calmly watched me chase my tail for a few more minutes, then reminded me that her favorite advice columnist says you don't have to tell your partner every darn thing you've ever done in your lifetime. Good ol' Nancy. What would I do without her? Or have I mentioned that already.

On my bus ride home that afternoon, I made a list of reasons why Paul shouldn't get upset over this. They rattled around in my head till I finally wrote them down:

- He wouldn't have to pretend he doesn't believe me, ever again.
- It will be so much better for my mental and physical health.
- I won't be afraid to go into the basement anymore.
- It won't cost him a cent.
- I won't keep whining for a dog to keep me company.
- Did I mention it wouldn't cost him a cent?

I hope and pray that Echo's cleansing ritual rids this poor little house of all the unseen inhabitants who reside within its walls, so I can live in peace. Most people find their homes to be soothing havens, places to escape from the stress of the workplace. They can come home, kick off their shoes, have some dinner, watch a little television or pick up a good book, and then eventually fall into bed for a restful night's sleep. My house has always been a source of stress. I've been the victim of psychic abuse for nearly three decades. To my knowledge, there is no support group for that. What would I have done without the friends who stood by me?

The big thing I need to do now is some old-fashioned house cleaning, and that will begin tonight. My sister wrote me an e-mail last night saying, "Don't clean too much, or your ghost will know the jig is up!" I thought that was hilarious. It reminded me of when my children were small. Whenever I'd get a burst of energy and start cleaning the entire house, invariably one of them would ask, "Who's coming over?"

October 6, 1997—A Day of Synchronicity

Echo said she would call for directions closer to the big day. Time was growing short, though, and I couldn't wait any longer for her. Type A—remember? I really was getting worried, so I made the proactive decision to check in with her instead. During our initial conversation, she had told me she was in the process of moving to a new house, so I had no choice but to call her old number. I sat at my desk, munching on my sandwich and chuckling to myself, wondering what my workmates would think if they knew that I was about to call a ghost buster. I picked up the phone and dialed. The familiar recording said, "That number has been changed to . . . ," so I grabbed a pen and wrote it down. I dialed the new one. A very hesitant voice on the other end of the line said, "Hellooooo?"

"Echo?"

"Yes?"

"This is Marlene."

You could hear the relief in her voice. "Oh, Marlene, I'm glad it's you. The phone company just this minute finished hooking up our new phone. You are the first call we've had." Then her voice abruptly changed. "How did you get this number, anyway?"

"From the information recording when I dialed your old number."

"This is my private number. They aren't supposed to give this one out."

I replied, "This is the one they gave me. Guess you'll have to call them again."

She replied, "You bet—as soon as we hang up." After that little piece of business was out of the way, Echo said she was glad I'd called, because during the move she had misplaced my phone number and since she didn't know my last name, she had no idea how to get in touch with me. She also casually mentioned that her editor was in her first trimester of pregnancy and suffering from morning sickness.

I silently wondered if Echo was backing out. I reinforced the fact that both Nancy and I had arranged to take vacation days even though this was a busy time of year, so I was hoping this would not fall through.

She reassured me they'd come out around one o'clock. "Now, your husband gets home at three, right?"

"Yes. It would be best if you could finish up before that."

"Oh, we will. It doesn't take very long at all," Echo said. "I'll call my editor to make sure everything is a go. What is your home phone? I'll call you tonight for directions to your house."

I provided it, and then we hung up. I sat at my desk, imagining all sorts of scenarios. Even though this was the realization of a plan that had been in the works for over half my lifetime, I again found myself having second thoughts. Granted, my life has been anything but dull, and though this ghostly activity bothers me, it is unique and humorous, which makes for good stories. I have to focus on the eerie feelings, the sleepless nights, the fear of being in the basement, and the disappearance of all the items over the years to bolster my resolve. I am definitely making the right decision, even though I'll miss the little guy.

Instead of napping on the bus ride home, I mulled over my day. Odd, wasn't it, that Echo had no way of contacting me tonight because she didn't know my last name and had misplaced my phone number during her move. And that in the meantime, my impatient nature had compelled me to contact her. And that when I dialed her old number, the information operator gave out her private number by mistake. Fate had intervened again by choosing me to be the first call Echo received, only minutes after her new phone was hooked up. This coincidence made it possible for her to correct the phone company's error and get my home phone number so she could call me. If I hadn't been her first call, the number on the recording would probably already have been changed to a business number by the time I called, and she may not have checked those messages before this evening. There are those who say there is no such thing as coincidence.

That evening while I waited for Echo's phone call, Nancy called to chat. She was excited about the upcoming adventure. I really felt bad having to chase her off the phone, but we don't have call waiting. I promised to call her early tomorrow morning. Echo phoned about twenty minutes later. "How do we get there from St. Paul?"

Augh! St. Paul? Being directionally challenged, I didn't have a clue how to direct her to my house from St. Paul. I replied, "I can only direct you from South Minneapolis. You take 35W north, take the Highway 10 exit, and proceed west till you pass the little general store . . ." The directions kept rolling off my tongue until she cut me off, laughed, and said, "That will do." I figured she'd find a way to hook up with 35W somewhere out there.

As I hung up the phone, I got a nervous feeling in the pit of my stomach, because my ghost hadn't bothered me since I'd hurled that salvo at it that Sunday evening. Did I finally succeed in scaring it away? After nearly thirty years, why would it choose to disappear now? I didn't tell Echo how quiet the house had become, because if history repeats itself, as it has many times over the years, *it* will return by the time she arrives.

Sneezing and Spiders and Dust, Oh My!

Over the past couple of weekends, I have thrown myself into a frenzy cleaning the whole house. Today I have to tackle the basement, because I think the ghost buster will spend a lot of time down there. I mopped that awful floor, which hadn't been properly done for quite a while. I washed down the cement walls, sending countless numbers of spiders packing their bags and fleeing for their lives. Over the years, I'd allowed a large colony of arachnids to spring up in that dungeon of a basement, giving the squatters down there a false sense of security. For all I know, word on the street is we have a "safe house." In many ways, it is; after all, I only go down there to do laundry. Since my husband doesn't think cleaning the basement is a priority or a guy thing, he doesn't clean it either. The basement space is a nightmare for anyone with allergies, since it has become a dusty catch-all for anything we didn't want upstairs.

On the main floor, I dusted, vacuumed, and spot-cleaned the carpeting. I folded a ton of clothes, cleaned the upstairs bedroom from top to bottom, and even washed the slipcover on the old wingback chair up there. I purchased a new accent rug for the living room too. My little house must have thought it was being put on the market, with all the attention it was getting. I had to smile, thinking if my mother-in-law *was* hovering around, she'd finally be proud of me. There is a first time for everything, even if approval has to come from beyond the grave.

October 8, 1997—At Long Last

The big day has finally come. I wanted it to be as low-key as possible. What a laugh! The prospect of anything being low-key in my life is pretty rare.

My alarm clock didn't go off this morning, so I overslept by two hours. Already my nerves were gearing up for quite a show. I showered, dressed, and prepared to drive into Minneapolis to pick up my partner in crime for what we were dubbing our adventure of a lifetime. I've always been more of a passenger than a driver, so anytime I have to drive downtown, I need to do some heavy-duty relaxation therapy. Positive self-talk and deep breaths have been a boon to me over the years, so I sat down for a moment to ground myself. Then, as promised, I gave Nancy a call. We decided on ten thirty as a good time to meet. I would pick up a tape recorder to tape the session, and we'd have lunch out here. Cool! Everything was set.

Well, not everything—there were a couple of unplanned trips to the bathroom. My bladder doesn't handle stress very well. Waiting around is very difficult for me, so I decided to vacuum and dust each room one more time. It was nervous energy and overkill, but I couldn't help myself. Then I threw a load of clothes in the washer and looked around the basement, thinking, "If you are hiding down here, you'd better pack your bags." I giggled again at my sister's clever statement about cleaning too much. Kathie has the day off and wanted to be here so badly. If she lived anywhere in Minnesota, she would have made the trip to Blaine. She is one of the reasons I am taping Echo's session: I want her to share in this experience the only way she can.

I did the breakfast dishes and then attempted to dry my hair. Despite the dryer's best efforts, all this activity, compounded by the hot flashes of menopause, stoked my inner furnace to the point where my hair had no recourse but to remain damp. I put on my makeup and checked the clock. Finally! It was time to leave.

I picked Nancy up at our office building. She was nice enough to bus downtown to meet me halfway, because I usually get lost on the way to her house and today had enough stress in it as it was. She was as nervous as I was. We were overcome with nervous giggles on the half-hour drive out to Blaine. We tried to talk about other things to keep our minds off the big event, but each time she said, "Just think—our dream from three years ago is coming true today." My stomach did another flip-flop. So did Nancy's.

I bought an inexpensive tape recorder and a package of audio-tapes at a local discount store; then we drove home. My hands were shaking as I ripped open the packages. I couldn't get the tape inserted correctly. The little door wouldn't close. I tried inserting the tape the other way. No, that was wrong too. A bossy voice bluntly demanded, "What the hell is going on?" Oh, sorry—that was me!

Nancy calmly took it out of my hands and said, "Here, let me try." She fumbled with it as well. I get very hyper when things don't work, and my patience flies out the window. I inherited this trait from my dad. Out of exasperation, I whined, "Damn, time is running short, and now I'll have to go back and get another one." Nancy tried to calm me down by saying there was plenty of time, but I knew better. Type A's always do. We hopped back in my vehicle to pick up a couple of sandwiches and exchange the tape recorder. When we were a few blocks away from the house, I realized I had forgotten the damaged recorder. That was par for the course today. This time at the store, I picked up a micro-cassette player without realizing I'd need different-sized tapes. Ack! My brain was going a mile a minute.

Too bad we couldn't set me on record; it would have saved us all this hassle.

We got back to the house with the new tape player before I noticed its package had already been opened. Our worst fears came true: this one didn't work either. A customer had obviously returned it at one time and an employee had put it back on the sales floor. Wonderful! I wonder what my blood pressure was at that very moment. *Oh well, I have no control over this,* I thought. *We're out of luck!*

Just then the phone rang. It was my daughter asking, "Where were you?"

I told her we had been out buying a tape recorder and that we'd ended up with two and neither of them worked. "Aren't you coming over?" I whined in desperation.

"I wasn't coming till I knew you were home" was her reply. At least now she was on her way. I checked to make sure there was film in my camera. I wanted to get a few pictures of Echo in action. Since the recorder idea had bombed out, a picture or two would have to do. All the little things going wrong today really bothered me. Was this an omen?

While I was eating my sandwich, I tried the first tape recorder again. This time, I noticed the play button had been pushed in. Oh, *that* was what had prevented the tape from going in all the way. Geez! Nancy and I had a good laugh; then we took turns saying stupid things into the microphone and giggling when we played them back. We were ready for action. What other emotions could we wring out of this day? So far, we'd had anxiety, stress, frustration, and anger, with a dose of elation and a bit of silliness thrown in for good measure. I think that about covers it, and the ghost busting hadn't even begun yet.

Kristen arrived at twelve thirty. She walked in holding a little ghost ornament high over her head. She declared that since Echo was going to chase out the real ghost, I should have one in the house that wouldn't be as much of a pest. We fastened it to the string on the ceiling fan in the kitchen.

Our ghost buster was due at one o'clock. One o'clock came and went, and no Echo. My stomach was churning. What if the directions I'd given her were wrong? They weren't, of course, but my guests still weren't here. Nancy left the house and paced up and down the street to pass the time. She's one of the most laid-back individuals I know, but today I could see she was nervous. Kristen seemed to be the most composed of all as she calmly sat on the couch. The only palpable presence in my house at that moment was tension—lots and lots of tension. The phone rang at ten minutes after one. I jumped a foot. "This is Echo. We're on our way. See you in a few minutes." I hung up the phone and relayed the message to Kristen. Then I yelled out the front door to Nancy, "She just called! They'll be here in a few minutes." Nancy raced back up to the house.

I'm afraid I gave our new reclining love seat quite a workout by sitting down, reclining back, then getting up and walking around a bit, and then sitting down and doing it all over again. We had finally purchased new living-room furniture, and here I was wearing it out already. I had worked myself up to the point of uncontrolled anxiety. *Take deep breaths, Marlene. Remember to breathe.*

When Kris first arrived, the three of us had chattered away like a flock of magpies. Now, except for an occasional remark, the house was silent. I guess no one had anything left to say that hadn't been said before. I finally banished myself to the family room, where I could nervously pace without bothering anyone. Suddenly, I heard my daughter announce, "They're here!" I raced into the living room just in time to see a small white station wagon roll to a stop in front of my house. I thought to myself, *Why, it's the Casper Mobile.* I uttered such a loud sigh, I was sure they heard it outside. Then Nancy jumped up from the couch and gave a little shout. I was positive they heard that. "Thanks a lot, Nancy," I said. "They probably think that was me." Geez, now I was being just plain rude. Fortunately, Nancy is a very understanding woman.

I just wanted to get this show on the road, but our guests didn't appear any too anxious to come in. Kris looked out the window and noted, "They are reading your letter and planning their strategy."

"Why would they be reading my letter?"

My daughter calmly replied, "To make sure they cover everything, I suppose." Who had made her the adult in this relationship? And not a moment too soon, I might add.

Did anybody care that I was about to throw up? I didn't even waste the energy of asking that revolting question.

Finally, my daughter said, "They're getting out of the car. Wow, Echo is really tan. She'd better watch it or she'll get skin cancer."

"Kris!" Oh, brother! Now I was correcting my adult daughter. What was with me today?

I greeted the two women at the front door, and introductions were made all around. I immediately liked Echo and her editor. Echo was as down to earth as she'd sounded on the phone. She wore a blue and white checked jumper with a white sleeveless T-shirt under it. Brown clogs and a black leather purse completed her outfit. There was no phony pretense, no long, flowing black dress, and no aura of mystique at all. I guess what impressed me the most was that she looked like a friend who had just dropped by for coffee. I finally took some deep breaths—better late than never, eh?

Echo's editor, "S.," interviewed me a bit. "How old is the house? How do you know the name of your ghost? Did he die in the house?" I answered all of her questions as best I could. The year this house was built escaped me, but I said it was probably sometime in the early fifties. They all thought maybe the late forties. They wanted to get background information, as well as examples of why I thought we had a ghost. During the interview, I mentioned twice that I was writing a book. I also added that I didn't remember what was in the letter I'd sent to Echo because it had been written a long time ago—even though that had no bearing on the questions being asked. I was repeating myself and couldn't help it. Stop me before I kill again!

I stumbled through describing a number of experiences from the first few years we lived here; then, thankfully, Echo put me out of my misery by saying, "I'll do my walk-through now." I asked if I could tape-record her trip through the house. Believe me, I was totally prepared to throw myself on her mercy after the difficult time we'd had getting the darn thing to work. She replied in a cheery voice, "Sure, that's no problem." Whew! Nancy and I had originally wanted to use a camcorder, but neither of us could get our hands on one. After the tape player debacle, it was a genuine blessing that we hadn't gone out to buy, borrow, or steal a camcorder. Since neither of us had ever used one, Lord only knows what damage we could have done with that piece of equipment.

Our little group of five left the living room and crowded into the short hallway. (Author's note: From here on, the conversation in quotes comes off the tape—word for word. Echo speaks rather softly and often spent much of her time talking to herself or her spirit guide. S. had a much stronger speaking voice, but she used hushed tones to model Echo's. I wish I had picked up on that unspoken cue. Nancy and Kristen had, so they were whispering, but I was far too nervous to whisper. I was chattering a mile a minute, and since I was the holding the tape recorder, my voice was dominant on the tape.)

Echo peeked into my office. "This room is clear," she said.

"Clear?" I squeaked in disbelief.

"Clear!"

What a letdown. I replied in a disappointed tone, "With all the noises heard in that room, I thought for sure something was in there."

Echo declared, "Whatever was in there is gone now."

She peered into Paul's darkened radio room for several seconds and softly said, "There's something questionable in here. We'll come back to this one." That familiar prickly feeling came over me again.

I turned on the light in the bathroom. Echo said, "I don't need the light. It's better if the lights are off."

I thought, *Oh, brother, even Echo thinks my bathroom looks horrible.* I flipped the switch off and apologized.

Echo laughed. "That's okay, a lot of people don't know." Then she added, "It's a funny thing that happens whenever I come into someone's home: they have every light in the place turned on, and I make them turn the lights back off."

I heard muffled laughter behind me, so I turned halfway around and looked at Kris. She was holding in a belly whopper of a laugh. I had worn myself out during the past couple of weeks, cleaning, polishing, vacuuming, shampooing, dusting, sweeping, mopping, and rearranging my entire house. My arthritic body ached so badly at the end of each weekend that I could barely climb on the bus on Monday morning. Of course, Kristen had heard about each and every thing I'd done around here. I had worked like a horse getting this place in tiptop condition because I didn't want Echo to think we lived in a pigsty. Now all that hard work appeared to be for nothing. But there's always an upside: all my fall housecleaning was done, so it wasn't a total loss. Echo peered into my tiny bathroom and said, "The bathroom is clear."

We walked into the kitchen, the site of all the crashing noises. "Clear!" It couldn't be. My fears were coming true. After all these years, there was nothing here. I was embarrassed and so very disappointed. On the drive out here this morning, Nancy told me she had a strong feeling Echo would find nothing. I shared with her that Kristen had the same thoughts. Last night, I dreamed that Echo made contact with Johnny. She asked him why he stayed here all these years. He replied, "Because she's fun, and she sings a lot." Oh yeah, little guy? Where are you when I need you? You'd better come out of hiding, or I'll kick your little ghost butt to the Other Side all by myself—I mean it!

Our group moved into the family room, and Echo stared deeply into this room for a few seconds. "Clear. Let's try the basement. You reported feeling very nervous when you are in the basement."

One by one, we walked down the steps. Normally, I never pay attention to the condition of these steps. As I mentioned earlier, this entire basement is a pit, because it's unfinished and we never use it. However, this afternoon I was seeing how bad it looked through fresh eyes. This was so embarrassing. The steps haven't been painted for many years. I am allergic to paint fumes, so the condition of this house is suffering terribly. You already know that my husband is *not* a handyman. He's also not a painter, wallpaper hanger, ceiling refinisher . . . the list is endless. He cooks, fixes cars, mows the lawn, and blows snow out of the driveway, however. That's why I keep him around!

We entered the laundry area through the ill-fitting door that divides the basement in half. Our little group wandered toward the vicinity of the dryer and ironing board. Paul's tool room is also in this area, as well as the furnace. Echo gazed into the darkened room for several seconds. I volunteered, "There's just a bunch of tools in there."

She cocked her head, whispered something to S., and then turned to her left. She was now facing the furnace and speaking in very low, hushed tones. I heard her say, "There used to be one." I repeated what the ghost buster said, because she was talking so softly I knew my tape wouldn't pick it up. The two women whispered together, and then I heard Echo say, "Yes. It's really strong." We all stood there like statues while Echo stared into the dark space behind the furnace and softly repeated, "Really strong." She motioned toward the back of the furnace with her right hand. "It was around here, but it's not here now."

I said, "That would explain why sometimes while ironing, I'd get this . . . sometimes I'd feel like I had to get out of here and go upstairs." My voice trailed off as I recalled the hair-raising moments I've had down here.

Kristen leaned toward me and whispered in a hesitating manner, "That's where . . . where Furnace Boy was." My body stiffened.

Echo said, "The energy is strong enough, so it hasn't been that long. It might just be in another part of the house."

Nancy whispered in my other ear, "It's upstairs."

Echo continued, "The psychic image is like he created a little fort in here. You know how little kids create forts?" I agreed that it was a perfect little space for a fort. She concluded, "This is where he lived. This is Johnny's fort."

My stomach was churning with waves of nausea. It was difficult to explain my feelings at that moment. I was being told a piece of information that I somehow had always known. I felt vindicated in

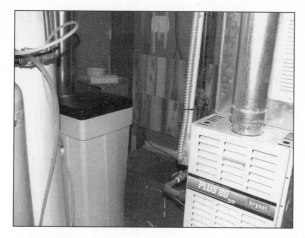

Furnace Boy's Fort
Echo Bodine helped to explain the terror that caused my
"non-basement days" by confirming that our little ghost
known as Furnace Boy lived in this spot.

a hollow sort of way. Our little ghost had lived down here because
he felt safe. Was it because upstairs I either ignored him or yelled at
him out of frustration? Was that any way to treat a ghost child? How
many nights did he cry down here? He was only six years old. Did he
come to me calling, "Mommy, mommy" because he missed his real
mother? Did he feel abandoned after Agnes wished him back into
their lives and then walked out on him? And why didn't he leave
when his family moved? Had his mother banished him because she
was tired of her little spirit boy? Is there such a thing as psychic
guilt? If so, I have a ton of it on my shoulders right now. I wonder
if his mother has any guilt over this. If not, she should! Standing by
the furnace, I found myself thinking back to the night Scott drew
a picture of his little friend who lived by the furnace. I was getting
goose bumps on top of goose bumps. Not from fear, mind you, but
from excitement. In my mind, this was proof that Furnace Boy was
not an imaginary child.

Echo compared impressions with her editor while Kris, Nancy,
and I exchanged a variety of looks. Echo told us there were two ways
to get rid of this energy: burn a white candle or burn sage. We joked

about the disadvantages of burning a candle by a gas furnace—ka-boom!—and decided on sage. The smoke from the smoldering sage apparently takes the negative energy with it as it drifts up the steps and out the door.

I paused again to reflect. Wow, thirty years of fear and uneasiness explained away in two short sentences: *"This is where he lived. This is Johnny's fort."* Shivers ran up and down my spine. My mind raced back to the frigid winter nights when the pilot light would go out on the old furnace. It always happened during the weeks Paul was on ma-neuvers with the Air National Guard. In my husband's absence, it was my responsibility to come down here in the dead of night to light that bloody pilot light so the kids and I wouldn't develop hypother-mia. Picture me at midnight, shivering in my nightgown and slippers, crawling into the creepy, confining space behind the furnace. After jockeying into position back there, I had to strike a farmer's match and insert it into the twisted end of a coat hanger, fashioned for just that purpose. It always took at least three matches before one would stay lit. Then I had to carefully extend it far enough into the black abyss in the hopes of making contact with the gas jet lurking in there. That part always scared the heck out of me. The thought of blowing us to bits, coupled with the feeling that *something* might be standing behind me, was terrifying. It's a darn good thing I didn't know my ghost child lived by the furnace back then. I'd always thought the cubbyhole was his home, and that is the only reason I could make myself come down here on those frigid nights. It's a wonder I didn't burn the house down. If nothing else, this bears out the old saying, "What you don't know can't hurt you."

Echo's validation made perfect sense out of how my son was able to play and talk with the little boy who lived by the furnace. It also explained why the ball my daughter was playing with had defied the laws of gravity. For a moment, I pictured this young ghost child glee-fully playing ball with the living girl who shared his house. What a kick to have someone interact with him. I could almost picture the little guy sitting on the basement steps, patiently waiting for a kid his age to come downstairs to play. And if he saw me as a mother figure, it made sense that he'd follow me around in the basement and upstairs while I was doing my housework. However, empathy for the little ghost will never heal the stress I've experienced, nor give me back the sleep I've lost over the years. It's best for all of us if he goes to the Other Side.

Our group moved over by the washer, which is actually located across the basement from the dryer. I know that configuration makes no sense, but that's how the laundry area was set up when we moved in, and the explanation for it is too long and too boring. Although this setup looks pretty silly, I decided to make that twenty-foot walk an innovative form of exercise.

Echo vaguely gestured toward my washer and said, "This area is clear over here."

Her editor quickly turned to her and with blatant disbelief, "It is?"

Then Echo fine-tuned her statement. "It is clear over there," she said, indicating the space under the stairs. "But over here," she said, again pointing to the washing machine, "there's a pocket of negative energy." This time, her sidekick agreed. Neither of the ladies explained what had caused the negative energy, and because of the excitement of the day, I completely forgot to ask them. However, I managed to ask S. if she could feel this extrasensory stuff too. She told me that she was a student of Echo's and that she was indeed getting the same vibrations.

We walked back through the door to the area opposite the laundry room, where the Millers had had their family room. This is the area that held the piano, which is long gone. It's also where Paul strung clotheslines for me in the pre-dryer days, when the weather was inclement. Echo proclaimed, "This area is clear."

I finally asked, "Do you feel a kind of 'heaviness' when an area is *not* clear?"

"Yeah," she replied.

I added, "I feel that too, and this side has never bothered me." Later, in retrospect, I remembered the time I'd heard that child crying at midnight, which sent me flying up the steps after damaging my knees. However, the day Echo was here, my mind drew a blank.

Echo said, "Let's go upstairs."

Nancy asked Echo if spirits could leave the house and then come back whenever they wish. Echo replied, "Oh yes. Once I get through the whole house, I'll be able to tell if he comes and goes. Yeah, sometimes they'll leave when they know that a ghost buster is coming."

That was my cue. I volunteered, "My sister said not to clean too much or else he'll think the jig is up!" Kathie's joke infused the atmosphere with a welcome humor break, and we shared a hearty laugh over the thought of a little spirit zipping out of here. Then we climbed the steps to the second floor.

Echo and I were standing on the small landing that faces the cubbyhole area while the others waited on the steps. I asked Echo if she wanted me to open the dreadful creaking door. She replied, "No, that's fine."

I opened it anyway and said, "I had my husband put a lock on the door years ago, because it swung open any time it wished—day or night—usually just as I was walking by. I'm getting creepy feelings up here now just from all the past stuff that happened."

Echo softly replied, "I'd say that's one of his places."

"I know it is, because of the stuff my neighbor found in here," I boasted. My nerves were showing. I was talking too loud and too much, and my asthma was acting up, causing me to cough a lot. My body was trying to tell me to be quiet by dropping major hints, and I was turning a deaf ear.

"Yeah, he liked these little caved-in spaces," Echo added in a very diplomatic tone.

"What kind of toys did they find?" asked Echo's editor.

"We found a temple of his glasses, couple of marbles, couple broken crayons—hang on a minute, I have asthma." Cough, cough. "There may have been a little broken truck as well. My neighbor found them. She might talk to you if you need some verification."

Echo said, "I can feel energy in this place too. He spent a lot of time up here, but his real fort was down in the basement, next to the furnace." She seemed very puzzled as to why his energy would remain so strong when his spirit seemed to be missing.

The two ghost busters walked the length of my bedroom. Echo asked again, "Who sleeps up here?"

I replied, "My husband sleeps up here all the time. I sleep up here once in a while, when my back doesn't hurt."

Echo stared at the junction of the walls in the northeast corner, and for a second or two I thought she looked mystified about something, so I asked her if there was anything up here. Her distracted voice trailed off, "No, it's . . . clear . . ." Her face had a peculiar look, as if she didn't quite believe the words that had just come out of her mouth. I didn't ask her again. I was being enough of a pest as it was.

We went back down to the main floor of the house. S. asked, "The office again?" They conferred for a second or two, and we followed Echo into Paul's radio room. She looked around for a moment, then concentrated on the northeast corner. She raised both her arms and motioned to that corner, "What's above this area? That cubbyhole?"

I explained that the cubbyhole ran the length of the house and that the space was directly above this corner. She said, "There is a really strong concentration of energy in this corner." Then she paused for a moment. "But there's no spirit there." She sounded perplexed, yet thoughtful, as she spoke those words.

Nancy, who was standing next to me, softly said, "I can feel it too."

Echo continued, "I would say that at one time something really traumatic happened in that corner, or above, or directly below. Maybe even outside, on that corner of the house. Your husband probably shouldn't be in here for long periods of time."

Her editor asked, "He's not sensitive to it?"

I replied, "He must block it out."

Echo said, "I hate to say this, but I don't think a woman or a man who is very sensitive can be in this room for very long. But if somebody can block out their feelings and just stay in their head, they could remain in this room. But after a while . . . after a while, the room wears on you. There's a real"—and here she uttered a heavy, defeated sigh—"sad feeling in the corner of the room. I think that anybody, any person who is really sensitive—if they spend any time in this room—would after a while become really sad. They could be in a good mood in the rest of the house, and when they come into this room, they'd want to cry, actually. Or they'd leave the room feeling, um, hopeless and discouraged. Like, why look forward to anything, why be excited about anything—because there's nothing to look forward to. And those feelings are so strong in that corner that they just permeate out into the rest of the room."

We stood there in silence. I was surprised to hear about the negative vibration of the room. It was certainly nothing I'd expected.

She reiterated, "So again, your husband, in order to remain in this room, would have to really work hard to block out all the feelings in here, because it is very, very strong . . . that hopeless feeling in here, a despairing kind of feeling." Her words stumbled a bit as she reached for this advice. "I don't think—I mean—I'd, uh . . . if you have any members of the family who are very sensitive, I wouldn't even let them be in this room."

"My son slept in this room for many years," I told her. "Maybe that's why he is the way he is. He's very—what would you say, Kris— rigid? Set in his ways?" My daughter nodded, then left the room, followed by Echo's editor.

Echo explained, "He probably had to be in order to survive in this room. He probably had to shut off all his feelings and just come in here. You know, it's like I want to say—which is so sexist—the only way you could survive in this room is if you were a guy!" Nervous giggles punctuated the silence.

I added, "And a guy that wasn't sensitive."

Echo said, "Yeah, yeah! And if you were sensitive, you would have to find a way to desensitize yourself in order to keep coming in here. What I'm surprised at is how strong it is, and how it's lasted for so long. It just lingers in that corner. It's like something either happened below this room in that corner, above the room, or right outside the house. But it's right in this area—very despairing."

Just then, I realized that my ironing board is right below that corner. That's interesting. I wondered to myself if this negative energy could be responsible for all the creepy times I've had while ironing over the years.

I mentioned that some nights I can't get on the Internet because my modem keeps reassigning itself. This renders my PC incapable of going online. Whenever this happens, I go into Paul's room and log on with his PC. I added, "I hate sitting in here." Although no specific area feels any more hostile than any other, it still feels like I'm intruding, like I don't belong in that room. I've heard that spirit energy is quite capable of messing with electronic toys, appliances, and anything else that runs on electricity. Human minds run on electric current, so when our bodies die, the soul, spirit, or energy survives, because energy cannot be destroyed. Neither Paul, Scott, nor I have an explanation for why my computer will reassign my modem like that. So maybe our ghost is doing it.

Echo went on, "You know what I'd suggest? When your husband is not here, or when he goes to sleep, I would bring a white candle in and I'd set it over here." She pointed to one of Paul's crowded shelves. "Put it someplace where it won't set anything on fire. Then ask an angel to come in here and start working on this room to clear out all the negativity in that corner to change and transform the room into a very positive room. I'd do that daily for at least thirty days."

She repeated the instructions for me, then said, "I would bet you anything that in a month's time you'd start to see a change in you and in your husband or anybody who comes in here. Something has to raise the vibration of this room. It's like the words I'm hearing are, 'The angels can come in and lift the vibrations.' But that's about it. I don't know what else can do it. If you burn sage in here, first of all your husband would just go nuts." I laughed. Echo grinned and said, "I would ask for the angels' help on this one. Sage smells like pot! I'd definitely use the candle in here." Then Echo joined Nancy and me in a good laugh.

All joking aside, I was quite disappointed. "So there is nothing here that you can dispel? Nothing you can send to the light, because there's no presence . . . just a vibration?" I'd secretly hoped she would send something to the light during her visit here.

Echo said again, "There's just 'energy.' Something awful happened here at some time, and it just stayed in the walls. And it just hovers over there." She pointed again to the northeast corner. It was a riveting experience to watch her face as she spoke of the negativity in the room. Her facial expressions looked as if she were trying to draw the secret out of the walls through pure concentration alone. Her eyes were darting back and forth as if searching for something that she knew was there but just couldn't locate. Of course, the rest of us couldn't see it. I wish I would have asked her what that negative energy looked like. My amateur psychic impression tells me the negative energy looks like a boiling, grayish brown vapor cloud.

Echo told us about a house in a South Minneapolis suburb where she had cleansed a bedroom. The former homeowners had lost their fourteen-year-old son to suicide, and the current owners' teenage son slept in the suicide bedroom. Soon after they'd moved in, they noticed their own son acting strangely. The mother contacted Echo and asked her to clean out the bedroom because her son's personality had changed so abruptly. He, too, was becoming despondent, and his mother feared for his life. "I went in and found the same sort of energy in that room. Very much like this. You could still see a little soul hanging there."

I felt such sadness at her remark that I blurted out, "Oooh!"

She continued, "This was seriously affecting their teenager. So I sent the kid spirit to the light." The mother called Echo a couple of weeks later and said that she was already noticing a difference in her son. His normal personality was returning. But after Echo finished her story, she repeated, "There is no spirit here for me to send to the light. There's no spirit over there."

"When Paul leaves this room, is he kinda sad?" Nancy asked.

"No, I don't think so." I laughed. "Paul is Paul. He doesn't actually seem any different." But I wondered to myself if the vibrations of that room were responsible for his adamant denial of a spirit in the house. It could also explain why Scott believes what he does. They might have both experienced that bad energy many times over the years. Since they had no idea what was causing it, they overcompensated by making up their minds to deny it. And while they believed their shield of denial protected them, I was left defenseless—left to face this stuff alone. Chivalry is dead.

After hearing Echo's diagnosis of the room, I was stunned. Her explanation of the negative energy accurately describes the Scott we know. I told her that this was his room from age three. When he was in his early teens, his whole disposition changed, and we never knew why. When he was nineteen, he had some kind of frightening episode during which he wouldn't talk to Paul and me. We called a friend of his to come and talk with him. Among other things, Scott told his buddy that no one in this house ever loved him. If that isn't genuine despair, I don't know what is.

My eyes welled up with tears for a moment. I thought about my son sleeping and playing in this room since he was a small child. He was surely affected by that strong negative energy. What kind of defense would a toddler have against it? He was scarcely out of diapers when we moved him into that room. And to make matters worse, his bed was placed in *that* corner. I had no way of knowing that anything would harm him in here, but after hearing Echo's assessment of this room, I fear it did. Although I'll never forget what she said, I can't do a blessed thing about it now.

I'll never know what kind of dark battles were waged in this room between Scott and this corrosive energy. Except for a near-self-destructive episode at the age of eight, he seemed to be a fairly normal kid. He had a very dry sense of humor as a small child. He was always cautious about trying dangerous things and didn't seem as fun-loving as his sister, but I just chalked that up to the difference in their personalities. She was the rambunctious one of the two; he was our little conservative. Maybe sleeping with that bad energy hovering around him made him that way. We didn't have money for a therapist when our son was younger, so worrying about it at this late date won't help matters.

I've decided not to tell Scott about what Echo found in his room. I'll let his sister do that. They were never close growing up, but they have become fairly good friends as adults. It will be interesting to find out what he thinks about today's discoveries. Knowing him, he'll think it is all garbage. The only thing I can do now is burn a white candle and ask angels to cleanse the room. We are leaving on a vacation shortly, so when we get back, I'll follow Echo's instructions and burn a candle for one hour each day for thirty days.

Echo, Nancy, and I joined the others in the living room. Echo said she would now get in touch with her spirit guide, and he would tell her why she saw what she saw. My tape recorder was running, because I wanted a blow-by-blow documentation of this. She closed her eyes and began speaking slowly in a deliberate manner, pausing periodically while listening as her guide relayed words to her. "Your home . . . was inhabited for many years . . . by various ghosts. There were five different ghosts . . . that lived in this home . . . from the time that you bought it. Now, they were not all here at the same time. One would live here for a time . . . then another would come. That was when there were more people in the home, more activity. Since the home has calmed down, there is less human activity, and it is less likely to attract visitors from the Other Side.

"You did have Johnny here for about ten years . . . from the time you bought the house. He has come and gone, but he has also grown. He has moved on now from his incarnation as Johnny. There was a child spirit here named Peter. There was a male spirit named Frank. There was a woman spirit named Arlene or Ardene, and another male named Jeremy. Jeremy was a teenage spirit who was around when your children were teenagers. Jeremy liked to . . . he was one of the mischievous ghosts . . . he liked to scare the kids. As of now, there are . . . no ghosts in this house. He says that there is a ghost that comes and goes. He doesn't dwell in this house." Echo then paused a long time, as if listening. "Okay, that's the ghost named Peter. He comes and goes, comes and goes, and the voice says he doesn't feel particularly attached to any one home in the area. There are several different homes that he goes to. He's a bit of a prankster, in that he likes to make noises. He laughs when you appear frightened. That was him, just recently, whom you told you weren't impressed [when he messed with the lamp], and he just moved on to another house."

I had never told Echo about that incident. If anything confirms the authenticity of what she said here, it would be that solitary statement.

"Okay . . . now the guide says that this house, as of now, is clear and will remain clear if that's how you want it to be. He says there are certain energies in your house. The energy by your furnace was little Johnny's energy, and it's where he lived for quite some time. He did not just stay there. He roamed throughout the house. He felt comfortable here. Then he was urged on to the Other Side by other souls."

Echo's spirit guide addressed her editor then. "Write this down. There is a squadron of souls, spirits from the Other Side, who go from area to area looking for ghosts. They work with ghosts to take them to the Other Side. It's important that people know about this squadron, that they can call on the squadron from the Other Side. It isn't just up to people on this side to clear out all the ghosts and spirits. So, Johnny was moved on to the Other Side by this squadron.

"All right! Ah . . . he says the reason that there were spirits here . . . is because you are a friendly person and you were open to them. You haven't really wanted them to reside in the house, but you hadn't been adamant about them not visiting either.

"He says to tell you about the technique of visualizing the outside of your house in a white light—drawing all around the outside of your house, like a caulking gun. What it does is seal up the house so that the spirits don't enter here. He says when a spirit floats by, it can look down and see that your house is sealed. Yup! The way we do it is, imagine yourself or an angel going with this white energy just around the entire frame of the house and sealing the doors and windows, however much you'd like to seal off, and then it is done. It's sealed. It is something that does not have to be continually done. Once it is sealed, it is sealed. It says to the ghosts floating by, '*This house is not open to entities!*'

"Now . . . okay, I get the name Fred, and a voice just said, 'Are you sure you want Fred out of here?' Hmm, I'm telling them, 'Yes.' We want the house sealed up to all spirits, all visitors. Now, just say that a visitor from the Other Side, a relative or loved one, wants to come visit—they can come and visit as long as they don't try to scare you, and as long as their visits are loving. But aside from that, no other spirits can enter this house." She was tracing the shape of my house in the air with her finger. "So, he says to reassure you. All the experiences that you have had were real—they weren't in your mind. Again, you had five different entities visiting you throughout the years."

Kris broke in, "How old is Peter?"

Echo replied, "Eight."

Then Kris asked, "Brown hair?"

Echo confirmed, "Brown hair."

I jumped in at this point, saying, "Johnny was blond."

Kris said, "The boy I saw was Peter." I looked at her in disbelief. This experience was one I did not know about. We have to have a serious talk one of these days.

Echo looked up and said, "He's just about done [referring to the spirit guide who was sealing up the house]. The voice says to use the experience in a positive way. Take from it all that you can—again, in a positive way. But he says, 'Don't mark it as an experience that hurts you or makes you feel crazy. It's like closing a door, closing a chapter in your life. Close it, and look back on it, and see what good you can take from this. If you are going to write a book about it, that's good. It will help others realize that what they are experiencing is real.' He says, 'Move on from here, doing something good with the experience.'"

I asked, "Does he have an example of that?"

"Just writing a book or a short story—something to help others understand," Echo said. "An example would be if you were at work, or some other place, and somebody started talking about sitting in the chair and then suddenly the lights went off. Instead of laughing and saying, 'Oh yeah, I've been through that,' be empathetic and help them see that it was real, so they don't have to go through life like you did, wondering if you were nuts. Help others understand."

She uttered a big sigh. "Okay . . . that's it!" She clapped her hands together, opened her eyes, and smiled.

We spent several minutes conversing about all the things that Echo's spirit guide had talked about. Her editor turned to me and asked again, "Where did the name Johnny come from?" I explained that the people who lived here before us were the ones who'd lost Johnny and that my next-door neighbor told me his name. S. had asked this question when they'd arrived as well, so I wondered if they were trying to determine if I was telling the truth.

At this point, Nancy decided to join in the conversation. Up until now, she was sitting very quietly, taking it all in. To reaffirm what she had just heard, she said, "And you said the little boy was named Peter." Echo nodded.

I mused, "The Frank visitor. I wonder if that was my father."

We then discussed whether Echo had said, "Are you sure you want Frank out of here?" or "Are you sure you want Fred out of here?" I was sure she'd said, "Hey, what about Frank?" in reference to sealing the house up from all spirits.

Echo said, "I don't know what I said. It was my spirit guide talking." We reached a consensus that she had said Frank, but in listening to this tape again, I clearly hear that she said Fred. Now I'm sad. My father's name was Frank, and I could easily have imagined him blurting out, "Hey, what about me?" He must have been hovering around me when Echo's spirit guide was talking, causing me to hear his name. I miss him a lot.

Echo reiterated that Johnny was only here for the first ten years we lived in this house. That certainly accounts for the numerous incidents from 1968 till 1978 and the hit-and-miss experiences from 1978 till today.

I asked, "If he isn't here, then who or what has been plaguing us since 1978?" Why did I ask that inane question after she had just spent ten minutes telling me who had been here? I belong in a home!

Her partner looked at her notes, then repeated, "Jeremy, Frank or Fred, Peter . . ."

Kris spoke up, "That's the boy I saw in my room!"

I interrupted Kris. "You saw Johnny upstairs."

"No, I saw Peter in my downstairs bedroom. I saw him many times."

I was stunned. "What?" How could she have kept this from me all these years? I explained to my daughter, "When you were five years old, you told me about a little boy who stood upstairs by your dresser and watched you sleeping in your bed. Now that would have been Johnny."

Kris replied, "I don't remember, but if I told you that, then I saw him. This boy was older and had brown hair." Kristen told the ladies she'd always loved the name Peter. That was her great grandpa's first name. She always wanted to name her first-born son Peter, but her husband didn't want him to get teased. Of course, when Echo first said Peter, I immediately thought of my little foster dog, Pete. I miss him a lot too.

Suddenly, the realization hit me that my house was now sealed up. I had been on the fence for years, but when I finally said, "Yes, go ahead and seal it up," I felt good about it. "I know it will be a lot more boring, and very, very quiet, but go ahead and do it," I said. I have had enough experiences to last a couple of lifetimes, and I was ready to have it come to an end. S. smiled at me and said, "You know you can be very interested in ghosts and read and write about them without living with them as well." I agreed.

In retrospect, I wish now that I had asked Echo to include my mother-in-law and father-in-law in the ghost blockade. They have both been back since they left this earth. The odor of the chair that lingered in my room and the stale whiskey and cigarette smell are pretty definite signs that they were hanging around. Perhaps they feel differently about me now that they have crossed over. Be that as it may, I do not wish to be bothered by either of them ever again.

The ladies left my house about 2:55, and a few minutes later, we met Paul as I was driving Kristen and Nancy home. I was under a time crunch, because my dinner group was meeting a few hours from then. When we all arrived at the restaurant that evening, I eagerly filled them in on what happened at the house. They were all disappointed that Echo didn't find any spirit in residence—all except Steve, the skeptic.

October 28, 1997—So I Guess the Party's Over

It's hard to believe that episode of my life is over. I've reached the end of my story. For decades, I have been dreaming and planning on how a ghost buster would kick the spirits out of my house. Instead of the dramatic expulsion I anticipated, my house was pronounced *clear*. At least I didn't break down in tears of disappointment. Maturity has its benefits.

Echo's spirit guide validated the years of emotional turmoil, and that helped me understand all the things that have happened here. My work isn't finished yet. I have the pockets of sad, negative energy to purge at some point. I'm not sure how I'll handle those areas in the basement. Maybe my friend Melissa will have some suggestions.

It's been three weeks since Echo's visit—since my house was pronounced clear. There have been a few taps here and there, which I can't explain. If Peter is gone, why would there be taps on the lampshade? There were only maybe three faint taps, then nothing. Maybe he somehow squeezed in under the white light to say good-bye, like my old dog Pete.

My house has become extremely quiet. I have not heard any more odd noises in the kitchen, which just amazes me. Now, when the refrigerator thermostat clicks in, I jump a mile, because my senses are not expecting noises of any kind—not even normal ones.

It would have been awesome if Echo had found a ghost in residence and we could have watched her send it to the light, like she does on television. Kristen and Nancy didn't say anything, but I'm sure they were hoping for that outcome as well. However, since they both felt the spirit was no longer within my walls, they may not have been expecting anything.

This must have been a boring visit for Echo. If only I had known about her in 1968! She would have had a field day at my house. If it's true that spirits are drawn to homes that bustle with activity, no wonder we have none here now. The party is over. Now it's time to get out the candle and prayers and clean out the bad energy. Will I ever get used to a dull, quiet, ordinary life? Only time will tell.

9: Peace and Quiet and ... What Was That?—1998

January 17, 1998—Peace and Quiet at Last

It's been over three months since my house was sealed against spiritual visitors. I have finally become accustomed to the stillness that permeates my house these days. Get this: I've even been ironing clothes in the basement at night, with or without Paul around. Nothing has disappeared for a long time. I am not carrying a flashlight around with me any longer. On a related note, I can walk with confidence into a dark room without feeling the hair stand up on the back of my neck. The biggest difference I've noticed is that I can now sit anywhere in the house, any time of day or night, without those annoying tapping sounds setting my nerves on edge. I can actually read a book or magazine at night without the jangling interference of the television. In the past, I'd often use the television to mask ghostly noises so I wouldn't jump out of my skin while I was trying to read. The delicious peace and quiet does wonders for my concentration. Last but not least, although I'll always be a night owl, falling asleep has been much easier without Peter's aggravating noises.

During the entire month of January 1998, I burned a white candle in Paul's radio room and asked the angels to lift the negative energy from the northeast corner. The room and Paul's personality seemed different afterward—lighter and less testy, in that order. As soon as it gets warmer outside, I'll burn the sage in the basement. My spiritual friend from work, Melissa, gave me some sage for that specific purpose. She, too, can rid homes of spirits. Kristen wants me to invite Melissa out so she can verify that the energy is gone for good; Missy said she could do that in the spring. She suffers from fibromyalgia and other health problems, so it is often difficult for her to get around. We'll do it at her convenience.

John-Paul stayed with us over Thanksgiving. On the morning I brought him home, he told me about the loud breathing in my office, where he'd slept. He heard it all three nights. It was so loud that it woke him up. Although it frightened him, he didn't come out to the living room to tell me. I secretly think that sound was my dad watching over him. Dad had severe emphysema, and his breathing was quite labored. Echo said relatives could visit as long as their visits were loving. My dad never lived to see my children grow to adulthood, so I believe he looks in on them from time to time. Kristen tells me that every once in a while she'll catch a whiff of white liniment in her house, even though she has nothing that resembles that distinctive odor in her home. She remembers it from when she was small, because my dad used white liniment every day for his aches and pains. I bet the drugstores don't even sell that old-fashioned pain remedy any longer, but my dad swore by it. Kristen also hears labored breathing around her from time to time. I wish Dad could have gotten to know his great-grandchildren. No wonder he sneaks an occasional peek at them. I just wish it wouldn't frighten the kids so much.

Camden spent a few days with us a week or so after J-P, except Cam ended up in the living room with me one night, very frightened. At about four in the morning, he said he heard ghosts and that they would not let him sleep. I have no idea what he heard, but I made a bed for him on the love seat and told him they weren't allowed in the living room. If sealing up our house worked, he shouldn't have heard a thing! Maybe he dreamed it, because the poor little guy thinks about stuff like that all the time. It's one of the offshoots of hearing too much about it.

Kari-Lynn spent the weekend after Christmas with us this year. She slept through the night, both on Friday and Saturday. But then she has never had a problem with my house.

All the second thoughts I had about missing my ghosts are gone. I enjoy sitting in my office till the wee hours of the morning with the soft clicking sounds of the PC keys instead of the annoying sounds of Peter's tapping. Occasionally, the furnace vents give off noises and my nerve endings spring back to life. Perhaps that knee-jerk reaction will subside someday as well, and wouldn't that be nice.

I've recently asked Kristen about her sightings of Peter in her bedroom. She said she saw him several times. He stood across from her bed, along the east wall that divides my office and Paul's radio room, and stared at her. That sounds just plain creepy to me. That area is where my desk and computer now sit. Could Peter have been the culprit messing with my modem? It's possible.

Here's one more interesting item to report. Just recently, Kristen attended a coffee party with some childhood friends out in Monticello, Minnesota, where they all reside. Two of the women were my former neighbor Martha's daughters. The minute Kristen walked in the door, L. asked her point blank, "Is your mom's house still haunted?" Kris was taken by surprise. Martha's kids never talked about the ghost years ago. Kris asked L. what made her think it was. Her friend replied, "Sometimes when I was over at your house, I would hear someone playing the piano in the basement. I always thought it was you down there, but when I'd go down to look, I didn't see anyone. That's when

I knew it was the ghost. Everyone knew your house was haunted, but no one wanted to say anything to you, because you might get scared." Kris laughed and told the group she had been seeing things in the house all her life—that it was no big deal. That must have surprised a few women at the party. How odd to think of those girls all grown up, reminiscing about my house some thirty years after they played there as children.

Echo's spirit guide said Peter would often spend time in other homes around here, so I wonder what stories I'd hear from my neighbors if I asked them. Maybe I'll approach a couple of them sometime and ask if inexplicable noises occur in their homes. Of course, the mood would have to be just right. Maybe I'll wait till Halloween night, when I can hide behind a mask. I'm such a coward. I still haven't told Paul about Echo's visit. But then, that gives me something to look forward to, doesn't it? Like I said, it's been pretty boring around here.

Oh No, Not Again . . .

In late August of 1998, I had arthroscopic surgery on my left knee. I was home alone after Paul went to work—or so I thought! My friend Melissa and her partner, Mike, drove out to visit me the day after my surgery. When I hobbled to the front door to let her in, the first thing she said was, "This house is clear." Every pore in my body gave a sigh of relief. Even though I only had the cartilage removed, the surgery was no piece of cake, and worrying about unseen guests was something I didn't need to deal with right now. Her verification was puzzling to me, however, because the sounds had clearly started up again.

Since watching television all day long had become horribly boring and I had read all the books I wanted to read, some afternoons I just sat around daydreaming. Prior to my convalescence, I thought the familiar kitchen noises were back, but I paid them no heed. My house was sealed, and I clung to that belief for dear life. However, with nothing to do all day but take naps and heal, those sounds were

almost impossible to ignore. In the days that followed, they continued to increase in number and volume. What the heck was going on
now?

Sometimes Truth Hurts

When I went back to work in late September, I confessed to Melissa
that I was still hearing noises and that it was getting to me. "How
can that be, when you said my house was clear?" She admitted that
she had lied to me the evening of her visit. I was totally blown out
of the water. Telling lies was completely out of character for Melissa,
so I demanded to know why she'd said everything was okay. I should
have known she had a good reason.

"Girlfriend, I wasn't about to tell you there was something in
your house," she said. "You needed all your strength to recover from
that surgery. I could feel the activity the minute I stepped onto your
property." Oh damn!

Between working, going to physical therapy, and keeping up the
house, I tried not to get too worked up over the newest sounds in
my life. The kitchen cacophony had moved back in, bringing with it
a few new playmates for the living room. These noises took the form
of staccato cracks and snaps and came from the vicinity of the television—and believe me, they raised the hair on the back of my neck at
night. I could almost ignore the bumps and fuzzy crashing sounds in
the kitchen, because they were the same old same old, but the new
noises invading my space were so loud I could barely stand it.

I was forced to share my misfortune with my daughter and Nancy.
Kristen didn't say too much, but Nancy claims that I have—either
consciously or unconsciously—invited my spiritual guests back into
my life. She might be right. But if I did, it was definitely not a conscious action. I had embraced the fact that my house was permanently sealed and hung on to that belief in good faith.

Missy thinks my hallway might be a portal or vortex through which
spirits come and go. Echo did not mention that. I won't fault her for
failing to mention that possibility, though, because I put her under a

time constraint. I wanted her to finish up before Paul got home from work, and I might not have gotten a full session with her because of that.

In the past year, I have managed to achieve a certain amount of spiritual growth, although it may not sound like it. I'm not the same frightened soul I was when I began writing this journal. Melissa has taught me how meditation can strengthen me both emotionally and spiritually. I owe her a debt of gratitude that will be impossible to repay. Her comforting guidance makes me feel like I can handle almost anything that comes along—the operative word being *almost*. Missy is several years younger than either of my children, but by her own admission, she is an old soul—a much appreciated old soul, and I have adopted her as another daughter.

10: Patience—1999

January through August 1999—Ignore 'Em While You Can

For most of the year, I did a fairly good job of ignoring the noises that were supposed to be sealed out of my home, but then something happened that jarred me out of that illusion. In the summer of 1999, I decided to keep closer tabs on each new episode as it occurred. One of my spiritual visitors is back in a noisy way, or maybe it's a new spirit altogether. I have no idea. If I've inadvertently broken the seal around my house, it could be anything.

Echo made the statement that family "drop-ins" can visit at any time, as long as their visits are nonthreatening. Perhaps one of them has moved in with me and has no idea how much anguish it's causing. Melissa has a strong hunch that it is a relative trying to get my attention. I keep wondering if it's my dad trying to convey something to me about my mother. She recently entered a nursing home and isn't very happy about the whole thing. As much as I loved my dad and my relatives when they were alive, I'd really rather they didn't try to get in touch with me now. Yes, I've gotten much stronger, but I'm still not at the level where I could comfortably converse with a spirit if one happened to drop in for a chat.

September 1999—I Remember Something Painful from My Past

Since my knee surgery in August 1998, I must occasionally resort to using a cane. My surgeon told me my knee would never be normal because he had to remove all the cartilage under my kneecap, which had fallen victim to arthritis. The way he explained it, tiny pieces of bone kept breaking off and embedding themselves in the cartilage, which shredded it to pieces. I'll need a knee replacement at some future time. Some years ago, I saw the replacement procedure on television, and all I can say is, they'll have to catch me first!

During my first consultation with the surgeon, he asked me when I had injured my knees. I couldn't remember all the times I had hurt my knees. I've fallen down stairs periodically since I was an infant, most recently in 1993; played in a ladies' softball league in the 1970s, where I might have twisted my knees a time or two; and more than once I've hurt them while raking the yard. As I mentioned before, I'm rather clumsy, so I could have injured them any number of times throughout my life. I was told it would have taken quite an impact to mess up the kneecap that badly, because the MRI showed an injury much more severe than a simple twist. Doctors' offices make me nervous, so I couldn't think of a specific incident when my knees had been severely injured.

However, almost a year later, the memory of one serious injury popped into my head. It was that frightful night I was hanging up clothes in the basement, when I first heard that mournful crying. In my fearful haste to get away, I tripped and fell on the stairs. I came down hard, with both knees hitting the edge of a step, which caused a numbing pain. I'm positive now that that debilitating injury began the process of cartilage disintegration. That damage healed over, and until I became older and put on more weight, both knees functioned fairly well. However, after a serious fall in February 1998 on the ice-covered steps of the office building where I worked, the inevitable couldn't be put off any longer, and so the arthroscopic procedure was done.

My Own Personal Cane Mutiny

Since my surgery, there are times when my left knee is quite swollen and painful, so I keep a cane in a handy spot just in case it's needed. Until late one Sunday afternoon, the cane had been hanging on the closet doorknob in my office for months. Paul had just returned home from his job at the airport and opened the door to go upstairs to change clothes. I was in my office when I heard him ask why I'd put the cane on the steps. I had no idea what he was talking about, because there was only one cane in the house and it was in my office.

Or was it? I glanced at the closet door, and it was gone.

I approached the stairway door and saw the missing cane positioned diagonally across the steps, with my turquoise T-shirt tied around the tip of it in a large, bulky knot. It was not there earlier that afternoon, when I'd gone upstairs to put away some freshly folded clothes. In fact, that T-shirt was in the clothes hamper behind my office door until Paul caught it having that illicit rendezvous with the cane. I have to admit the sight shocked me. Normally, visual things don't alarm me, but this was so brazen. Of course, I knew my husband would never believe the cane got there under paranormal circumstances, so I took a proactive stance and, in a confident tone, stated, "I didn't put it there."

He dismissed the incident by saying, "Of course you didn't." Augh! Then, without skipping a beat, he handed the cane to me and added, "Don't forget to pack this for vacation in case you need it." Oh great! We're back to the denial stage, with just a whiff of sarcasm for good measure. The frustration is starting all over again. To plead my case would only have started an argument. I wish my husband would not judge me because of his own fears and beliefs. It seems I'm trapped again.

October 1999—Back from Vacation

We had a relaxing trip to the East Coast until one lazy afternoon in Wells, Maine, when the cell phone rang. It was my sister informing me that our mom had broken her hip. The bane of the elderly had finally caught up with her. I told Kathie we'd start driving back tomorrow morning and arrive home in two days. Thankfully, Kristen and my brother's wife's sister were around to check on Mom in the hospital. (More on this later.)

New England is always gorgeous in the fall. We've made that trip many times over the years and never tire of the sights. The red leaves, rolling hills, and small, picturesque towns with their white church spires make Vermont my favorite vacation state for scenery. The rugged coasts of Maine and Massachusetts also get high marks from both of us. Over the years, Paul has become a gregarious sort and loves to meet people and take long bike rides. I have changed too, often keeping to myself, working on a manuscript, or communing with the ocean. My job is full of personal contact, interruptions, and deadlines, and I find the ocean waves to be the perfect drug-free remedy for stress reduction. This year, in addition to some fine sightseeing, we had a fun dinner and a visit with good friends in Connecticut that ended way too soon. We also met my new Internet pen pal from New York and had dinner with her and her significant other. However, as soon as we got back, all the responsibilities and aggravations were here to meet me. And worst of all, my pesky house ghost was at it again.

The first hint of post-vacation tomfoolery occurred when I realized my everyday watch and a beautiful fourteen-karat gold bracelet had disappeared from my desk. I had worn a ring watch on vacation but brought my wristwatch along as well. When I unpacked, I left all my pieces of jewelry on the desk to be put away at a later time. As soon as I noticed the watch and bracelet were missing, I immediately launched into a frenzied search. The gold bracelet was a gift from a former manager, and I wear it quite often. As far as the watch goes, I feel naked when I'm not wearing a timepiece. Like it or not, I'm an inveterate clock watcher. When I couldn't find the wristwatch, I was forced to go out and buy a new one. Unfortunately, I can't afford to replace the bracelet. So this paranormal prankster, the one Paul claims doesn't exist, is costing me hard-earned cash once again.

While in Hebron, Connecticut, visiting with my dear friends Bea and her son, Dan, I purchased a cute silver-tone ghost pin. I planned on wearing it to work each day till Halloween. Actually, this pin could be my signature jewelry piece, couldn't it? I also purchased ghost pins for Melissa, Kristen, and Nancy—my triad of strength. Predictably, my pin disappeared off my desk at home on or around October 16. So until it floats back into my life (and it darn well better), I am ghostless—in that respect, at least. After checking a couple of that national chain's other stores, I was told that the pin was a seasonal item and that they were completely sold out. They weren't getting any more in until possibly the next Halloween season. That bummed me out, because it was the cutest little pin. I wonder if or when it will turn up.

I searched every day for my missing jewelry, but to no avail. One Saturday, while digging through my jewelry box one more time, I picked up the velveteen pouch in which I store my good turquoise and lapis necklace, which at the moment needs to be repaired. There was no reason to check inside, because this pouch hadn't been opened for three years. Or had it? Voila! My ghost pin was hiding in there, nestled among the beads and strings of the broken necklace. Strangely enough, I found the missing pin just in time to wear it to work on Halloween day. I checked to see if the watch and bracelet were in there as well, but that would have made the game too easy.

Trying to keep track of my belongings is like being on a never-ending scavenger hunt. Apparently, my unseen friends delight in watching me scurry throughout the house, cussing and tearing my hair out. Do you suppose these pesky spirits have entered a *Funniest Humans Home Videos* contest in their dimension? If so, they're getting some great footage at my expense. (Note to the ghosts: If you win, I demand my cut of the prize money!)

December 1999—Lost and Found

One night in December, I needed to trim my bangs, which were getting a bit unruly. Usually, Kristen, who is a cosmetologist, takes care of my hair, but occasionally I have to snip here and there between haircuts. In the bathroom, I began digging in a small woven basket that my father made for me many years ago, looking for the barber scissors. As I picked through the old makeup and hair clips, I found my watch and gold bracelet in a tattered sandwich bag under the clutter. Aha, the return of the odd couple. I didn't share this discovery with Paul, for obvious reasons. He'd only say I had put the filthy tattered bag in there and forgotten about it. If I was the one who hid these items, I would have put my jewelry in a clean bag!

More Jewelry Plays Hide and Seek

A couple of weeks later, a garnet ring and a sterling silver square band ran away, taking a pair of simulated ruby hoops along on their adventure. They were last worn to a church program on December 6. These rings are two of my favorites. I have dozens of rings, but I wear the garnet band in honor of my father. It was his birthstone. The square band ring is the perfect complement to it. I wear these rings together often, but *someone* has momentarily put a stop to that.

What Else We Can Lose Before Year-End?

In November, I purchased four pair of high-tech ear warmers from my favorite shopping channel. I planned to give them to my daughter, my son-in-law, my husband, and my son for Christmas. These items had been stored for several weeks in a pigeonhole in my desk while waiting to be wrapped. This proved to be a big mistake.

The grandkids were coming for a visit, so I hid them in my storage closet. On Christmas Eve morning, when I took them out to wrap them, I could find only three pair. I took everything out of that closet to look for the missing pair, but it was gone. I found the shipping invoice showing the purchase of four pair, so I knew I wasn't hallucinating. That fourth pair could have already been missing when I'd crammed the others into the closet that day: they were all clipped together, and I didn't take the time to separate them. What incredibly bad timing! I had to quickly come up with another gift idea before we left for our Christmas Eve celebration in Monticello.

11: A New Century Begins—2000

January 2000—The New Millennium

At least Y2K didn't spring any surprises on us. The planet didn't explode, the World Wide Web didn't collapse, and it's status quo in this house as well. Nothing has changed. I can see that the saga of missing items is going to follow me into the year 2000. The dead have no concept of time, so they don't know or even care that we've entered a new millennium.

Good news! During the last week of January, I came across my missing rings in the pocket of a red linen blazer. I had retrieved it from the dry cleaner in November and then managed to get an ink stain all over the front of it the first day I wore it. Having to pay for another cleaning after wearing it only once is just wrong. Each weekend, I'd drag the blazer out of the closet on Saturday, fully intending to take it to the cleaners; then I'd hang it back up on Sunday. This is called avoidance. I was just thrilled to find the pieces of jewelry, because it would have been costly to replace them. It would be interesting to see how much money I have spent over the years replacing missing items.

It's February and the List of the Missing Grows

It's February 13th, and the ear warmers are still missing. So is a favorite meditation tape that always resides in the recliner's armrest compartment when I'm not using it. My tape walked off sometime in January. I don't care about the ear warmers any longer, but I listen to the tape nearly every night, so it had to be replaced as soon as possible. After a thorough search of my house, I placed a call to Barnes & Noble. They had to special-order it. In the interim, I continued my search.

Since I am quite familiar with the habits of my ghost(s), I made the rounds every day to look for my lost items. The evening before Barnes & Noble notified me that the replacement tape was in, the old one happened to show up on a shelf in the entertainment center, wedged in between some books. Is this annoying, or is it just me?

Paranormal Pandemonium—Oh, Poo!

Prior to Echo Bodine's visit to my home in October 1997, my house was alive with noises. Sometimes they were so irritating that I had to turn up the television or wear earplugs at night. As I mentioned earlier, after she pronounced my home clear of any visiting spirits, it became almost as quiet as a tomb here. I finally got used to that stillness. My kitchen still tosses me an odd sound now and again, but thankfully not every night. These noises occur just often enough to make sure I don't forget them—like that's possible.

I've also begun to hear noises behind me again when I'm sitting in the family room and checking my blood sugar. And the new staccato cracks in the living room are becoming more frequent and much louder. They begin their performance at night when I'm trying to watch television, and they grow even louder when I'm trying to fall asleep. They also seem to travel around the room. I first heard them in the area of the bay window; then, a few days later, they moved behind the television set. Next, I heard them over by the front door and adjacent coat closet. The traveling noises finally put down roots behind some knickknack shelves in the corner of the room near the hallway arch. These new noises could be described as the type of cracks one might hear on a frigid night in the dead of winter, when the house is snapping from the cold. So far, this winter has not been cold enough to warrant those sounds. Over the years, we've heard those cracks in the vicinity of the front door, but only when the temperature had plunged way below zero. At no time were they ever heard behind the television or near the hallway, so I'm positive someone new from the Other Side is vying for my attention.

I have also been hearing noises in my office again—always behind me, and usually at night. This would fill Peter's need for attention. A couple of psychic friends have told me to pray for the spirits to return to the light. I did that for several nights, and they seemed to take a break. However, there appears to be a palpable uneasiness in almost every room of the house, almost like it's getting ready to explode. It is not the calm structure it was in 1997 when Echo walked out my front door. I find it difficult to deal with this situation, and that dreaded theme from *Jaws* has started playing over and over in my head again.

February 14, 2000—Scents and More Nonsense

Since the living room recliner has become my permanent bed, I've moved all my stuff downstairs for convenience. I get dressed in my office, so I keep my clothes, fragrances, and jewelry in there. This morning while getting ready for work, I noticed my bottle of White Shoulders cologne was missing from my desk hutch. As usual, I was running late, so I quickly dashed into the bathroom to see if I had brought it in with me earlier. Surprise, surprise! It wasn't in there either. It's an exercise in futility. I had tidied up my desk the evening before, so I knew the cologne was in one of the pigeonholes. I had no time to play *their* game this morning, but, as is my custom, I ran back into my office to check one more time before heading out to the Northtown park-and-ride. I sat down in my chair to begin looking around again. Ah, isn't this cute? My White Shoulders was now sitting directly in front of me.

There Would Be More Disappearances to Follow

When I first met Paul, he told me he had been stationed in Scotland for a year when he was in the Air Force, and he often talked about that beautiful country. I finally got my own chance to fall in love with its lush green countryside during our first vacation there, in 1996. After we returned home, I purchased a Scotland travelogue video. This video has been a godsend to me whenever my job gets too stressful or this house gets on my nerves. As soon as I pop it in the VCR, I'm there once more, enjoying the sights and sounds of that delightful country.

On Friday, February 11, I sent a box of goodies out to Bea and Danny in Connecticut. Shortly afterward, my life went haywire, and I needed the rugged landscape, quaint villages, and lilting music to soothe my stressed-out psyche. The evening I chose to take this armchair holiday, my Scotland tape was nowhere to be found. I jumped on the Internet and e-mailed my friend and her son, asking if, by any chance, the tapes had ended up inside the box they'd just received. The next day, I received Bea's reply: "Nope, we don't have them." In the days that followed, I continued looking and began wondering if I might have misplaced them. That's often the consensus around here, but in this case, Paul couldn't find them either. So I'm still waiting to see if they return.

February 29, 2000—Happy Leap Day!

Well, I found both the England and Scotland videotapes on a shelf in my entertainment center. Paul and I had searched that very area a couple of weeks ago, so if they had been there then, one of us would have seen them. I don't bother sharing these incidents with anyone any longer. Everyone thinks I'm the woman who cried wolf.

Wolf! Wolf! Do you hear me? *Wolf!*

March 2000—I'm Not Feeling Up to Par

It's been a very depressing month. It has been almost one year since we had to put my mother in a nursing home because she could no longer care for herself. After a four-month period in the nursing home in my hometown, I moved her down to a care facility near me. She fell and broke her hip while living there, and after she was released from the hospital, she was sent to another local nursing home to recuperate, where she still resides.

With tight budgets and rising costs, many nursing homes are closing their doors, leaving anxious families to worry about new accommodations for their loved ones. My mom's nursing home is one that will close in a matter of weeks, and it's a terrible strain wondering where I will place her. In a state of panic, several families have already pulled their loved ones out of that facility and taken them into their own homes. Paul and I have full-time jobs, so taking in Mom is not doable on any level. Her wheelchair would not fit through the eighteen-inch opening between the kitchen and hall. Wheelchair access to the toilet is also impossible, because of the size of the bathroom. Our finances simply won't stretch far enough to remodel our home.

With all that I have on my mind lately, I have not been writing things in my journal as they have been happening around the house. Suffice to say, I am still hearing noises in the kitchen and living room late at night—we'll let it go at that. If anything else has gone missing, in this frame of mind, I might never know it or care.

Work isn't going well either. Our company is downsizing, and there is talk of a merger. My manager was reassigned to another area, and our department was disbanded. I have become an outdated dinosaur waiting to fall into the corporate tar pit. It's a sad truth—the business world has no room for low-level employees who are fast approaching retirement age.

My brother lives in northern Minnesota, and my sister lives in Colorado, so finding a new place for our mother is my sole responsibility. Losing sleep, being tormented by all the stupid noises in this house, and facing early retirement is bad enough—and now this. It's almost too much for me to handle. I've called numerous nursing homes in our county, and the answer is always the same: "Sorry, we don't have room at the moment, but we'd be happy to put your mother on a waiting list."

"About how long is the wait to get into your facility?"

"About two and a half years."

Augh! I'd like to hand this assignment off to someone else and disappear. Being the oldest child was never easy when I was young, but these days it's just plain unbearable.

Extreme emotional anguish finally got the best of me, and on Sunday, March 12, I became so despondent that I found myself contemplating the benefits of suicide. Half of me wanted to do away with myself while the other half tearfully protested, "No! I can't do that." This internal argument continued nearly the entire day. Paul was working at the airport, so I was alone. I didn't want to bother my kids with this either. It isn't their problem. Thank God nothing ghostly happened. Although this sounds lame, I couldn't even think clearly enough to figure out a way to dispatch myself to the Other Side. We don't own any guns. We have kitchen knives, but slashing my wrists didn't pop into my mind. I didn't have enough of the right kind of pills to do any damage, and I doubt the ant poison under the sink would have done the trick.

Some of my friends maintain that I really didn't want to kill myself, because if I had, nothing would have stopped me. They might be right. However, I prefer to believe that my angels kept careful watch over me by bombarding my tortured mind with enough positive messages to keep me in limbo till my husband came home. I made a doctor's appointment the following day, because I knew I needed help.

March 19, 2000—What a Difference a Week Makes

This Sunday, I feel more emotionally secure, because I'm back on an antidepressant that I used some years ago. As soon as the drug reaches optimum level in my system, things will be fine. However, I noticed I'm having trouble making decisions. This drug might be messing up my thought processes, but as long as it keeps me from running headlong into the traffic, I will work with it as best I can.

Today I should have painted my bathroom ceiling. It's been waiting patiently for two whole years. The paint is downstairs, but this felt like a very strong non-basement day to me. I overslept this morning anyway, and so I'd already lost two and a half hours of productive work time. These excuses were as good as any to keep me from starting the painting project.

By eleven thirty, I had to do my laundry. While dabbing a stain lifter onto a favorite shirt, I heard a distinct metallic ringing or buzzing noise. It came from the area behind the furnace, or maybe from Paul's workroom. It sounded like an oven rack had fallen on the cement floor—kind of a fuzzy, metallic *boi-oing-oing* sound. I quickly stuffed the shirt in the washer and then dashed out of the laundry room with my heart stuck in my throat. This was something new; my stressed-out nerves didn't need this. I slammed the chain lock on the kitchen door. This was a non-basement day, and I should have heeded my instincts.

I want to take a shower and wash my hair, but since I heard that awful noise, there is no way I'm going to get into that shower now. My whole day is shot! I can't go shopping, because I have to take the chain lock off the kitchen door to get outside, and I'm not opening that door until Paul comes home. I cannot even finish my laundry, and I can't meet a friend for lunch either—and all because I heard a freakin' noise in the basement. I feel stupid, silly, powerless, and paranoid, but on the bright side, I don't feel suicidal.

Logic tells me there is no way anyone could be down there. I'm asleep when Paul leaves for the airport at six forty-five in the morning, but he always locks the back door behind him. Unless I go somewhere, the door is kept locked up until the time he gets home. Now, I suppose the argument could be made that something simply fell down and I was overreacting. I know there is an old oven rack hanging up on a nail over by Paul's workroom door. It's been hanging there for God knows how many years. What would make it jump off the nail today, eh? Something must have knocked it down. And what, pray tell, would that be? I don't want to know what it was—human or supernatural. All I know is, I'm trapped in my own home for the remainder of the day. Paul will get home about forty-five minutes later than usual tonight, because he's picking up Chinese food from our favorite takeout place.

What a crappy Sunday! A week ago, I wanted to kill myself because I was so depressed, and today I am paralyzed with fear. I wish someone from the real world would drop in for a change. At least then I would have another person on the premises and I could nonchalantly excuse myself to put another load of clothes in the washer. I won't call a neighbor to come over, because I look deranged right now, and I don't want anyone to get the wrong idea. I might be shell-shocked, but *I'm not crazy*. Part of my problem is that I have been exposed to this haunted house for thirty-two years and just can't take it anymore. I could call my son. He thinks I'm unbalanced anyway, but at least he's family. He lives about four minutes away. I'd have to listen to his rhetoric about how I imagine everything, but it might be worth it to be able to finish up what I wanted to do today. Paul won't be home for five hours. If there *is* a ghost down there, it would be helpful if the darn thing would put my clothes in the dryer and start another load. Hint, hint!

March 26, 2000—*The Kitchen Noises Strike Again*

This morning, I'm meeting my friend Lu for breakfast. After I got out of the shower, I opened the bathroom door to make a dash for my office when I heard a sharp *crack*, as if something very brittle had snapped in the kitchen. I was in a hurry because I had dawdled earlier while picking out an outfit, so I paid it no mind. In running between my office and the bathroom, I noticed a piece of something dark lying on the floor by my desk, but in my haste I ignored it. I flew in and out of my office two or three more times.

Finally, my curiosity got the better of me and I picked up the mysterious item. It was a good-sized piece of wicker that had apparently broken off the new basket hanging on my kitchen wall. The ghost must have broken it off when I got out of the shower and tossed it in here or, worse yet, walked into my office while I was getting dressed. What does a lady have to do around here to get some privacy?

April 14, 2000—Echo Gives Advice

I got an e-mail from Echo Bodine today. What a pleasant surprise. I had recently written to her about the new noises in the kitchen and basement, but she's a very busy woman, so I didn't expect to hear from her for a long time. She said I should ask the Spirit Squadron to come and take these ghosts out of my house. I've tried that a time or two, but the noises remain. She said that it is usually young spirits who take a lot of pleasure in scaring people and that my worry, stress, and suicidal thoughts have made me a prime target. Sure, kick me when I'm down! Over the years, I have learned that spirits feed on fear, and unfortunately, I'm serving up big portions these days. Isn't that just like me—generous to a fault.

April 2000—What the Heck Was That?

My night life has been invaded by loud, crashing, knocking, banging noises in the kitchen and living room. When am I supposed to get any sleep around here? With each noise, my eyes pop open just to make sure that nothing is standing there. Early one morning on the way back from the bathroom, I saw a horrible creature in my mind's eye. It was flying directly at my back. It looked like a huge bat with a contorted, humanlike face and long, thin, oddly bent appendages resembling arms and legs. I took Melissa's advice and telepathically instructed it to stop. Then I told it, "I'm more powerful than you are. You cannot hurt me." It vanished in an instant. After that jolting episode, I tried to get some sleep, surrounded by the usual noises that refuse to be scared away.

The following day, I asked Melissa about this. She said, "Girl, you are starting to see the other world. You are growing more powerful every day." I know I am. I can feel it. I believe the meditation tapes I've been using each night are responsible for enhancing this unusual gift. I have always had paranormal experiences; however, as a small child, I didn't understand what they were. By the time I married and began raising children, I was too busy to tune in to much of anything. Like any other skill, one has to keep using it to make it work; therefore, my paranormal talents fell by the wayside. Other than sensing and seeing the ghostly occurrences when we moved into this house, I didn't venture too far down the paranormal path.

One Big Problem Is Solved

During the past couple of weeks, I've been attending evening meetings at the nursing home. We have a state senator who is working with us to keep Mom's home open. After months of worry and distress for the residents, their families, and the staff, we got word that another corporation had purchased the crowded facility, which would remain open until it could build a new one. Whew! That's one heavy burden lifted off my shoulders. My mother has dementia and osteoporosis, but other than that, her overall health is good. I believe all her siblings died in their nineties, the last one at age ninety-six. Since my mom is only eighty-eight, it's a relief to know she will have a place to live till her time comes.

May 2, 2000—What Goes Around, Comes Around

I rarely go down in the basement these days—again—unless Paul is home and awake. Looks like I've come full circle. This evening I had no choice, because I was running out of pressed garments and by no stretch of the imagination would wrinkled clothing fit the corporate definition of business casual. After plugging in the iron, I threw some clothes in the washer just to have some noise to keep me company.

While the washer was filling up, I heard that metallic *boi-oing-oing* sound again, coming once more from back of the furnace. I was able to take a more rational approach to it this time: it must be the new hot-water heater we installed a few weeks ago, because the noise seems to occur when the washer is filling up. It's a great feeling to discover the source of that nerve-racking noise. I finished some ironing and came upstairs feeling quite proud of myself.

Two Days Later—Déjà Vu

I had to make another foray into the dreaded bowels of my home to iron something for the next day. Paul had gone up to bed already, and I couldn't run the washer, because there was nothing left in the house to wash. It was just me, the ironing board, and whatever else was lurking in the shadows. As I began pressing a shirt, I heard quiet footsteps walking across the floor above me in Paul's room. I had only heard those noises on two previous occasions, both decades ago. In those instances, little Johnny was messing around upstairs.

The back of my neck began to tingle, but I declared in a resolute voice, "God is here with me, and He is bigger and more powerful than anything in this house—even whatever is making the noise!" I finished pressing one leg of my khaki trousers. When I set the iron down to readjust the garment, that *boi-oing-oing* noise struck again. The sound wasn't coming from the water heater, though, which is located several feet behind me and to my left; it had come up from the floor next to my right leg. I looked down at that spot. Of course, there was nothing there. I quickly pressed the second leg, unplugged the iron, took my clothes, and ran upstairs. While hanging up my khakis, I noticed the crease on one leg was way off center, but I thought, "I am not going back down tonight for any reason. I may never go down there again."

I wore the pants to work the following day and showed Nancy L. how badly I'd ironed them after hearing that mysterious noise. She said, "You gotta call the Spirit Squadron to come and collect whatever is doing that."

I replied, "I have been asking the Spirit Squadron to remove every spirit in my house. But this stuff continues to happen." She asked me to bring a tape recorder the next time I go downstairs so she could hear it. In a flippant manner, I replied, "What makes you think I'm ever going to iron again?" Nancy grinned. God love her, she understands me and my moods completely, and I truly appreciate her for it. By the way, I asked the "head of the house" if he had ever heard that noise, and he said, "No, I don't understand what you are describing." Damn! Even if he *had* heard it, he'd probably never admit it.

(A postscript: A few months after this incident, Paul said he found the source of the sound. It was the new water heater, and the noise occurred when the hot water was running. He said it was probably some mechanical malfunction that caused the sound. Okay, I'd guessed as much already, and that explanation works 99.99 percent of the time; however, it doesn't explain the night it occurred adjacent to my right leg. That night, I wasn't even running the hot water. I believe our spirit was mimicking that noise because it loved to scare me. Cheeky little devil.)

Sunday, May 5, 2000—Some Kitchen Interaction

On Sundays, while Paul is working, I usually try to do one big cleaning project. Today I am looking for my old blender. While removing the items to get at the blender, today's project became obvious. After realizing how long it had been since I had cleaned these cupboards, I rolled up my sleeves and jumped in. The whole process took over two hours. I've never been able to reach to the back of this base cupboard without taking a flashlight and practically crawling halfway into it. This has always been a deterrent to keeping it neat and clean. When I was younger, more limber, not as chubby, and had better knees, this chore wasn't as much of a bother.

Soon today's job became kind of fun. During the archaeological dig, I spotted the extra blades for my food processor. I had put them in a zippered storage bag to keep them away from the grandkids when they were very small. Apparently, over the years they'd gotten pushed farther and farther back into the black hole. I fished out the well-worn bag and tucked it behind the food processor, which sits on a bottom shelf in the other base cupboard unit. Then I returned to my task. A few seconds later, I heard a soft, dull sound, like something had fallen behind me. I turned around and saw the dilapidated bag of blades lying on the kitchen floor. I must not have shoved them in far enough, and they just popped back out. This time I really wedged them in, and then returned to pulling things out from the far reaches of the other cupboard. After a few more seconds, I heard the same quiet sound. For a second time, the bag of blades had flopped out on the floor. *Okay, what's going on here?*

Of course I knew what was happening. I was annoyed because there were kettles and plastic containers of all sizes sitting around me on the floor, and Paul would be home in an hour or so. To test the pest, I put the blades back one more time and watched the shelf to see what would happen. Sure thing, nothing did! I gave up the pointless vigil, and as soon as my back was turned, the bag flew out onto the floor again. I picked it up and said, "I don't know who you are and why you want my attention, but I'm getting tired of your game." I tossed the bag in a drawer and slammed it shut. This time they stayed put.

Since I was working in the kitchen, I baked some muffins. While they were baking, I washed and dried all the kettles that had been in seclusion for such a long time. While separating out the items to give to charity, I decided to update my journal with this bag-of-blades incident. I grabbed a warm muffin and sat down at my PC. After catching up with my journal entries, I returned to the kitchen for a cup of coffee. While standing out there pouring my coffee, it felt like something touched the back of my neck. I was wearing a bandana to keep my perspiration at bay, so I thought the dangling tails were responsible. Reaching around the back of my neck, I realized the tails were not located anywhere near the area where the touch took place. It hadn't felt like cloth anyway; it was more like the soft caress of a hand. So I'm entering that incident in my journal as well. With my kitchen all cleaned up, the only thing I have to do now is find something to wear to work tomorrow. I'll iron it as soon as Paul comes home from work. Hey, I'm no dummy.

A Few Days Later

After my ordeal with the strange noise in the basement a week or so ago, I ordered a clothes steamer from QVC, and it arrived yesterday. Great! No more nights in the basement for this kid. I can steam my clothes up here. Funny how much peace of mind a little thirty-dollar item can do for a bad case of nerves.

Summer 2000—My Drop-Ins Have Dropped Out . . . For the Time Being

As of June, it's been very quiet. I love these periods of silence. Since the ghostly hand touched the back of my neck, nothing of any substance has taken place. The noises in the kitchen still continue to happen, but even they have become hit-or-miss.

September 16, 2000—Kari-Lynn's TV Trick (Reprise)

My project for the day was painting the ceiling and the cabinets in the bathroom. When I stopped for a bite of lunch, I watched my favorite shopping channel. When I finished eating, I was in no hurry to get back to my paint job, because they were showing some beautiful sterling silver rings. My favorite! Oh well, duty calls. As I gathered my plate and glass and got up from the table, I heard a *click*. Whoa! The television went off *before* I'd even reached for the remote. I guess my phantom foreman was encouraging me to get back to work. I grabbed the remote and clicked the television back on and off just to make sure that's what had happened. My daily meditation keeps me from jumping out of my skin when things like this happen. I still get prickly feelings in my nerve endings, but at least I don't run screaming from the house—not that I ever did, but I often wished I could.

Sleep Paralysis? You Be the Judge

Ever heard of sleep paralysis? This is no textbook definition, but I'll try to explain this phenomenon as I understand it. This condition occurs when a person is first drifting off to sleep. Over the years, many explanations have been given for it, ranging from alien abductions and heart attacks to the legend of a mysterious old hag who stops your breathing by sitting on your chest.

In spite of all the folklore associated with it, sleep paralysis actually serves a useful function. I've heard when we start our initial sleep cycle, the paralysis shuts down our nervous systems so that we won't flail about and injure ourselves when we act out our dreams. Most of the sleeping public is not aware of this condition, even though some scientists say it happens to most of us each night. I've been aware of many episodes in my lifetime. The paralysis doesn't last very long, but while you are in its grip, it can be a very frightening experience. Every muscle in the body is frozen, which means you cannot even cry out or move for several seconds. Once you realize you won't be injured by this paralysis, it's no big deal.

Another common nighttime occurrence is the OBE (out-of-body experience). Prior to the surrender of sleep, the body becomes rigid (sleep paralysis) and the astral body starts to rise up to go on its nocturnal journey. Those who study this phenomenon believe each of us goes traveling at night into other planes of existence, which is one explanation for dreams. Some researchers claim our dreams are happening in real time, only in a different dimension. Those who have OBEs say they can go anywhere they wish via the astral plane. For example, out-of-body travel can take a sleeping person through walls or ceilings, across bodies of water, and over stretches of land. Some even claim they've gone to other worlds, and still others tell of dropping in on friends and watching them sleep. While some night travelers have had dramatic astral trips to faraway locations, others go no farther than their own bedroom ceiling. Over forty years ago, a roommate of mine had an out-of-body experience one night. We shared the only bedroom in that small apartment. At breakfast, she told me that she had stood by the window in our bedroom and watched us sleep. It gave her the creeps. I was jealous, because it sounded pretty interesting and she obviously hadn't appreciated the experience. Of course, I was eighteen years old at the time.

Anyone can learn how to experience OBEs. Between the Internet and bookstores, there are many opportunities to get step-by-step instructions for personal flights of fancy. While this phenomenon still sounds interesting, I no longer wish to try it. When correctly executed, it can be an incredible experience. However, if terminated prematurely, the astral body will slam back into its sleeping twin, causing quite a jolt. This is what I believe happened to me recently.

I had finished my meditation and was drifting off to sleep when all of a sudden I was aware of a floating sensation. My right arm, which had been resting on the arm of the recliner, had nothing beneath it. This was the first time in my life this had happened to me, and I became alarmed. I reached down to grab something solid and found myself back in my original position—toot sweet. It felt like I had been body-slammed back to the recliner by a huge invisible wrestler. My body was jarred against the recliner so hard that it actually hurt. I wondered if those brave souls who go flying at night do so after they are sound asleep—or are they just a more adventurous lot? My OBE might have jumped the gun a bit, leaping off when my conscious mind wasn't quite asleep. Since I inadvertently aborted my first OBE, I'll never know if my astral body would have floated up to the ceiling or through it, but that's okay with me. Although it still sounds exhilarating to this old girl, I have no plans to consciously attempt it at another time. Unfortunately, I have no control over my subconscious mind, so who knows? I might take off again one of these nights.

One bout with sleep paralysis—if indeed it was sleep paralysis—happened on a night when I swear I was awake. I had tucked myself in and was about to say my evening prayers. All of a sudden, it felt like someone had grabbed my upper right arm and was pulling on my shoulder joint. It was a slight pressure at first, but it steadily increased till it felt like my shoulder would rip out of its socket. The pain was excruciating, and I couldn't utter a sound. It nearly took my breath away. If this had occurred on my left side, this would have been the heart attack I've been expecting all my adult life.

My right forearm seemed to be plastered against my stomach, as though a small being was standing on it while pulling on my shoulder joint. Sleep paralysis? Maybe. However, I can't accept that verdict. I will have to do some research to find out if paralysis can occur while the victim is awake. My eyes were open during this whole painful episode, and I could see the light from the kitchen stove as well as shadows on the living-room wall made by our neighbors' yard light. I was relieved to find I could move my eyes. I slowly shifted them to the right, expecting to see some short, weird thing yanking on my arm, but there was nothing there. I telepathically cried out to God to please stop whatever was doing this, and immediately the pressure released. I could move again, but I was in terrible, terrible pain. After the episode was over, I wondered if that hideous batlike creature might have been the culprit.

My right shoulder was extremely sore for a couple weeks. I could barely lift my right arm to dress myself. It was difficult to do my job at the office as well. I considered going to my doctor for some high-powered pain pills, but I had no idea how I'd explain what had caused it. She'd probably say it was bursitis. I've had bursitis in the past but definitely didn't get it this way—or this quickly. Usually, bursitis pain starts out slowly and gets progressively worse over days, not minutes, and it occurs after some repetitive injury to a specific joint. I've never read about a case like mine, where the effects of sleep paralysis continue for a number of days after the incident.

The night after that painful experience, I decided to sleep upstairs, because if it happened again, at least then Paul would be within earshot. That didn't protect me from another frightening episode, however. This time it involved my left side. It felt like someone had a viselike grip on my left forearm and was trying to pull me off the bed. I was completely rigid, like the night before, but this time I couldn't turn my head to see if anything was there. It felt like my body actually moved toward the edge of the bed while I prayed silently to please make it stop. Again, whatever was holding my arm released its grip. I hope this isn't going to become routine, because I don't get much sleep as it is. After these episodes, I was afraid to go to sleep for several weeks.

The last months of the year 2000 found the staccato noises in the living room taunting me each evening while I stoically ignored them. I think they are back for good now. Nancy still claims that I've wished them back. It's beyond belief that I secretly enjoy being tortured by the phantom noises and unusual happenings I endure night after night. Am I that much of a masochist?

November 2000—A Friend Has a Tale to Tell

November was my month to choose a restaurant for my dinner group. Our dinner outings occur once a month, as they have for several years. This is my only night out, and I eagerly look forward to it. We always dine in restaurants, and when our conversations get too lengthy or our laughter gets too loud, we get dirty looks from the wait staff and the other patrons. For a change of pace, I decided to make a nice supper for us so we could visit here as long as we wished. Everyone was okay with that arrangement. I was excited, because it had been years since I'd had friends over to dinner.

The night of the dinner, it began to snow. My friends are scattered across the metropolitan area and none of them enjoys driving in severe weather or blinding snowstorms, so I was hoping the snowfall wouldn't increase in intensity. My dinner was ready and I was getting anxious, because no one had shown up yet. Finally, a pair of headlights appeared in the driveway, so I flew to the back door to greet my first guests, Ellen and Vicki. When I opened the door, Ellen had a very strange look on her face. She actually jumped when I said, "Hi, come on in!" I must have frightened her. This is not a good thing to do to a guest.

Eventually, both the guys showed up and we had a fun supper. Paul said good night to everyone and went upstairs at his regular time. After we ate, I showed them around the house. They all knew about the occurrences in my home, but they had never walked through it to see where these events took place. While the rest of us went down into the basement, Vicki preferred to remain in the family room. She was clearly ill at ease. Three of the dinner group members believe in hauntings; however, Steve avidly denies that such things exist. He reminds me of Paul and Scott. After Ellen, Steve, Dave, and I finished the tour, we sat down in the living room, except for Vicki. Later, she told me she was too uncomfortable to relax. I think it's a real shame that my house has this effect on people, and that it is socially crippling to us as well.

A couple of days later, I got an e-mail from Dave, who asked if Ellen had given me an explanation for what happened to her at the back door. I was totally intrigued by his comment. Ellen had not said anything to me, so I asked Dave what happened. He wrote back, "I think you should ask Ellen about it." Now, Ellen has also experienced many ghostly happenings in her lifetime, so Dave's comment raised a big red flag.

At the office the following day, I sent my friend an e-mail to ask what had happened to her. Ellen told the following story. She hadn't been to my house before and wasn't sure if they were at the right place. When they drove in, she told Vicki, "I'll go to the door and see if this is her house." Just before she knocked, a threatening male voice strongly warned her not to enter my house. She said it was a telepathic message but was very loud and rude. It really shook her up. That explains why she had looked so frightened when I opened the door.

I have no idea who or what sent her that message. She said the voice had an ominous sound to it. I remembered the night when a hostile male voice spoke to me as I was falling asleep, and I wondered if it was the same disembodied entity that had frightened Ellen. In all the years we've lived here, no one else has ever mentioned hearing a voice outside my back door. I wonder if some did but then kept it to themselves because they didn't wish to appear as if they'd taken leave of their senses.

Tidbits from an Unexpected Source

A visit to my dentist's office today proved to be very informative. My favorite hygenist left the practice and was replaced with a young man named Larry. He read my file and noticed my home address. We'd been chatting for a couple of minutes about my neighborhood when I remarked, "Sounds like you know my street pretty well. Do you live around here?" He grinned and said his older sister used to run around with one of the girls who lived in my house. Oh my gosh—dare I ask? He'd heard all about the Miller family from his sister. Larry was easy to talk to and had an open, honest face. I asked him if he believed in ghosts. He said he did, without batting an eye, so I started telling him a little about my experiences in the house. He nodded while listening; he'd heard a lot of this before from his sister. I asked him if he would mind checking a few things out with his sister for me. I told him I was writing a book and wanted it to be as truthful as possible. He promised when I came back for my six-month checkup that he'd have the answers I needed.

12: Retirement Can't Come Soon Enough—2001

January through May 2001—Same Old Stuff, Different Year

I wish I had a dog. The nights aren't quite as bad when one has a furry friend to hold. Damn those allergies. I am planning on retiring June 1, because my job has been dissolved and I don't feel up to learning a new position after so many years. My health is suffering from lack of sleep. Getting up to go to work is all but impossible some mornings. I have been taking a couple of drugs for pain, but I still don't sleep very well. The sleeplessness is taking a dreadful toll on me, and most nights, it's caused by those damn noises.

It's almost a given that telling your health care provider you hear ghosts in your house would result in a one-way ticket to a rubber room. What American medical schools need is a course called Paranormal 101. Hearing voices and noises automatically brands a person as schizophrenic. Most members of the AMA can't or won't take the time to learn and understand that there truly *are* things that go bump in the night. The problem is, these phenomena are not easily proven, which gives the skeptics the upper hand. Therefore, most of us suffer with loss of sleep and all the ills and isolation that accompanies it. My rheumatologist is from Pakistan, so he might be open to a conversation about paranormal noises. Americans seem to be the only people on the planet who consistently deny the paranormal, and that's a real shame.

June 1, 2001—I'm Free

Yesterday, after nearly twenty-three years of gainful employment, I reached my last day. I am officially retired. From now on, I'll be broke but hopefully well rested. People tell me I'll get bored being home all day—and maybe I will—but until that happens, I plan on enjoying every day away from the business world. I have projects to keep me busy, such as working in my garden, catching up on my reading and sewing, and working on all my writing projects. I can visit my mother at her nursing home during the week, which is so much nicer than cramming visits in on the weekends. I have dreamed of retirement for years, and now I'm finally sleeping late, wearing whatever I want to wear, and doing whatever I want to do. Somebody pinch me. Somebody from the real world, that is.

From June 5th till the 16th, my oldest grandson, John-Paul, and their family dog, Willie, stayed with us while our daughter, her husband, and their younger children went on vacation. It was really nice having John-Paul around, and their Westie was a hoot! We went up to Duluth one Saturday and had a great time. J-P loved being an only child for a couple of weeks. He was allowed to eat as much as he wanted, stay up all night, and sleep late the following day. Grandma M's house is a teenager's dream—when the atmosphere is normal, that is.

It really meant a lot to have J-P and Willie around, especially at night, because it helped keep my mind off things. I seem to have hit a dry spell with the noises and ghosts. You don't hear me complaining. Each night when I meditate, I ask the angels to keep whatever walks through my house away from John-Paul and Willie. I can't have *it* bothering my guests.

He Kept His Word

Most people do not enjoy visiting their dentist. I do, however. Today I was excited to show up for my appointment, wondering what I'd hear from the new hygienist. While he was busy working on my teeth, he told me that when Johnny was hurt or upset he'd usually go to one of his sisters for comfort, not his mother. So maybe the disembodied voice I heard calling, "Mommy" in my ear was that of Peter, the other ghost child. While my mole was digging up information for me, he learned that many years ago Johnny's family had burned all of his toys that were stored upstairs in a cubbyhole, in the hopes of freeing his spirit. So the fact that Johnny was bothering me had completely confused them: as far as they were concerned, he was not there any longer.

That was an eye opener. I wondered if Joan had helped the Millers in freeing their ghost child, since that was the same method she'd suggested when helping me. That might explain how she knew where to locate the little items she found on that blisteringly hot day. It always puzzled me how she knew where to find them. I wish I could share this piece of information with Martha and Joan. They'd get a laugh out of it. However, Martha died some time ago, and Joan sold her house and moved from the neighborhood. Since she and I never spoke after the day she was in the cubbyhole, I had no idea where she went. If I could tell her face to face about how the Millers got rid of their son's ghost, her expression would reveal if she'd had anything to do with it.

Johnny may not have bothered the Millers after they got rid of his toys, but he definitely didn't leave the premises. He must have felt deeply betrayed by his family. It's my belief that he hid some of his things before his family ditched the rest of them and then languished upstairs or in the basement while waiting for a new family to move in. Later, I came along and threw out what was left of his former life. I was relieved to hear he'd moved to the Other Side. I thanked Larry for his help and said I'd see him in six months.

July 2001—A Spirit Plays Spin the Bottle

July lived up to its reputation of being a very hot, humid month. My plan to divide the perennials and relocate my front flower garden was put on hold after the day I nearly passed out while moving a hundred irises in ninety-degree heat. I was home alone, because Paul was working one of his other part-time jobs. After that scare, I resigned myself to the boring job of pulling weeds during the cooler mornings—*cooler* being a relative term. During the piping-hot afternoons, I stayed inside my air-conditioned house and read a lot.

My days and nights are still quiet. I've been enjoying the ghostly hiatus; however, one night while watching television, I heard a soft thud in the kitchen, prompting me to get up to investigate. This was a sound I hadn't heard before. After making my way through the dark kitchen to the light switch by the back door, I found a gallon bottle of drinking water in the middle of the floor, spinning around and around. Only seconds before, it had been sitting against a wall two feet away atop a twelve-pack of Diet Rite. I put the plastic jug back, and that was the end of the tricks that night.

Midway through July, I broke the little toe on my right foot. My doctor and I had a good laugh over it. You see, I promised her I'd restore my health upon retirement. I worked for the past fifteen years in a lot of pain—the last four without much sleep. My main objective these days is to take care of myself: to rest, heal, and meditate. Now, as I limped out of her office, I promised to do better.

Since I had to stay off my feet for a couple weeks, it was time to catch up on some reading. Before I left work, Melissa had given me several of her books on healing and other metaphysical topics. Up until this accident, I hadn't taken the time to seriously dig in to them. Now I could. Each afternoon, I'd burrow into the pillows on the comfy couch in my office with my bottle of water, my book for the day, another pillow to elevate my foot, and the phone. This was the life! My days were my own. Retirement wasn't so bad—even with a broken toe. However, about the time my toe healed up, I went through another life change.

I Become a Mom Again

One morning in August, I was weeding a small patch of flowers in the back of the house when my daughter and her two youngest kids showed up unexpectedly. Kris had a big grin on her face and a little bulge in the bib of her overalls. Paul had been up on the roof working on a radio antenna, and when the gang arrived, we were intently peering into the lilac bushes trying to find his safety glasses, which had fallen there.

I had not been expecting my daughter and her kids, so I had to ask, "What brings you guys here today, and what is that lump in your bibs?" She smiled and pulled out a tiny white puppy. My hands were full of mud, so I couldn't take the little guy, but I did the next best thing: I gushed all over the little animal. "Oh, isn't he cute! Did you guys get another dog?"

I kissed the tiny pooch on the top of his head while she held him for me and replied, "Nope, this is *your* dog."

A puppy? Did I hear that right? She's really giving me a puppy? I almost fainted. I had not planned on getting a pet ever again because of the breathing problems my allergies cause. The years since Pete died were sad and empty for me, and I really missed having a companion at night; however, on the plus side, I no longer had to mess up my system with antihistamines and allergy shots. Still, Pete was about six years old when he came to live with us, so he didn't take a lot of work. But I was in shock: *It's my puppy? Oh dear!* I looked at the adorable sleeping pup and wondered if Kristen was pulling my leg. After all, she had been talking about getting another dog to keep her Westie company. The bichon-poodle mix was just about the cutest thing I'd ever seen. He was so helpless and sweet. He looked like a miniature Pete snoozing away in Kris's hand.

Kristen knew how much I wanted a dog to keep me company during my scary evenings. And the funny thing is, she had been telling me about this puppy for the past couple of weeks. He was part of a litter bred by her friend's brother-in-law. She kept suggesting that I take the runt because all his siblings had been adopted. I answered her with my typical indecisive repartee: "I don't think so. I'd like a dog, but I don't think so. If I ever get a dog, I'll get a Scottie. I've wanted a Scottie dog all my life." Kids never change—not even when they become adults. They still hear what they want to hear. My daughter took my ambiguous rambling as a yes. She and Paul schemed to present me with this retirement gift. Let's be honest: a new pup is not really a practical retirement gift, is it? It's a little bit like finding out you are pregnant the day your AARP card arrives in the mail. I said, "He's adorable, but what about my allergies?"

She replied, "Oh, you don't have to worry about calling in sick anymore, so you can have a dog." Her heart's in the right place, but her logic is slightly flawed. However, I immediately fell in love with this two-month-old sweetie, who weighed less than three pounds and could be carried in one hand. Boy, were our lives about to change!

All the dog books I've ever read have stated that bichons and poodles shed very little, if at all. Therefore, they are fairly safe for people who are allergic to dogs. Armed with that knowledge, Kristen figured this puppy would be perfect for me. Apparently, my system wasn't aware of that piece of information, because I began sneezing the day the pup moved in. After a few weeks of misery, I went to see an allergist, who reluctantly prescribed a couple of medications. I tested very high for dog dander, so he said up front that I should get rid of the puppy. I told him that was not an option. The pooch had stolen my heart and solidly bonded with my husband. I told the doctor if Paul had a choice, he'd probably give me away and keep the puppy. I was semi-serious. Of course, so was my doctor.

**My Pup's
Paranormal Powers**
From when he was just
a puppy, Max has always
been able to track our
house's "visitors."

My Dog Sees Dead People—He Really Does!

Max was about three months old when I first noticed that he followed things with his eyes—things I couldn't see. The first time I observed this, he was sound asleep on the couch. I was sitting across the room waiting for him to open those precious kohl-rimmed eyes. Watching him sleep was a soothing throwback to my younger days, when I spent hours watching my first baby sleep. The little guy's short legs were twitching. He was having puppy dreams. How adorable!

All of a sudden, for no apparent reason, Max woke up from his snooze. He sat bolt upright and began looking toward the living-room archway. Then he slowly followed *something* into the room, over to the couch where I was sitting. Apparently, it stopped right in front of me. I strained my eyes, trying to see if it was an insect that held his undivided attention. But there was nothing else in the living room, only Max and me. Even when I called his name, Max never broke his intense gaze. Whatever was in the room commanded his attention after it had wrenched him out of his deep slumber. An insect couldn't have done that. My neck bristled again. Now this could get interesting.

I'm Not as Young as I Thought I Was

I got very little done around the house the first few months after Max moved in with us. Potty training was a lot more difficult than it was when Shaggy lived here decades ago. By the time Max was four months old, his voice was changing, and he would emit a raspy, puppy-sized growl whenever he saw *something*.

The first time he let loose with that growl, it gave me the heebie-jeebies. He was snoozing on my chest early one morning when suddenly I felt him begin to stiffen up and then shiver. He broke the predawn silence with that raspy growl. I pried one eye open to see what was going on. Max was staring into the far corner of the living room by the hallway—the corner that is inhabited by those awful sharp, cracking noises. Twice I turned his little body back to face me, but he'd rotate himself around again, stare at the corner, and continue growling. Fascinating! I knew there was something over there but wished it wouldn't bother my little pup so much. His growling is raising goose bumps on my body—as well as my stress level.

Max started retrieving his jingle ball between three and four months of age. It's his favorite toy, and you rarely see him without it. We thought he was very smart, because he would intuitively return the ball to us without prompting. The only time he'd refuse is when his ball would end up in that scary corner. He'd make several attempts to get it, but each time he'd stop dead in his tracks and growl. Eventually, Max would give up, surrendering his favorite toy to whatever was standing there. That's when I would retrieve it. Paul thought I should stop spoiling the pup. He insisted I leave the ball where it was and make Max get it himself. I didn't agree. Paul wouldn't believe the reason Max was frightened, so I kept it to myself. Max's reaction to this corner wasn't scary during the day, but in the wee hours of the morning, when he was snoozing on my chest, it was just plain creepy. Since Max can actually see or sense spirits and confirm that one inhabits that corner, it would be perfect if he could explain what he sees to Paul.

Max Is Sprung by a Spirit

File this story under Totally Unbelievable. When my bouncy pup was around four and a half months old, he had a strange experience. I had put Max in his kennel for the night and then settled down in the living room to read. Having a puppy is akin to having a toddler, and we frazzled moms have to make time for ourselves whenever we can. I had just gotten comfortable with my can of Diet Rite and an interesting magazine when Max came prancing into the living room looking especially proud of himself. For several seconds, I stared at him in utter disbelief. I knew I had locked the kennel door. I always check the upper and lower latches, because I don't want Max getting out and peeing on the carpeting during the night.

"How did you get out?" I asked. I could have sworn Max smiled up at me. Much to his chagrin, I picked him up and brought him back into the family room. As if Max's escape wasn't mysterious enough, when I reached down to pull open the kennel door, my fingers slipped off the handle with a painful snap. The kennel door was still locked tight. I turned the kennel around to see if there was a hole on the back wall that Max could have squeezed through. There wasn't. Who let the dog out? I had the perfect answer to that popular rap song's question, but who would believe me? I deposited the escapee back in the slammer and locked it again. I checked it twice before going back to the living room, wondering how often this was going to occur. Max hadn't earned his stripes in the potty department yet. If the ghost continued to let him out, maybe the ghost would like to clean up after him. It was only fair.

The next morning, I felt compelled to share that strange experience with Paul, because it was so unbelievable. He might never accept the things I tell him about what goes on in this house when I'm the only one involved, but maybe with Max caught up in the strange goings-on, he'll pay attention. Paul was going to puppy-sit while I ran some errands. I told him about the kennel incident before I left. He said, "Oh, you probably didn't have the door securely fastened."

"If that is the reason he got out," I went on to say, "how do you explain the fact that the door was locked tight when I went to put him back? Do you think he shut and locked the door behind him?"

No answer. No kidding!

When I got back from the store, I was in for the surprise of my life. Paul called me into his office and said, "You know what happened to you last night? Well, it happened to me today. I locked Max up in his kennel so I could vacuum my office without him being underfoot, and while I was going through some stuff on my desk, he walked into the room."

God help me, I blurted out, "Oh, you probably didn't have the door securely fastened." Ouch! The sarcastic reply flew out of my mouth before I could stop it, because I was in shock.

It was Paul's turn to defend himself. "Yes, I did! I even checked the entire kennel to see if he squeezed out another way."

I asked, "How do you think he keeps getting out then?"

My bewildered husband shook his head and replied, "I don't know." Although I could have explained it to him, I held my tongue. To be honest, I was very proud that Paul had told me about the incident, because logic rules his life with an iron fist, and he could have kept this occurrence to himself and left me to ponder my kennel experience all alone.

A couple of weeks after the kennel caper, Max learned to go potty outside. During our October vacation, he stayed at Kristen's house with his dog cousins, Willie and Joey. They showed him how it's done. He doesn't really have to be locked up at night any longer, but since we think of the kennel as Max's bedroom, that's where he sleeps. Kris feels sorry for Max and keeps insisting that we should let him sleep wherever he wants now that he's housebroken. I explained to her that as long as he sees spirits, I'd rather he growled in his kennel instead of next to me in the living room. Besides that, he isn't suffering. Since I'm still sleeping in the recliner, I can hear him if he needs to go out during the night.

13: Max and Mom—2002

January 2002—I Try to Shoot a Ghost

Max is now seven months old, weighs twelve pounds, and is full of the dickens. I thought he'd grow out of it, but he still growls and watches things walk through the house. I keep telling him, "Relax, Max, the ghostie can't hurt you." I wish he could understand me. It's so hard watching him try to warn me about something only he can see. He is a nervous animal. I know genetics have a lot to do with Max's behavior. His daddy is a high-strung poodle and his bichon mother contributed her share of anxious traits as well. Unfortunately, my puppy also has a strong sensitivity to the paranormal, which exacerbates this jumpy behavior. There is no way this Type A dog will ever be mellow like Pete.

Max and I always relax in the living room prior to his bedtime. He usually falls asleep on my lap around eight o'clock, and then at nine

I deposit him in his kennel. It has become a ritual with us. Everyone says he's spoiled, and I won't argue the point. This is our time of night to unwind. He snoozes, and I get a chance to catch up on my reading. During this lazy time, Max often wakes from a sound sleep to watch *something* enter the living room and then drift over to the bookcase located against the south wall. This doesn't happen every night, but I've decided to take a few pictures of that area when it does, just to see if anything shows up on film. Articles on ghosts claim that it doesn't make any difference what kind of camera is used, so I'm going to give this a try to see what transpires.

Nancy, Kristen, and Melissa have been kept up to date on these happenings. Melissa thinks I could clear the unwanted energy from my house by myself, because I'm strong enough to do it, but I don't share her confidence in my ability. I'd rather try it when someone—besides Max—is here with me. Kristen, since she's fearless, would be an excellent companion; however, she lives forty-five minutes away from us now, so it's not convenient for her.

The Camera Takes a Picture and Takes a Powder

I'm not sure I'm ready to become a card-carrying, ghost-seeking paparazzi, but just the same I've begun to tote my 35-millimeter camera night and day. I never know when Max is going to go into his ghost-detecting mode. I have taken several shots of my little guardian watching an invisible entity slip into the living room and stop over by the bookcase. This occurs almost every night now. One night, the little guy even jumped down from the recliner and up onto the love seat next to that bookcase. He braced his little body against the arm and growled while perhaps a foot away from whatever was there. I snapped that picture. I was so proud of myself until I realized that it might never prove that Max was eyeballing a spirit. All that could show up on the print is a little white dog hanging over an armrest and staring at a bookcase. I just hope the spirit is cooperative and shows itself on some of these snapshots.

On the morning of January 14, I neglected to take my camera into the family room while I ate breakfast, and Max began growling in the direction of the refrigerator. This has been a hot spot for years. By the time I retrieved the camera, Max had lost interest and dozed off. Asleep at his post, the little soldier! I'll have to wait till he draws a bead on the fridge another time. I left my camera sitting on the table when I finished eating. Then I put some clothes in the washer, did my dishes, and read and answered my e-mail—pretty much my usual morning around here—and I didn't give the camera another thought until that evening. About eight thirty, Max again picked up on the spirit that drifts into the living room each night to watch television with us. I got up from the recliner and went into the family room to grab my camera, but it wasn't there. I searched the entire room, then quickly checked the kitchen, my office, the bathroom, Paul's office, and the living room, but it was nowhere to be found. I just shook my head. *It* has got me on the run again.

The following morning, I e-mailed this incident to my support group and then checked the upstairs bedroom for the heck of it. Max, my constant companion, toddled up the steps behind me. I didn't really think it would be up there, but when things go missing, every inch of living space is searched before I give up. I wondered out loud if the unseen being that walks through my house hid the camera because it didn't want its picture taken. While I was searching the bedroom, Max homed in on something and growled. I scolded him by saying, "That's enough, Max. Give it a flippin' rest." On that day, my patience was wearing thin. My little pooch stood his ground and continued to growl in the direction of the closet door.

When Paul got home from work later that afternoon, I asked if by any chance he'd seen my camera. He said, "No . . . where did you leave it last?"

"On the table in the family room," I replied.

He said, "It wasn't there this morning when I ate breakfast."

I silently answered, "I know, I know!" His question prompted me to recall the countless pairs of scissors that disappeared after we first moved here, and how those disappearances were followed by missing flashlights and, most recently, umbrellas. When I was working full time, I had the means to replace the objects that were spirited away. But now I can't easily replace my camera, since my pension check doesn't stretch that far. If it doesn't reappear, I will be one unhappy woman.

January 23, 2002—The Lost Is Found

On this sleepy Sunday afternoon, I plopped down in the recliner to check out the ads from the Sunday paper. Max was napping on the couch across the room from me. For the past ten days, I've been doing spot checks on the couches and recliner and coming up empty-handed. Out of habit, I absentmindedly slid my left hand down between the arm and the seat of the recliner. My fingers closed around something smooth and cold. Well, what do you know? My camera wasn't there yesterday. Looks like I'm in business again. Somehow it left the table in the family room, traveled in limbo for several days, and then finally came to rest in the recliner. I had to laugh, because a week ago I asked Melissa if she could see where the camera had gone. She said, "It's in another dimension at the moment, but you'll find it in an odd place when it returns to you." Is she good or what? I took the film to be developed that afternoon but haven't picked it up yet. I know Max sees something; I just hope my camera lens sees the same thing.

February 1, 2002—My Ghost Is a No-Show

Nothing appeared on the film. I'm bummed, because I wanted some proof of existence to show my husband. I asked Melissa if she knew why nothing showed up. She replied, "The spirit you are trying to capture doesn't wish to be photographed. And if you are completely honest with yourself, you'll admit you don't really want to see it either. With those conflicting energies working against each other, you'll never get anything on film."

She's right, you know. I don't think I'd be emotionally prepared to see the ghostly face of my father or any other dead relative, but it would have been nice to get a glimpse of a white streak or blob across the photos, like I've seen in *FATE* magazine. Max continues to let me know when he sees a spirit, but I no longer waste my film.

Many afternoons when I'm sitting at my PC, Max is sleeping on the couch behind me. All of a sudden, he'll break the silence with that low growl. When I turn to see where he's looking, he'll be staring into the hallway. Many times, he will station himself on the threshold of my office doorway and growl into empty space. That raises the hackles on my neck. Other times, he'll be on the couch, looking up at something standing directly in front of him, which means it's directly behind me. It's just plain eerie.

I wanted a dog to keep me company so I wouldn't be so afraid, and Max doesn't always fill that need. In fact, most of the time he makes the situation worse, but that's due to my inability to deal with the spirit activity. For the record, I still adore him. Max is just making me aware of them. Learning to deal with it is up to me.

March 2002—Some Nighttime Shenanigans

When most people get ready for bed, they get a glass of water, pull out the alarm, and crawl under the covers—period. How nice for *them*! My nights are never that simple, so I freely admit to being envious of everyone who falls asleep without a care in the world. Don't get me wrong: not all my nights are as bad as the following example—but many are.

Every night between midnight and one o'clock in the morning, I prepare for bed in this way. I do my bathroom chores, then adjust the recliner so I can lean all the way back comfortably. Next, I set up a TV tray and bring in my basket of inhalers and meds, along with a snack to satisfy the "take with food" directive on the labels. I turn on my white-noise machine to help me sleep and start the fan to ward off hot flashes. Then I gather my flashlight, lip balm, foot cream, ice bag, tissues, bottle of water, and my little radio and headphones.

Finally, I open the living-room curtains, adjust the blinds in the bay window, grab my comforter and pillows out of the closet, and finally tuck myself in.

My daughter once told me I resemble a turtle on its back when I struggle to get out of the recliner. Is that any way to talk to the woman who brought you into the world—a breech birth, yet? She is very honest, so the description is probably right on.

Well, one night after I was settled in, I realized the room was too quiet. In a fit of temper, this turtle kicked the pillows off the footrest, threw the comforter on the floor, returned the recliner to the upright position, and then got up and turned on the white-noise machine, which sits across the room from the recliner. This indispensable piece of equipment helps to deaden the nightly noises I hate so much. As long as I was up, I figured I would return my empty snack plate to the kitchen. I had taken most of my pills and needed to refill my water bottle, but I forgot to grab it. Welcome to my world!

Walking back into the living room, I noticed the curtains were still closed. I require some light in the room at night, and opening the curtains takes care of that obsession—unless I forget to open them, like on this night. When I made these curtains a few years ago, the placket turned out to be too narrow to be easy to move, so it's a real struggle to coax them open or closed. Paul closes them in the late afternoon to keep out the sun, which means I have to open them before I can go to sleep. He's taller and has a longer reach, so it isn't as much of an effort for him as it is for me.

And so the Great Curtain Snafu began. I frantically tugged at the folds of fabric but couldn't get the curtains to budge. The wrought-iron rod is permanently affixed to the wall, but this style has a removable extension in the middle that slides back and forth to allow the curtains to glide on and off easily. Did I say "easily"? I lied. I forgot that the extension can only move so far, and after tugging with more and more determination, I managed to pull the heavy curtains off the rod. Dang! I had no choice but to go back to the kitchen and get the step stool, because I couldn't stand on my tiptoes any longer and keep raising my aching arms. I wedged the step stool in place and

An Insomniac's Outpost
When I tuck myself in at night in the recliner in
our living room, my complicated routine often
lets me forget about my paranormal pest—but it
doesn't forget about me.

then climbed up. With some difficulty and a couple of cuss words, I
managed to slide the two ninety-inch sections back onto the rod.
When finished with that irritating interruption, I snapped the step
stool shut, then predictably tripped over it. Now my shin hurt. Geez,
was there a full moon out there? I guess I could have answered my
own silly question, since the curtains were open now—duh!

From childhood on, I've envisioned my life as a movie. I still think
of it that way. On this night, I must have been starring in a masoch-
istic comedy of errors. I looked up at the ceiling, shook my little fist,
and wheezed, "As God is my witness, I'll sew rings on those damn
curtains if it's the last thing I ever do." Yes, I really said that. I often
channel Scarlett O'Hara, minus the accent, and occasionally I'm loud
enough for the neighbors to hear.

With the step stool back in the kitchen, I returned to the recliner
and got all tucked in again—a procedure that needs no laugh track.
When settled once more, I grabbed my three inhalers out of the basket and put them in my lap. I took the prescribed two puffs of one
then picked up another and took two puffs. At that point, I glanced
over at the TV tray and spied one of the nine pills I have to take each
night. Missed one, dang it! I washed it down with a giant swig of

water. Now the bottle was completely empty and I'd have to refill it after I used my last inhaler. Perish the thought I'd wake up during the night and have no water nearby.

I reached for the Nasonex inhaler, which allows me to remain as allergy-free as possible while living with Max, but it was missing. I madly groped around in the hills and valleys of the comforter and couldn't find it. It wasn't in the meds basket either. I kicked the pillows and comforter off for the second time that night and then checked around the cushion and down both sides of the recliner, but I couldn't find the inhaler. Cue the turtle again! I struggled to my feet once more, wheezing and grunting, and then grabbed the comforter, which was crumpled up in a heap on the floor, and gave it a crisp snap. Still no inhaler. I carefully checked all the items on the TV tray as well as inside the tissue box. The inhaler was simply gone.

Okay, I'm way past being angry now. I'm fuming. Heck, *fuming* is much too wimpy a word. Tell it like it is, Marlene! Okay . . . I'm stark, staring, up-the-wall *mad*! Only a mad woman would tip a recliner up first on one side and then the other to see if her missing inhaler was hiding underneath it. Augh!

I am supposed to use that medication, without fail, twice a day. Since I couldn't find it, I resigned myself to hoping it would show up in the morning. If it didn't, I'd have no alternative but to go back, hat in hand, to my allergist's office and ask for a new prescription. He'd ask what happened, and I'd have to come up with a good story. They don't just hand those things out like candy on Halloween, you know. For some reason, insurance companies and physicians have formed a tight alliance to make sure patients don't end up with duplicates of the same drug. Hey, guys, don't worry about whether we might need a spare in case of an emergency, like tonight! I sat back in the recliner again, just about to tuck the pillows under my knees, when I realized my water bottle was still patiently waiting for a refill. I dragged myself out into the kitchen one more time and pulled the water jug out of the fridge. At this point, I'd had it. If anything else went wrong tonight, it would just have to go wrong. To respectfully quote Popeye, a cartoon hero of my childhood, "Ah stands all ah can stands, and ah can't stands no more!"

Back in the living room, I parked the full water bottle on the TV tray and tucked myself in. All this activity had brought on the mother of all hot flashes, and I really needed to cool off, so I reached for my water. Hel-lo! My missing inhaler was nonchalantly leaning up *against* the bottle, as sassy as you please. For some silly reason, the position of that little container reminded me of Gene Kelly casually leaning against the lamppost just before he began singin' and dancin' in the rain. So help me, if that inhaler pulls out a wee umbrella and kicks up its heels, I'm going to throw it across the room. "Where the heck have you been? As if I need to ask." Before the inhaler could answer, I grabbed it and squirted it up my nose. Then I said my prayers, put on my headphones, fine-tuned Coast to Coast AM on my little radio, turned off my lamp, and finally called it a night. It was past one a.m. My mind was racing, my adrenalin was pumping, and it would be a miracle if I got any sleep.

Since I'm a victim of raging insomnia, I read nearly everything I can find on the subject. I especially love all those self-help articles that suggest in a patronizing tone, "If you have trouble sleeping, why not try a relaxing routine before bedtime? Meditation or yoga works wonders to lower stress levels. Another foolproof method to ensure a good night's sleep is to dissolve all the cares and worries of the day in a soothing herbal bath. Or, try a glass of warm milk. Pamper yourself. Make your bedroom a sanctuary of serenity, a tranquil space, a safe haven in which you can drift off to dreamland on lavender-scented sheets." Yeah, yeah, yeah! In my house, there is no such thing as a relaxing, peaceful routine before bedtime, due to my paranormal pest.

April 2002—Peek-a-boo, I See You!

Ever since Max was a couple months old, he and I have gone many places together. Paul and I want to make sure our little dog is comfortable with car trips, in case we want to travel with him when he calms down a bit. He loves riding in a car, so when I have a quick errand to run, I pop him into my station wagon and off we go.

One morning after a trip to the post office, I had quite a surprise when we got home. As Max and I entered the kitchen, I watched in amazement while a large, pale brown shape, human in form, hurried from the kitchen into the hall. It glided away quickly, as if it had been caught with its spectral hand in the cookie jar. This was an incredible sight. Just for fun, I called out, "I see you, and it's okay to be here." I mean, if we are going to share the same space, at least we can do it on a friendly basis. What surprised me was the fact that Max didn't stop and growl at it. He may not have noticed the entity, because he went straight to his water dish for a quick drink and then dashed off to find his jingle ball. Or perhaps since I spoke to it, he thought it was okay for it to be in the house. Maybe I should start speaking to all the things he barks at, so he will think they are all friends. It couldn't hurt.

May 2002—The Heartbreak of Old Age

Several years ago, we noticed that Mom was missing a beat here and there, such as identifying the wrong person in a picture or bringing up an unrelated subject in the midst of a telephone conversation. I'll never forget the night we were chatting about Thanksgiving dinner when she began telling me she wanted ham and cold roast beef and buns. I blurted out, "What?" She went on to say that she also wanted Jell-O with fruit cocktail and some cold salads and lots of coffee and cake. Again I asked what she was talking about. She ignored my question and said, "And I want you and your brother and sister to take home the leftovers. I don't want a thing to go to waste." This time I got stern with her and demanded to know what that had to do with Thanksgiving dinner. She said, "What Thanksgiving dinner? I'm talking about my funeral lunch." Yikes!

Things weren't serious enough by any means to put her in a nursing facility yet. She still maintained her huge yard, cared for a big vegetable and flower garden, cleaned her house, shopped for her own groceries, and drove "old people" to church on Sundays. At the time, she was in her early eighties. In 1997, my sister, Kathie, spent a week with Mom, since she couldn't visit as often as the rest of us. She was able to get a better perspective on our mother's condition, because our visits were always so brief. One morning, Kathie came down to breakfast and caught Mom holding the newspaper upside down. Of course, when asked what the paper said, Mom knew all the answers, because she'd already heard the news on the radio. Kathie's visit was a reality check for all of us.

By the year 1999, old age and dementia had my eighty-seven-year-old mother on the ropes. She could no longer care for herself properly. We found out long after the incidents had occurred that she had fallen down the basement steps and broken ribs, blacked out in the snow, and showed up for church after soiling herself. Townspeople would just call the paramedics for Mom, and for some reason the news never reached us. We must have looked like villains in the eyes of those who watched us grow up. *Those nice Cook kids are ignoring their poor mother. How can they be so cruel?*

We tried to talk Mom into moving to an assisted-living apartment, but no dice; she insisted on staying in her home. So, for the past year, my daughter and her family drove up to help out twice a week. I went up each Saturday and Sunday, and my brother drove down from his home in northern Minnesota whenever he could. He and his wife contributed to Mom's care by handling all the financial and legal responsibilities—a daunting task. We had discussed Mom's future living arrangements many times; however, we always gave in to her obstinate demands to stay put in her house. Mom had ruled the roost when we were kids, and she could still be pretty intimidating.

Back in 1976 when my father died, Mom made me promise I'd never put her in a nursing home. She stressed the word *"never."* She told me that when her time came, she wanted to die alone in her own house, like he had. (Dad dropped dead in their kitchen from a massive heart attack. He always said he wanted to die alone. It seems he got his wish.) I truly meant to keep my promise to her, and could have if Mom had died with her boots on—perhaps gardening or mowing her sizable lawn. However, her life was to take a different tack.

We all knew when the day came that she could no longer care for herself, the decision would be taken out of our hands and she'd be forced to move. We dreaded that day, because our mother is one of the stubbornest humans on earth. Case in point: in her mid-eighties, she had several fender-benders we didn't know about. I discovered this one Saturday when I noticed a long row of magnets from a local collision repair company on her fridge. When I questioned her about them, she laughed a little and said, "Well, I get a magnet each time I bring the car in to have a dent pounded out. I just decided to put them all on the fridge, because they're so colorful." I gave her a lecture on the danger to herself and others—and to her insurance premiums. She replied, "I don't report those accidents. I don't want my insurance to go sky high." The next weekend, I noticed she had taken the magnets off the fridge. She's a wily one.

My mother had been driving since the age of twelve, an accomplishment that makes her quite proud. Think of it: behind the wheel for seventy-five years! Although this wouldn't be easy, it was time for Mom to relinquish her car keys. Now, who would tell her? I finally asked her doctor to intervene, because she might take the news from him much easier than she would from one of her kids.

Well, Mom was sitting in his office the day he delivered the news. Her strong personality, compounded by dementia, caused Mom to explode like a bomb. She became so upset and indignant that she stood up, shook her knobby finger at him, and loudly ordered him to "Get out of my house!" When he called me that evening to tell me that the task had been accomplished, he said, "I can't believe she tried to kick me out of my own office."

I laughed and replied, "I can." Whenever we'd drive up to see her, she'd go to great lengths to fool us into thinking she was just fine. But despite her best efforts, the dementia continued to worsen. Mom had finally reached the point where she could no longer maintain herself or her home.

Our Prayers Are Answered

One June morning in 1999, Kristen called me at work to ask if I could take a day off to help clean Grandma's house. I took the vacation day, and as luck would have it, my brother and his wife planned to drive down from Eveleth that day as well. All the way up to Foley, I kept asking my dad's spirit to intervene and convince my mother it was time for her to go to a place where someone could care for her. If anyone could convince her, Dad could—even if it meant reaching out to her from the Other Side. Since she still talked to him all the time, I felt she had a psychic bond with him. And for all I know, his spirit could reside in his old home, which would explain why Mom stubbornly refused to leave it.

When Kris and I arrived at the house that morning, we discovered Mom lying on the floor in a pool of urine, in almost the same place where Dad had died twenty-two years earlier. That was kind of eerie. Apparently, she'd passed out from one of her chronic dizzy spells and was too weak to get back on her feet. If none of us had shown up on her doorstep that morning, she would have surely died. Mom pleaded with Kris not to call the paramedics, but this was our sign, the opportunity we had prayed for. My daughter placed the call, and her grandmother became so incensed that she never spoke respectfully to her oldest granddaughter again. The paramedics arrived, stabilized her, and then loaded her into the ambulance. Kris sent her kids home with her husband and rode to the hospital with her grandmother. Mom was whisked away. It was the last time she'd see her home of fifty years.

I waited at the house for my brother and his wife and cleaned up what I could until they arrived. The doctors concluded that Mom had been down on the floor for at least twenty-four hours, maybe more. She might have fallen right after Kris had left two days before. After almost a week of hospital care and IVs, she was strong enough to go to rehab, and that's when her nursing-home days began. At that time, all of us went through another life change.

As I previously mentioned, prior to our vacation that year, I moved my mother down to a facility closer to Kristen and me. While there, the poor lady fell and broke her hip while Paul and I were in Maine, and she had surgery before we could return. Our family believes she had a stroke during her hip operation, because prior to that day she had had no problem letting us know what she thought about things, but after her surgery, she rarely spoke. We could see that our once-energetic mother was fading away ever so slowly. Her mental condition was poor, and by the time her body healed, she had lost the will to walk around. It broke our hearts.

After a Long, Rocky Voyage, My Ship Comes In

My siblings and I knew Mom would never return to her home. We kept up the property for a couple of years, but the well-loved structure was becoming an albatross around our necks. Last October, we finally put her house on the market. It was time. After several false starts, the house finally sold in May. Since the deed was put in the names of Mom and her three children many years ago, we each got one-fourth of the sale price after all the incidentals were paid. With my share, I decided to put up a picket fence and do some refurbishing inside the house. Paul is finally turning into a handyman after all these years. There is a God!

I thought the picket fence would set off my front yard's flower garden just beautifully. I envisioned it connecting with a privacy fence in the backyard so Max could romp outside with his dog cousins when they come to visit. The fence builders teased me about putting up "one damn expensive dog run," and I had to agree. The fence was completed in July. The first time I saw the finished project, I thought of how bad the property looked back in 1968. It pays to hang on to a dream. I can't believe how nice the yard looks now. Even neighbors I don't know stop by to tell me how beautiful everything looks. It was worth the long wait.

Our house has changed a great deal since we bought the place. The Millers wouldn't even recognize it anymore. It is slowly becoming the vision I had when I first saw it. But even though the outside looks inviting and the inside will soon be completed, all the paint and gardening techniques detailed on Home & Garden Television can't do a thing about the invisible spirits who drift in and out of our home whenever they feel like it.

Max Spots a Spirit

John-Paul helped me out this summer with tilling and other odd jobs. On the afternoon I drove J-P home to Monticello, we ran into a traffic jam on Highway 10. The traffic slowed to a complete stop, and my vehicle ended up next to a cemetery. J-P had the passenger seat tilted all the way down so he could snooze on the way home, and Max was sitting on J-P's stomach. All of a sudden, I heard Max utter his ghost growl. The sound startled me. My dog has ridden out to Monticello many times in his young life, but this was a first. He had gazed out the window from the time he was tall enough and had never registered any bark or growl along the entire route. Like all dogs, he barks excitedly when he sees a cat or a squirrel. He always announces when someone comes to the door, and he has a delightful growl when we play tug of war with him. But his ghost growl is unmistakable. He hasn't seen anything around the house lately, and I have been enjoying the peace and quiet.

My little pooch was staring intently in the direction of the cemetery with his front paws resting on the window and his tiptoes digging into John-Paul's stomach. There were at least a dozen sprays of flowers positioned all around one of the gravesites. I said, "J-P, sit up and see if you can spot a critter near that grave."

He stared for a second or two and then lay back down, saying, "Nope, nothing there, just those flowers."

Max continued growling and didn't take his eyes off the grave until traffic started moving again. The whole incident lasted less than five minutes, but it proved to me for once and for all that he truly sees spirits. We drive by that cemetery every time we go to see Kristen and her family, and Max never made a sound at that grave again. If his lack of interest is any indication, that spirit has moved on.

July through October 2002—Mischief and Mystery

Although much of the ghostly activity in the house seems to have gone underground, little fragments remain. For example, I often find the basement light turned on when I've made a point of turning it off, and I'll find it on when I return from running errands. On many days when I haven't even been down in the basement, the switch will occasionally be flipped up in the on position. And a nice complement to the basement-light mischief is the kitchen-door mystery. Over the years, when returning from a quick trip to the grocery store, I've often found it closed when it was left it open, or vice versa. It isn't partially closed either, but actually latched. Finding the door open or closed when I'm sure I left it the opposite way doesn't really bother me. I just tuck it away in the back of my mind. I realize I must be the culprit some of the time, but I know it can't be me all of the time.

Kristen gave me a perm at the end of September this year. I've always loved curly perms, because on the inside I'm kind of a "wild child." Max and I left the house just before lunchtime. When we returned home at about four fifteen that afternoon, the kitchen door was standing wide open. I know I'd closed it when we'd left, because when I pulled the door shut, my jacket got caught in it and I had to close it a second time. Paul always returns from the airport at around four thirty on Sunday, and I was so convinced that Paul had beat us home that I called out his name twice as I entered the kitchen. Upon hearing no answer, I walked back to his office, and he wasn't there. Just then, he drove into the driveway.

The basement light was on that afternoon as well. Our drop-in visitors are still messing with us. I'd love to know what goes on here when we're not home.

November 11, 2002—Where Oh Where Has His Jingle Ball Gone?

Max's jingle ball has been missing for a couple of days. He rarely lets it out of his sight, because it's his favorite toy. It has never gotten lost—until now. It's quite possible I moved every piece of furniture in this house during the past few days, but to no avail. I was running out of places to look. Max was acting very glum, because he missed his ball so much. He was even helping to search for it. Paul or I would say, "Get your jingle ball!" and he'd look all over the house and then return with that pitiful look in his eyes. He has tennis balls to play with, but they don't jingle, so he doesn't really enjoy them as much.

Whoever spirited Max's prized possession away was in no hurry to return it. This morning, I finally decided to pick up a new ball for him, but before going to the store, I wanted to take care of a few things on my to-do list. At the top of the list was fixing the wicker basket that holds my kitchen tools. I plugged in my hot-glue gun and began removing the basket's contents. Whoa, Mama! There was Max's ball, smack dab in the middle of the utensils in the back section. I just shook my head in disbelief. Paul and I used items from this basket several times a day, and neither of us noticed it in there before that very minute. "Hey, Max! Come here!" I tossed the ball to a very happy dog.

When Paul got home, I told him where I'd found the ball. He looked very puzzled. Then I added, "With all the things that happen in this house, it doesn't surprise me that it was hidden in there." I turned and left him to mull over my words alone, in the hopes it would occur to him that some outside force must have hidden that ball, as neither of us had.

November 24, 2002—Max Chases a Ghost

Today I have a miserable intestinal flu. No need to discuss that any further, except to say that during one mad dash this morning I didn't have time to close the bathroom door. Max and I were home alone, so it didn't matter. My little buddy followed me into the bathroom and then jumped into the tub with his favorite ball firmly between his teeth. He loves to play in the tub, for reasons known only to him.

While sitting there, I suddenly felt like I was being watched. The feeling was so strong that I wondered for a split second if I had forgotten to lock the back door and my son or possibly a neighbor had actually entered my home. Under ordinary circumstances, that would be disturbing, but today it was even worse, due to my embarrassing circumstances. I slowly turned my head to the left and, out in the hallway, saw a transparent intruder between five and six feet tall. It was standing directly in front of the bathroom doorway and seemed to be peering in at me. This faceless spirit had a nearly perfect human form and a much more defined outline than the shapeless brown entity that dashed out of the kitchen some months ago. If the ghostly voyeur planned to scare the you-know-what out of me, rest assured, it was too late!

While I was staring at this figure in utter amazement, Max, who was completely hidden from view by the shower curtain, began his eerie growl. He's not tall enough to see over the rim of the tub and certainly couldn't see through the double shower curtains, but when I pulled the curtains aside, there he stood, nose pointed directly at the doorway. His radar is amazing. Suddenly, my little pooch jumped out of the tub, lowered his chest almost to the floor, and began inching his way toward the figure, growling in a menacing way. The figure began to drift. Max's growl gave way to a barrage of barking as he marched out of the bathroom and into the hall. It was quite obvious that my canine bodyguard was on a mission. He chased the ghostly figure into my office. When I caught up with Max, he was standing in the middle of the room and looking quite proud of himself, because the spirit had vanished.

"Good dog, Max!"

14: A New Attitude—2003

January 2003—How Times Have Changed

Some time ago, Melissa said that as the veil between this world and the next grows thinner, more people will have paranormal experiences. I believe that's true. Hauntings are more widely accepted these days than they were in back 1968, when I collided head-on with this house and its invisible inhabitants. As recently as a decade ago, one might find a token television show about ghosts aired during Halloween week. Times have really changed. Between surfing the major networks and cable channels, one can find a documentary on many aspects of the paranormal almost any day of the year. Movie theaters offer supernatural films for the public's enjoyment all year long, and video stores have entire sections of supernatural movies ready to go home with you. There are dozens of books on paranormal topics available in libraries and bookstores all over the country. My daughter and I have found that most people now are quite open to talking about ghosts and hauntings once the topic has been broached. Many communities across America offer tours, by bus or by foot, where they proudly promote the spirits residing in their period homes, businesses, and graveyards. All I can say is, "Where the heck were you people when I needed you thirty-five years ago?"

When I began writing this book, I spent many a nervous night struggling to get words down on paper while surrounded by inexplicable noises and the unseen visitors who caused them. I was one terrified young woman back then. I can finally say that the years I've spent working on this project have been a catharsis—a true healing and learning experience for me. The sheer panic of those early days has diminished considerably as the years have rolled by. I've developed a maturity and an understanding of what causes spirits to stay on this plane when they should have moved on to the next. This doesn't mean that I'm completely comfortable with the whole thing, just that I've come to realize that we share this world with many things we can't see or fully explain. Noises still bother me, but not to the extent that they once did. And believe it or not, I'm actually able to go down into the basement again without any fear—most nights, anyway.

I was delighted that Echo Bodine chose to have a look around my modest home. After watching her many times on television, I thought I'd be awestruck seeing her in person, but that wasn't the case. She is a charming woman with exceptional abilities and a down-to-earth personality. She's also a very hard-working author, healer, and lecturer, so I wonder if she ever wrote the book that prompted that phone call to me back in 1997. I hope so, because I'm eager to read it. Even if she doesn't use my letter in her book, it was a great honor to be asked.

I very much appreciate my good friend Melissa. During a recent visit to my home, she validated much of what Echo found. In addition to what I learned from Ms. Bodine, Missy was able to elaborate further on a few things. She said the negative energy by the washer was left over from some violent deed that occurred long years ago, quite possibly before the house was built. The energy under the basement steps marks the site where the victim died. Now, if this had happened on the other side of the house, it could have easily explained the sad energy in my husband's radio room. Would you believe I forgot to have Missy check that room? Paul was working in his room during her visit, so I didn't even give it a thought. Now I may never find out what hangs around in there. Speaking of Paul's room, I'm thinking about burning another white candle in there to see if it will scare away the occasional spirit that floats in and out of our home. I have to admit the atmosphere felt much lighter after that procedure a few years ago.

On a lighthearted note, Max connected with Melissa in the cutest way. While she and I were chatting at the table, he trotted into the family room, sat down by her feet, and looked up at her. She glanced down at him for a few seconds and then said, "Oh, you are, are you?" Then she giggled and grinned at him. I asked her what he said. She replied, "He told me he's very sensitive."

February 2003—Exciting Things Are Happening

There is a lot of noise going on around here these days, and I'm pleased to say that almost all of it is from this side of the veil. We had a new kitchen floor installed two months ago. The family room and entryway are next on the list to be redecorated. Perhaps this coming summer I'll get around to that. Paul is now finishing off the living space in the basement with his beloved paneling. His work looks quite professional. He's also putting in a drop ceiling with recessed lighting. When the construction is completed, we'll carpet the area. It is going to be a very cozy-looking space. Our neighbor Maynard occasionally drops in to see how Paul is doing or to lend his expertise. When he suggested I move my office down into the new basement room because it would be the perfect location to write books, I agreed—in theory. However, as lovely as the space will be when it's finished, I am not mentally prepared to do that. The exercise equipment will go down there, along with a television and some furniture as well as a space heater, but I'll leave my office up here, at least for the time being. Of course, I couldn't explain why to Maynard, any more than I could have all those years ago when we talked on the phone until the wee hours of the morning. He might understand, but what if he doesn't?

Since we moved into the house, it has been redecorated several times. The living room shrugged off that horrid coat of brown in the early seventies. Either this spring or next year, the living-room walls will get another new coat of paint. I'm still deciding what shade to use in there. For the most part, the room has a soothing aura, unless *something* decides to make noises in there at night. I finally sewed wrought-iron rings on my curtains, so there shouldn't be any more midnight madness—relating to the curtains, that is. I'm grateful that the cracking noises have finally vanished. Some nights, while watching television in there, I try to remember how loud those noises were.

The kitchen has been redecorated several times since 1968, and this past summer it went through another face-lift. I worked very hard refinishing the cupboards, and even harder trying to decide on the wall color and wallpaper border. I settled on an Old World painting technique. My daughter and her oldest son joined forces to make that happen. The past couple of weeks, Max and I have been hearing noises in the kitchen at night, so all the work being done in this house must have attracted a nosy spirit or two. All I can say is, "Booga, booga!" I'm enjoying my new house, and they can just permanently move to the Other Side if they don't like it.

I can credit my spiritual growth to both Melissa and Nancy M., an Internet pen pal, good friend, and psychic from San Diego. Their wisdom, advice, and concern have made my excursion through the twists and turns of the paranormal a time of true enlightenment.

And best of all (fanfare!), skeptics no longer bother me. I have finally reached a comfort level with everything I've seen and heard in my house. Although my husband, son, and some of my friends will probably never believe a word of it, that's okay. Of course, I haven't spoken with Paul about everything that has happened here. That's his choice. I bet he'll never read this book either, since he has no desire to know anything more about the house, but I can accept that because I've learned to respect his boundaries.

April 2003—Something Saves My Neck

I could have had a nasty accident today while stenciling my kitchen door. Whenever I'm using a step stool, I often get frustrated, because my arthritis causes me to drop things. This morning, I had already dropped my brush and sponge two or three times while dabbing paint over the stencil. It bugged me each time I had to climb down to retrieve the items. When I finally finished the project, I stepped back to see how it looked, completely forgetting I was on the top step. The minute I felt nothing under me, something intervened. Either my guardian angel or one of my spirits must have caught me in mid-air, spun me around, and shoved me up against the fridge so quickly I didn't even realize it. All I remember is being plastered up against the refrigerator, facing the opposite direction. My heart began pounding in my ears. After that close call, I had to sit down for a few minutes to catch my breath and offer a prayer of thanks. I'm still grateful I didn't break my neck!

June 2003—My Mother Leaves Us

My mother passed away in the early morning on June 24, at the age of ninety-one. It was nearly four years to the day since she'd first entered a nursing home. I was called a week earlier, because my mother had lapsed into a coma. The staff at the nursing home told me she wouldn't last more than a day or two, so I immediately called my sister and brother. Kathie flew in the following day to join my daughter and me as we kept our death vigil. My brother was teaching summer school and had to first find a replacement. Mom had been losing ground for several weeks. She was finally going to leave the world of nursing homes, which she hated so much, to join her husband and the beloved son she lost sixty years ago. We got the call at 12:40 a.m.

I immediately notified my brother. I waited till ten o'clock the following morning to call Kristen, because she had to get up early for work and I didn't want to disturb her sleep.

Grandma's Gone but Not Forgotten

When Kris and I finally talked, she told me a call wasn't really necessary. It seems my mother's spirit had dropped in on Kris while she was getting ready to go to work. About six o'clock, while drinking her morning cup of coffee, one of her kitchen drawers suddenly shot open. Kris took it in stride and immediately knew her grandma had died. Around noon that day, she met a friend for lunch. While waiting for their food to arrive, they witnessed the salt and pepper shakers suddenly fly off the booth and onto the floor. She also told me the lights in her house and van blinked on and off several times that day.

My niece Erika e-mailed me a few days after she arrived home from the funeral. She filled me in on a couple of unusual incidents that had happened to her. The first occurred when she was outdoors grilling some chops for dinner. Her young daughters were playing at the neighbors' house, so Erika took this opportunity to quietly read for a few minutes. She lost track of the time until something hit her on the foot. She looked to see what it was: a unique pebble that she'd noticed on the ground by her lawn chair when she first sat down. Erika decided that her grandma threw the pebble to remind her to turn the chops so they wouldn't overcook. We laughed about that, because my mother always overcooked meat. She was famous for it. My friends and workmates have been regaled over the years with stories about my mother's culinary catastrophes. She made most foods very well but always had trouble fixing meats for a meal. I'll never forget the holiday dinners when we had to wash down her famous "dry as dust" beef roasts with sips of water to keep from choking. Guess she didn't want her granddaughter to end up with the same reputation.

A few days later, in the presence of her mother and some neighbors, Erika had another visit from her grandmother. She and her two daughters, Lauren and Katie, joined my sister to watch the fireworks on the Fourth of July. Erika got her girls settled; then she opened her can of soda while holding it away from her body in case it fizzed when she popped the top. It didn't fizz—then. However, a while later, while she was chatting with the neighbors, soda suddenly bubbled up and gushed all over her hand and lap. She had not shaken the can, so there was no logical explanation for that. She decided that it must have been Grandma again.

Then Erika commented on how my mother would never take a trip to Colorado to visit while alive but apparently had no qualms about flying out there now that she's dead. Everyone knew our mother still talked to Dad constantly and never wanted to leave her home after he died. Even her great-grandchildren had witnessed her gabbing away with him when they were visiting. She'd actually face an empty chair as if looking straight at Dad. We wondered if he'd ever appeared to her. Perhaps that's why she never wanted to leave the house for more than a day at a time. Now we'll never know for sure if that was the case or not.

Erika also told me that the lights in their hotel rooms blinked slowly on and off several times, especially on the day of the funeral. Danielle and Erika discussed the phenomenon and decided it was Grandma Cook letting them know she was glad they were there. After Erika returned home, the lights in her house blinked on and off each evening. She asked if Grandma had visited me yet, and I wondered why she hadn't.

My turn came a few weeks after my mother's death. We had recently purchased a nifty remote control fan for the living room so I don't have to move a muscle to change the setting once I've tucked myself in. One warm night while having an intense hot flash, I set the control on high and adjusted the air stream to blow directly on me. Even though it wasn't a prudent idea, it felt heavenly. I dozed off. After sleeping for about an hour, I felt awfully warm again. The extreme warmth actually woke me up. When I checked the fan, I found that it had been turned off. It was Mom. I'm sure of it. She dispensed many old wives' tales in her lifetime, one of which addressed this very subject: "Don't ever fall asleep with a fan blowing directly on you, or you'll wake up stiffer than a dead mackerel." I softly said, "Thanks, Mom!"

About that same time, I saw Mom in a vision just as I was falling asleep. She was young and pretty, perhaps in her thirties, and she stood there smiling and waving at me. The vision was in full color, and the dress she was wearing was from a honeymoon photo. She looked so happy that my eyes welled up with tears. To see her healthy, well, and energetic again made my heart sing. I haven't *seen* her since.

September 2003—A New Sound in the Night

During a trip to Duluth with our two youngest grandchildren this past spring, we stopped at an antique shop. Both the kids are amateur collectors, so we all had a good time walking through the rooms bursting with treasures. For years I've collected cats in all forms—except real ones. I spied a unique pottery whistle in the shape of a cat for ten dollars. Paul thought it was pricey, but I had never seen one like it, so I coughed up the cash. When you blow into the stubby tail, a reedlike sound comes out the cat's mouth. I doubt it's an antique, but it's mine, and that's all that counts. Fast-forward a few months. About two o'clock on a September morning, I was concentrating on my radio show when I was suddenly aware of a sound that didn't seem to match the program. I removed my headphones and heard it again, three times. There is an old recorder from my school days displayed on my fireplace, so I figured one of my drop-ins had picked it up and tooted on it. Later that morning, I blew on the old plastic horn. The sound was too sharp and grainy to match the low, mellow tone I'd heard eight hours earlier.

A couple of days later, while dusting and rearranging my cat collection, my eyes fell upon the whistle. The recent nighttime sound prompted me to blow on the whistle just for the heck of it. It was the exact same tone that had pierced through my headphones. Apparently, Max didn't hear it. I haven't heard it since that night either.

The subject of spirits that attach themselves to garage-sale and antique-shop items came up one night on Coast to Coast. The female guest said she never buys anything from those places because of the various energies that cling to those old, cast-off pieces. After recalling that program, I wondered if the cat whistle had an energy attached to it. I have since read articles stating it's a common belief that spirits often attach themselves to pieces of furniture or clothing that belonged to them in life. I can see that. Many of my mother's items are stored in the basement, along with items that belonged to her elders. However, I don't believe that my mother's items are causing the noises that Max and I hear around the house. Maybe I'm being naive.

October 2, 2003—Good Grief, I Could Have Used His Real Name!

For years I've worried about what Paul would think if he ever found out I was writing a book about our house, as he's a very private person. On the other hand, I'm not. He doesn't care to have ghosts in his life, while I seem to have no choice in the matter. Today I asked Paul if he wanted to read my story now that it's almost finished. He already knew the subject matter, because he had to save my text on his computer when my old machine was about to crash. He replied, "No, I don't want to read any ghostly stories. That kind of stuff scares me."

"Even if it's about our house?" I teased.

He shook his head no and walked out of my office. I suppose I could change his name in these pages back to the one his parents gave him, but I won't.

October 7, 2003—A Bark in the Dark

Tonight, as is my habit, I dozed off on the couch after Paul went up to bed. It makes up for the sleep I lose during the later nighttime hours. Articles on sleep disorders state that naps interfere with normal sleep cycles. To get back on a regular sleep schedule, an insomniac must stay awake in spite of heavy eyelids. Guess I'm not willing to make that effort. When the television volume is turned down and I'm feeling drowsy, I can't fight it. Max either climbs up and rests his little head on my legs or lies on the floor next to the couch and snoozes along with his mama.

Around eight thirty, a barrage of incredibly loud barking jarred me awake from a deep, cozy sleep. Max was standing in the living room and staring up at something in the hall, barking his little heart out. For a second, I hoped someone hadn't walked in the back door while I was asleep. Paul locks it when he goes upstairs every night, but that's not to say one night he might forget. Max was really upset. Each forceful expulsion of air moved his small, rigid body back a fraction of an inch, making him resemble one of those annoying mechanical dogs you see in the malls during the Christmas season. I got up from the couch. From what I could see, the hallway was empty, so I scooped up my apparition alarm. "Do you see something out there, Max? Is it a ghostie?" He continued to stare into the dark kitchen and bark with such passion that he nearly threw himself out of my arms. Typically when I pick him up, he feels safe and stops barking immediately. There was *something* in the hallway or kitchen that he didn't like. I spent several seconds trying to get a glimpse of it, but to no avail. This was the loudest demonstration Max has ever given while seeing or sensing a spirit in this house. It took several minutes to calm him down. It took a bit longer for me.

October 19, 2003—They're Gone Again

Our house feels almost normal these days. However, because Max had that loud episode couple of weeks ago, I know this blissful feeling won't last.

November 2003—Ghost Stories from Other Places

This past November, Paul and I drove out to San Diego to visit Nancy M., a pen pal and friend who loves ghost stories as much as I do. When I e-mailed her that we were driving out to San Diego, she immediately mentioned visiting the Hotel del Coronado. At Nancy's suggestion, Paul called the hotel and made lunch reservations for the three of us well in advance.

We arrived a month later. After we got settled at our own hotel, we picked Nancy up at her apartment building and took off in search of the Hotel del Coronado. As we drove up to the massive building, the sight of it took my breath away. It's awesome. A sprawling edifice that might look more at home in the famous seaside city of Brighton, England, it was originally built in 1888 and has had several additions over the years. It is often referred to as "The Castle by the Sea," and when staring up at it, it's easy to see why. Its red roof and white turrets seem to pop up from all sorts of interesting angles, giving this building plenty of Victorian character. This playground of the rich and famous contains seven hundred rooms—all of which are quite incompatible with our budget. And the Hotel Del has another claim to fame: it has been reported to be the home of many ghosts, the most famous of which is Kate Morgan.

Upon entering the hotel, we noticed several signs posted in the impressive lobby warning that only guests were allowed to access the upper floors. The magnificent oak-paneled bar, elegant hallways, and ritzy shops on the ground floor all displayed cautionary signage. For the management to post all these warnings, they must have a lot of trouble with the curious trying to catch a glimpse of the ghosts who live here. My heart sank as I read each new sign. I so badly wanted to photograph the hall and the door to the haunted room. Kate Morgan's ghost has been spotted in the hallways of the hotel as well as standing by the door of the room she occupied prior to her death. I can definitely understand the inconvenience suffered by the hotel staff and patrons because of determined ghost hunters, but when I weighed that concern against my desire to get Nancy and me up to that room, I won. We were going to give it a try.

Nancy, Paul, and I dined on the sunny outdoor terrace. This place was really busy, bustling with locals, tourists, and wait staff alike. The day was warm, and the umbrella-covered tables filled up fast. Nancy knew what she was talking about when she told us to make reservations. I told my lunch mates to pick out whatever they wanted—my treat. Even though the food was good and the service outstanding to the point of being intrusive, all I could think about was Kate. After we finished our lunch, the three of us were ready to find Kate's room or die trying. But first we each had to make a stop at the restroom. While getting directions, I spied an elevator. Aha, our transportation to the third floor. On the way back from the luxurious ladies' room, I filled Nancy in on the plan I had just hatched. She was ecstatic. We discussed the warning signs once more, then threw caution to the wind. Nancy was game, and my husband has more nerve than I ever will, so I knew he'd be up for it. Over the years, Paul and I have gotten into some odd places that were clearly posted "Do Not Trespass," and it's never bothered him. My law-abiding conscience has always objected, and my audacious husband would chide me by saying, "What do you think they're going to do if they catch us?" I could come up with lots of ideas (getting arrested comes to mind), but I always went along with him. Today, for a change, he'd go along with me. As soon as Paul joined us, we were off—a trio of intrepid interlopers.

The elevator operator was a middle-aged Asian man with a kind face. I could almost hear Paul's voice reverberating in my head: "This is your baby, so let's get the show on the road." I asked if the operator knew which room was haunted. He peered around behind us, as if to see if anyone else was listening, then motioned to us to quickly board the elevator. For a moment or two, I wondered if he was embarrassed at my question, but then I realized he was making sure no other patrons were waiting. As the door closed behind us, the operator leaned close to my face and asked in a demanding tone of voice, "Do you believe in ghosts?"

I stood my ground, looked him straight in the eye, and replied with a smile, "You bet I do. Don't you?" He shook his head, but he brought us up to the third floor in spite of his skepticism, then gave us directions to the haunted room.

When we left the elevator, Nancy and I were on cloud nine. Being senior citizens didn't prevent us from giggling like young schoolgirls as we nervously made our way down the corridors of the famous hotel. Good ol' Paul remained in complete control of his emotions, but then this wasn't his quest, so he could afford to act like a grownup. Someone had to anchor this expedition. I expected to see guests coming and going, but oddly enough, we had the corridors to ourselves.

Although ghosts don't appear on demand, we were hoping Kate would make an exception for us. Paul kept his camcorder and digital camera ready, just in case. I took my trusty 35 millimeter out of my bag, so I was all set. Nancy didn't have a camera with her, but she was armed with the correct room number and a brochure that contained a synopsis of the Kate Morgan story.

According to Nancy's information, both Kate and her husband, Tom, were con artists who traveled around the country by train in the late 1800s, earning their living at the expense of others. Kate, who presented herself as Tom's sister, attracted the "marks," and Tom fleeced them. The scam went something like this: Tom invited the gentleman who wanted to woo his sister into a friendly game of cards under the pretense of getting to know him better. Soon the gullible mark had no girlfriend and no money in his wallet, and the pair had moved on to another train and another victim. Apparently, at some point Kate became pregnant, which probably caused a big fight between the footloose cardsharp and his beautiful "sister." After all, how could she put the moves on a future quarry if she was carrying a child? Somewhere along the line, they split up, and she took the train to San Diego, where they were to meet again at a later date. However, as far as anyone knows, her cad of a husband never showed up.

Kate was a woman of mystery at the Hotel Del. According to a program I had seen on television, the staff said she seemed sad and appeared to be ailing. Kate stayed in her room most of the time. After a brief stay, she was discovered dead of a single gunshot while apparently on her way to the beach. The verdict was suicide. The weapon, a small handgun, was discovered next to her body. Upon searching her room, authorities found very little, because Kate had had no luggage. However, they did find bottles of quinine water, a substance that was believed to induce miscarriages. So apparently Kate had been trying to abort her baby. It is such a sad story. She was believed to be twenty-four years old when she died. Since Kate registered under another name, the hotel staff didn't know her real name until another guest came forward to say he had seen her and a man arguing just before she boarded a train bound for San Diego. He knew her as Kate Morgan. No one ever claimed the body. If that wouldn't cause a spirit to hang around, I don't know what would!

After a couple of wrong turns, we eventually found *the room*. As we stood there discussing the ghost, a maid approached us, pushing her cleaning cart. We asked if this was the haunted room, just to make conversation, and she nodded in the affirmative. Then she did the unthinkable: she asked if we wanted to have a look inside. While my inner child gleefully jumped up and down shouting, "Oh boy, oh boy, oh boy," I calmly replied, "That would be wonderful, thank you." Nancy and I looked at each other and quietly giggled again. When I first spied the maid walking toward us, I hoped at the very least that she would answer a question or two about Kate, but I feared she'd ask us to show our room key to prove we were guests. Inviting us to enter the room wasn't even on my radar. The maid knocked loudly on the door a couple of times, and when no one answered, she unlocked it and stepped back so we could go in. Be still my heart . . . I mean it!

The room was warm and stuffy and smaller than I had envisioned. Both Nancy and I had seen the Kate Morgan Room on a television program that featured haunted hotels. For some reason, rooms always look larger when they are professionally filmed. Although I knew that, I was still surprised. Paul turned on his camcorder. I brought my camera out of my handbag but decided since Paul was getting video footage, I wouldn't take any pictures. After making a sweep of the room, Paul handed me the camcorder while he took a few still shots with his digital camera. Nancy walked around the room to feel the vibrations in it. She peered in the closet and bathroom and then mentioned that she sensed something in the room.

Nancy thinks the suicide story is bogus and that's the reason Kate remains trapped here. She is positive that Kate was murdered. It's possible her husband showed up early that morning in 1892 and decided that Kate was a liability to his questionable lifestyle. He dispatched her to the hereafter and then went on his merry way. Although Nancy was soaking up the atmosphere of the room, I wasn't getting any supernatural vibrations. I was too busy savoring our victory. We were actually standing inside the haunted room. What a rush!

After taking several pictures, we thanked the maid for giving us this opportunity. She waited patiently for us to get our pictures and never once hurried us. I'm sure both of the hotel employees would be royally reprimanded or worse for their part in our caper if anyone ever found out. Outside the room, I took a couple shots of the hall, hoping to get something on film. That would make the visit perfect. Darn, it was time to leave. On our way out, Nancy and I were walking on air.

The following day belonged to Paul. He and I took a harbor cruise (his choice). On the way to the dock, we also watched part of a Veteran's Day celebration. Paul was in his glory. Being a former Air Force man, he loves talking with military people. After filming part of the parade, we continued on to get our tickets for the cruise. En route, we spotted a trolley car which had an ad for an Old Town Ghost Tour plastered all over it. Paul picked up a brochure for the tour, and then we boarded the boat.

It was a relaxing two-hour ride, even though the cool wind whipped around us on the sunny November day. The co-captains of this cruise functioned as the tour guides. They were really funny, and their patter made the time fly by. As we passed many military vessels of all classes and sizes, we were given facts and statistics about them all.

When we returned to the hotel, I called Nancy to tell her about the Old Town Ghost Tour. She laughed and said that was the tour she had suggested we take when she learned we'd be coming out to see her. We decided to go on the tour if Paul would drive us there and wait for us till it was over. He was a good sport and agreed.

When we arrived in Old Town that evening, he did even better than that. He paid for our tickets and took the tour with us. I almost demanded, "Who are you and what have you done with my husband?" We were each handed tiny, illuminated ghost pins, which served as tour IDs, and then got on the bus.

We stopped at many lovely old homes that had interesting stories connected with them. None of them felt haunted to me, so it was more of a historical tour than a ghost tour in my estimation. Nancy felt the same way, and so did Paul.

We also stopped at the oldest cemetery in Old Town. While walking around the tombstones, I met a lovely Greek woman who told me she had a ghost in her home. She and her daughter had named him George. She couldn't elaborate on his tricks, though, because the tour guide was chatting away and it would have been rude for us to continue whispering. However, she did say her family was not afraid of him. I enjoyed our short conversation. Nancy was somewhere else in the group, and Paul was bringing up the rear. Since he had paid for this tour, I hoped he was enjoying himself, at least a little.

I had one heart-stopping moment that night. The Whaley House was the last home we visited on the tour. This house is officially documented as being an authentic haunted house. When we walked into the house, the figure of a woman dressed in a long black dress, wearing a hat and heavy veil, sat just inside the front door on the right. The daytime tours couldn't have this feature, because the effect would have been lost in the bright light of day. For just a second, I lost my breath and couldn't speak. When I realized it was a real person, that still didn't quiet my pulse or soothe my nerve endings. Since this was an evening tour, the only illumination in the house came from the original gaslights. Talk about an eerie ambiance. The lack of light prevented us from seeing clearly into the various rooms on the ground floor; however, I'd seen them two years earlier on a previous visit.

We were prevented from going upstairs by a tall figure in a black dress and wig standing on the seventh step. This is a spot where a spirit is reported to linger—where people often report feeling like they are being pushed. The only scary thing here was that the figure reminded me of "Mother" from the original *Psycho* movie. Out in the garden, we heard the story about a playmate of the youngest Whaley children. While playing a game, she ran headlong into a low-hanging clothesline in the backyard and later died on the kitchen table from injuries to her neck. Her ghost is reported to be hanging around here too. (No pun intended, believe me. I don't make fun of ghosts!)

At the end of the tour, our group had a chance to examine perhaps forty or more photographs that were laid out on a table in the court-room attached to the house. These shots had been taken on previous tours. Many of the photos had orbs in them, just like the photos I had taken there a couple of years before. Some were taken in the same rooms as mine. Interesting . . .

Holy Cow!

When we returned from our vacation, Paul uploaded the digital pho-tos to his computer. I asked him to save the shots from the Hotel Del onto a disk so I could examine them more closely. Oh my God, I can't believe it. *I found an orb!* What a thrill. Actually, I found two orbs! One was located in the area of the bathroom door, and the other was in front of the window frame in the Kate Morgan Room. There were no orbs in the pictures taken either prior to or after that window shot. I enlarged the window orb up to maximum magnifica-tion and found a face in it—two eyes and a mouth! I couldn't get the other orb into range where I could bring it to the highest magnifica-tion, so I'll never know if that one contained a face as well.

My pulse began to race. I called Paul into my office to confirm what I was staring at. He admitted he could plainly see the face in it too; then he quickly left the room. This man might be my partner in life, but I seriously doubt he'll ever be my partner in the fine art of ghost hunting. I shouldn't be too hard on him, though. He really surprised me on this vacation by going on that tour, so there might be hope for him yet.

I shipped a CD with those haunted-room photos on it to Nancy. She was ecstatic when she saw the face. In her e-mail, she said, "I knew there was a spirit in that room. I could feel it."

My other good buddy, Nancy L., always used to tease that she and I should become ghost-busting grandmas after she retires. That would be a ball. We could go out to San Diego to join Nancy M. on ghost-hunting gigs. Who knows what we'd find? Each year on vacation I purchase books of local folklore. The books I bought in San Diego contain countless stories of hauntings, because it's a very old city. We'd surely have our pick of places to investigate. Old Town has a lot of hauntings, as it was the first settlement there. It would keep the three of us busy for quite some time. Since I don't enjoy driving—I always get lost—and neither of my Nancy friends drive, we'd have to drag Paul along to haul us around. Surely I'm the only one in our household who finds that humorous. Wonder if he'd consider it? It wouldn't hurt to ask.

15: Stick with What You Know—2004

January 2004—To Move or Not to Move

My life in this house has always been challenging. During the early years, it was an exercise in futility and fear. Although stress was a constant companion back in the day, followed by poor health in later years, my home has provided me with a wealth of experiences, ranging from humorous to heartbreaking and everything in between.

From time to time, our daughter suggests that we move to a nicer, newer house—a house that doesn't need as much upkeep, now that we are senior citizens. I have to admit that some days the idea is tempting, but our home is paid for and we're finally getting this place to where it's looking good. Some friends our age have given up single-family dwellings to move into condos and townhouses, where the yard work and upkeep is done for them. I think it would break my heart if

Quite a Difference from 1968!
While life here has always been a challenge, this house
has become my home, and though its supernatural
guests are still unsettling, at least they're familiar.

we moved to a place where I couldn't have a garden. Even though
working the earth with my bare hands often results in painful muscles
and joints, it is good therapy for my soul. It grounds me. The compli-
ments from neighbors who walk by when I'm weeding tell me that
they enjoy my flowers too. My mother enjoyed working in her large
garden till she went into a nursing home at the age of eighty-seven.
My grandmother worked in her flower garden until she was placed in
a facility as well. I plan to keep that gardening tradition going as long
as God will let me.

The odd occurrences and eerie noises that have terrified me over
the years have often been cyclical in nature, which would confirm
the findings of Echo Bodine and her spirit guide. If indeed we have
drop-ins, it would make sense that our house would be peaceful in
between their visits. I'm currently enjoying another dry spell. It's
wonderful! When the peaceful atmosphere hangs around for several weeks, I often wonder if the house is beginning to mellow, to
let go of its past. I think it's safe to say it will never be the hotbed
of supernatural activity that it was all those years ago. When we
first moved in, the only thing I could think of was getting out—the

sooner, the better—and now I won't even consider it. Besides that, another house might have a whole new set of supernatural experiences for me to deal with, so I'm sticking with what I know.

February 2004—Update on Max

Max is nearly three years old now. He hasn't lost any of his playful puppy enthusiasm or ghost-detecting skills. The pendulum is swinging again, and the kitchen noises have returned. Faithful little Max keeps tabs on the sounds, both loud and soft, and cuts loose when he feels it's appropriate. During the day, Paul has heard Max's ghost growl a time or two and probably has no idea why our dog goes into that mode. Unfortunately, since my husband doesn't want to hear anything about ghosts, my pooch and I are forced to live a secret life.

When Max was quite young, I taught him the word *ghostie*, so any time he growls and goes into that staring mode, I ask, "Do you see ghosties?" He looks at me and then quickly turns back and follows something invisible as it moves from place to place. It's the closest I'll ever get to a confirmation from him. If he's just staring to rest his eyes, which animals sometimes do, he quickly returns to the business at hand, be it taking a nap or chewing a toy or a bone. I know it sounds silly, but I can differentiate between the stares.

One thing I want to do this spring when it warms up a bit is bring him to the cemetery where my parents and older brother are buried. Ever since the day he noticed that ghost in the cemetery on the way to Monticello, I've wanted to test him again. If Max notices any spirits out in that little country graveyard, it will prove quite satisfying to me. Kristen, Melissa, my two Nancys, and other close friends will find it interesting as well. When we go up to my hometown, I'll take a digital camera with me to see if I can capture any possible streaks or shapes out there. It's possible he won't see a thing. If he doesn't, it's no big deal. If he does, I'll let Max drive the car and I'll turn cartwheels all the way home.

Max Grows Up

Forty-one years ago, I surrendered the gift of deep, restful sleep when I became a mother. Unless I'm exhausted way past the breaking point, I wake up at the slightest sound, even to this day. I always knew if Max ever slept with me, he'd wake me up with that creepy ghost growl. This has happened several times since November, because when we returned from our latest vacation, things really changed around here. He flatly refused to sleep in his kennel. Kids grow up; so do dogs, I guess. He's been snuggling in with me ever since, and he sleeps quite contentedly by my legs until something wakes him. Something besides my sneezing, that is.

One evening in late March, a weather system rolled into our area, bringing with it very strong winds. In the wee hours of the morning, Max woke up growling, which in turn caused me to wake up too. I reluctantly opened my eyes. My recliner partner was staring at the shadows that were dancing across the living-room wall. After a few seconds, he moved his head to the right, toward the bookcase, like he always does when a spirit drifts over to that corner of the room. While Max was bird-dogging his quarry, I asked him if he saw a ghostie. He gave me his confirmation look, then quickly turned back to stare at the empty air until I gave him a hug and told him it was okay. We both settled down and went back to sleep, leaving the ghostie hanging around the bookcase while the shadows danced and the wind howled.

I do wish I could read my dog's mind. I'd love to know if the spirits he stares at so attentively just dissipate or if he simply ignores them after I tell him it's okay. I e-mailed Melissa the next day and asked her what the little stinker sees, since he confides only in her. She said Max is easily bored, so he loses interest in the spirits after a while.

April through July 2004—Spaghetti to Go

Back in the spring of 1968, I certainly didn't believe I'd still be experiencing some form of haunting in the year 2004. There has always been an uneasy truce in this house. Max and I never know when the odd little noises from the Other Side will come crashing back into our lives, upsetting the quietude that fills the time and space in between. At least now the ghostly noises no longer frighten me.

There were no noises connected with this recent occurrence—this one has me truly baffled. Although it sounds impossible, a bowl of leftover spaghetti sauce recently disappeared from my kitchen counter. I make tasty spaghetti sauce, but this is ridiculous, because as far as I know, spirits can't even enjoy human food. The bowl of sauce wasn't on the counter when I did the dishes after dinner, so I assumed Paul had already put it in the fridge. The following day when I was going to package the sauce for freezing, I couldn't find it. Trust me, I took everything out of the refrigerator, because I just couldn't believe it wasn't in there. I checked the freezer compartment, and it wasn't there either. Nor was it in the little chest freezer in the basement. Even though I knew what his answer would be, I still asked Paul if he had used it up. The answer was negative, but he added, "I thought you put it away last night." I immediately launched a massive search around the house, because in the hot July weather, God only knows how ripe that sauce could get. I even dug through the garbage—ugh! After hunting for days wherever one could hide a medium-sized bowl, I had to give up and admit it was gone. So far it hasn't returned. Neither of us detected any rotten smells, so I know it's nowhere in this dimension. This is the first time real food has disappeared, so Paul is as puzzled as I am. The sauce was in a favorite Tupperware bowl of mine, and I'd like to have that back; however, it's probably in limbo with the other objects that have disappeared over the decades.

August 2004—*Kristen Helps Me Out*

When we put Mom's house up for sale in 2001, our basement filled up with some of her furniture, as well as other belongings that were too good to toss. My siblings went through most of the stuff that summer and took home what they wanted to keep. This still left many boxes and a few furniture pieces. For the last couple of years, I've been trying to get rid of Mom's items, because ever since Paul remodeled half the basement, we've wanted to tidy up the other half too. Digging through those old boxes made me think about how sad it is that folks spend an entire lifetime collecting items that mean a lot to them only to have their treasures tossed out by the next generation. My parents were not prosperous. They didn't have money, jewelry, nice furniture, or antiques. When items have no monetary value, they often become junk in a box for a family member to pitch. I managed to put many items in a church sale, but there was still a lot of stuff to throw.

Now, I can't say there was a presence stopping me, but there was a definite heavy feeling in the basement whenever I spent time going through Mom's belongings. The feeling held me hostage each time I attempted to get rid of her beloved things. I'd put items in the "throw" pile only to second-guess my actions and return them to their musty cartons. Therefore, the remaining three large boxes and several smaller containers were never emptied out.

One evening, I called my daughter and filled her in on my aborted efforts. "In the past two weeks, I've only managed to throw away one small sack of stuff. At this rate, I'll be dead before I get through these boxes, and you'll end up getting rid of Grandma's belongings as well as mine." I must have scared her, because she offered to take the remaining boxes and go through them. She is a good kid and said she'd salvage what interested her and toss the rest.

That weekend, I packed up my station wagon and drove out to her home in Buffalo. Kristen, Dan, and her kids had moved into this larger home nine months ago and still had boxes of their own to unpack, so Kristen said it was no big deal to go through her grandmother's stuff at the same time. We stacked the boxes in her living room. The following week, she started the project. She weeded out the items that were damaged and moth-eaten but saved much of the baby clothes from decades ago. While she was stuffing discards into a garbage bag, her heavy front door suddenly flew shut with an ear-splitting slam. There was no breeze going through the house, and she was the only one in the living room.

A day or so later, we were exchanging instant messages and she told me about it. I asked her what she thought caused the door to slam. She said, "Grandma is probably upset because I'm tossing out her stuff. She is still mad at me for calling the paramedics when she fell." It's possible, I guess. Mom would find it difficult to believe how one person's treasure is another person's trash. I'm so sorry that my mother's dementia turned her against her oldest granddaughter. Kristen did so much for my mom in her last years, from personal care to picking up groceries, but dementia robbed her of those memories. My mother adored our kids and grandkids, so it was quite uncharacteristic of her to become angry with them. Another explanation of the slamming door could be that other spirits in Kristen's current home may have resented my mom's stuff in their space. The house was built in the 1920s and more than likely harbors many lingering spirits. We've seen orbs in pictures of various rooms, so who knows?

Erika's Question

Lately, I've been experiencing odd and frustrating circumstances when attempting to save my text to a disk. Two disks became corrupted and unusable within the last month alone, giving me another mystery to contemplate. I have no idea what happened, but I know it meant I had to remember the recent changes so I could get up to speed again. Believe me, I had a good cry first.

A couple of weeks ago, my niece Erika asked me how I was coming on my book. I told her about the disks and the lost data and, above all, how discouraged I was at that point. She asked, "Is there someone or something in your house that doesn't want that book published?" The same question had been rattling around in my head ever since I began writing this book, but I've hesitated to verbalize it. That kind of stuff only happens in movies, right?

mber 2004—A Fan Tale

Just before we left on vacation this year, I had a bizarre experience with our fan. While doing my pre-vacation cleaning in the living room, I prepared the fan for storage by placing the remote control in the flip-up compartment located on the top of the appliance. When I returned to the living room after lunch to put the fan in its storage box, I noticed something on the floor a few feet away from it. I thought it was one of the many dead leaves that Max drags into the house at this time of year. But guess what? It was the remote control that I had tucked away inside the fan's compartment before my lunch break. See what I mean?

Christmas Day, 2004

After dinner tonight, Kristen's dog was alone in the family room while the other dogs and family members were in the living room. I was washing dishes in the kitchen when I heard Willie begin to growl. I looked into the family room and saw the Westie engaged in the same curious behavior that Max goes through when he's tracking a ghost. Willie's eyes were following *something*, which appeared to be moving around the room. Every couple of seconds, he would emit a low growl and stare off in another direction. When Kris walked into the kitchen, I told her about her dog's odd behavior. She said, "Oh, he sees the ghosts in our kitchen all the time. He's always barking at them." I wonder if Willie locked eyes on my parents, who just might have dropped by for the family Christmas.

16: Enough Already!

January through August 2005

Almost every evening when Max and I sit on the couch watching the television, we hear some commotion going on in the kitchen. When these sounds occur, both Max and I look at the archway at the same time. It would be pretty humorous if it didn't scare him so much. Max continues to carefully watch invisible beings move around in the house, which fascinates me. As long as he isn't growling or barking at these entities, it's okay with me. But the minute he gets irritated to the point of becoming vocal, my nerves begin twitching. If he didn't react to these psychic disturbances, it wouldn't bother me; however, at this rate, the two of us will end up on Valium or on a couch somewhere babbling to a psychologist.

June 2005—The Tuna Can

Max is now four years old, and his mama spoils him terribly, which is bad for his health. One thing Max adores is canned tuna. Whenever I make tuna salad sandwiches for lunch, he stations himself at my feet and then watches and waits till a tidbit drops on the floor. Against the vet's wishes, I slip Max the tuna can when I'm finished with it. It's one of his favorite treats. I put the can down on the rug in front of the bench under the kitchen window, and he dives in. His curly white head doesn't come up until every particle of fish has been gobbled up.

Today, after putting the can on the floor, I returned to mixing up the tuna salad. Suddenly, I heard a loud metallic thump. It sounded like someone had kicked the tuna can or hit it with something. At the exact same time I heard the thump, Max beat it out of the kitchen and into the hall. I looked at the spot where I'd left the can, and it wasn't there. My curiosity got the better of me, so I walked into the family room and there, about nine feet away from its original location, sat the tuna can. Oh boy! Even if he'd possessed the physical attributes to do so, I knew my pooch hadn't thrown or kicked that tuna can. He wouldn't part with something that yummy for anything in the world. I called Max back into the kitchen and held the can out to him, coaxing him to finish the tidbits. He stood a few feet away from me and refused to budge. His normally curled-up tail was even drooping. I dug the tidbits out and placed them in his dog dish. He still wouldn't touch them. Only after I put them in my hand and offered them to him would he lick them up. He was one scared little guy. I suppose the ghost of a dead vet could have dropped in and kicked the can as a way of showing its displeasure at what Max was eating.

A couple of weeks later at lunchtime, Max had plopped himself down in the hallway with his head in the kitchen to watch every move I made. He was probably thinking, "Maybe today the old girl will drop a piece of cheese. . . . " After several minutes, I realized that his brown eyes were no longer boring into my soul. Max had silently abandoned his vigil in the hallway. I hadn't even heard his dog tags jingle; yet I found him sitting in the living room with his back to me, watching an invisible quarry flit around the room. Max loves to eat and never leaves the room when there's food to be had. So something drew his attention into the living room, and it was so strong that he abandoned the prospect of goodies to watch it. I called his name two or three times, and even that didn't break his concentration. Only after I walked into the living room and patted his head did he look up at me—and then only for an instant.

Please, Not the Old Shattered-Glass Trick Again!

It's a good thing Max isn't a cat, because with all the times he's been scared out of his wits, he'd have used up nearly all his lives by now. Poor dog! Late one night in July, yet another occurrence took aim at Max. He was snoozing behind Paul's recliner in the corner of the living room. This recliner is positioned in front of a shelving unit that holds all our British souvenirs, books on England, and so on. There are three cup and saucer sets made from paper-thin china on those shelves. They were a Christmas gift from my brother and his wife. The three sets are actually stacked one upon the other due to the lack of space. Someday they'll probably fall over and I'll hate myself, but for right now, they are holding their own.

I was dozing in my recliner a few feet away from Paul's chair, listening to Coast to Coast AM. Around two in the morning, I heard the sickening sound of glass breaking in the vicinity of the shelving unit. At that very moment, Max shot out from behind the recliner and ran behind the couch. This unit stands on carpeting and, if bumped, will rock slightly because we've never anchored it to the wall. We love to live dangerously in this house. I concluded that my pudgy pooch must have changed sleeping positions and, in doing so, bumped up against that shelving unit, causing the cups to topple over.

I turned on a lamp, put my earphones down, and pulled on my slippers to avoid stepping on broken glass. Then I turned on a second and third lamp to get a better look at the destruction. Imagine my surprise when I found absolutely nothing out of place in that shelf unit at all. The cups were still at their post, standing tall and proud.

None of the little glass knickknacks had fallen over. The books were all lined up as well. Only Max knows what made that noise, and he isn't talking. I haven't heard breaking glass in this house for decades, and if it's all the same to my house ghosts, it's a heart-stopping sound that I'd rather not hear ever again.

Kari-Lynn and the TV (Reprise)

Thirteen years ago, Kari-Lynn had her first strange experience with the television set in the living room. At that time, she didn't want to go home until the show she was watching was over. On her sixteenth birthday this year, she was watching her favorite show in our family room with her mother when another experience occurred. Dan walked into the room and told Kristen they had better get going because it was getting late and it takes an hour to drive home. Both Kristen and Kari-Lynn reached for the remote, but before either of them touched it, the TV clicked off. This is a new television with a new remote, and to my knowledge, this set had never pulled a stunt like before this night.

My startled granddaughter's eyes opened wide in surprise. She immediately looked at her mom and asked, "What just happened, Mom?"

Kris laughed and replied, "The ghost beat me to it again."

I looked up from the article I was reading when I heard the word "ghost." I looked over at my daughter with raised eyebrows. She explained, "The TV went off by itself before either of us had a chance to pick up the remote." I just shook my head. Then, without skipping a beat, Kris told her daughter about the time the TV kept popping back on when she was little because she didn't want to miss her show.

February 2006—Guess What?

While searching for a seldom-used platter in the black hole that masquerades as a base cupboard, I found a long-lost item stashed in the least accessible corner of that unit. Without my trusty flashlight, it would certainly have escaped detection. Voila! It was the spaghetti sauce bowl that disappeared a couple years ago. I shook my head in disbelief, totally afraid of what I'd find in it. I had visions of crusted green sauce permanently bonded to the bowl. With a yardstick, I carefully snagged it out of its hiding place. Believe it or not, it was clean as a whistle. I hope the spirit who sneaked it off my counter that hot summer evening enjoyed the contents. I thanked the invisible pest for washing it up. Now I'd like to ask when the bowl came back, but something tells me I'll never know the answer to that one.

May 2006—It's a Wrap!

Paul still refuses to discuss any paranormal occurrences that happen around here. Scott has finally stated that he can neither prove nor disprove that ghosts exist. That's a big step for him. Once upon a time, their apathy nearly drove me to the brink, but thankfully I've grown. These days, I'm content to allow every skeptic their sphere of comfort, since I've found mine. One thing that will always bother me, however, is the way Max stares and growls at the thin air.

I've worked on this project for over half my life. Wow! That fact blows me away. Whenever I'm asked why it's taken such a long time to finish my book, I just reply, "How would *you* end a story about a house that is still actively haunted?" It was certainly never my intention to make this journal my entire life's work. The plain truth is, I've tried to put it to bed several times but have always failed in the attempt. Having a ghost buster come to my uneasy home was a priority. It took me years to get up the courage to find one. I thought that after Echo's visit the house would finally be peaceful and quiet. Unfortunately, after my house was sealed up against entities and noisy happenings, things continued to happen. I couldn't very well stop writing about them. One thing has always led to another, but now I'm finally calling it quits.

Though dwell I here till my days cease, I promise I shall rest in peace.
I shall not sing a ghostly song, nor haunt these rooms when I have gone.
If I can help it!

—M. L. Woelm, 1968